Tom Graves is by profession
but he is perhaps best kn
teacher and an historian of
Stone, the whole realm of Ea
examination of the work
Underwood and Alfred Wa

Also by Tom Graves

Dowsing: Techniques and Applications

Tom Graves

Needles of Stone

A PANTHER BOOK

GRANADA
London Toronto Sydney New York

Published by Granada Publishing Limited in 1980

ISBN 0 586 04965 7

First published in Great Britain by
Turnstone Press Ltd 1978
Copyright © Tom Graves 1978

Granada Publishing Limited
Frogmore, St Albans, Herts AL2 2NF
and
3 Upper James Street, London W1R 4BP
866 United Nations Plaza, New York, NY 10017, USA
117 York Street, Sydney, NSW 2000, Australia
100 Skyway Avenue, Rexdale, Ontario, M9W 3A6, Canada
PO Box 84165, Greenside, 2034 Johannesburg, South Africa
61 Beach Road, Auckland New Zealand

Set, printed and bound in Great Britain by
Cox & Wyman Ltd, Reading

Set in Times

Contents

Acknowledgment is made to Oxford University Press for permission to quote from *Megalithic Sites in Britain* by Alexander Thom; to S.P.C.K. for permission to quote from *Exorcism* edited by Dom Robert Petitpierre OSB; and to Darton Longman and Todd for permission to quote from *But Deliver Us From Evil* by John Richards.

Author's Note

This book is a study in ideas, an attempt to put some of the ideas that have arisen in the 'earth mysteries' field into a coherent shape or form, to place them in a context that makes practical sense at the present time. This is not a thesis: I'm not trying to prove anything conclusively. Rather, I've tried to show where those ideas seem to lead us now, and where some have misled us in the past. Some of these ideas may prove to be wrong, and many will and must change as new information arises: they can only be based on the present state of research into the 'earth mysteries'. But the underlying theme of the study, the idea that the earth itself is alive, is ageless and is more likely to be reinforced than proved false as time goes by.

Much of the information on which this study is based comes from my own research and fieldwork; but much has necessarily come from other sources. In most cases the detailed information on the sources is given in the notes at the end of the book; but in some cases, particularly among dowsers, information was only forthcoming on the promise that the source would not be published. The 'Dod' cartoons were drawn and kindly provided by Ian Thomson, art editor of *The Ley Hunter* magazine.

And to all those who've helped me in this study, named and unnamed, known and unknown, many thanks.

Tom Graves   London, December 1977

1

Introduction

The earth is alive: living, breathing, pulsing.

It lives, but sleeps, stirring at times: and the people of the cities try to ignore it, hoping it will stay asleep.

It breathes: and the wind batters the grimy arrogance of the townsman, who dreams of 'Man's increasing control over the blind forces of nature'.

It pulses, its seasons and cycles turning in all their subtleties: and those pulses are accepted and realized in the lives of everyone and everything in the countryside.

Our problem is that we've become too civilized to accept that the earth is alive. Our whole way of life is civilized, 'citified': we think of cities and towns as the normal places to be, to work and to live. To our culture, the countryside is a sort of inter-urban space, partly just 'pretty' landscapes and partly areas where food-production for our cities goes on, now greatly improved by the resourcefulness of modern science, technology and economics. The country is a place to get away from the cares of the city when we want to: just for a drive, perhaps, or – if we're rich enough – to our nicely modernized country cottages for the weekend. Apart from some minor problems – soon, no doubt, to be solved by the constant progress of science, technology and economics – our world, and our view of the world, is secure: nature is tamed, and does what it is told by us to do. The old, near-forgotten war between *civis* and *pagus*, the world-views of the city and of the village, seems indisputably to have been settled in favour of the city and its Law and Order: and the victory is symbolized by the power in our culture of the schoolroom, the law-court, the laboratory and the bank.

But for all the apparent power of that image of Order, it is only an image: and a very tenuous one at that. Even in our culture, the veneer of 'civilization' is thin: behind it, the real forces represented by the *religio paganorum*, the religion of the villagers, are still at work, no matter how hard we try to deny their existence. Those forces are the subtle and not-so-subtle forces of nature: pagan cultures were based on an acceptance of those forces, while our civilization is based on an artificial 'separation' from nature, based on the belief that we can be 'above' those forces and can control them to suit our whims. In some ways that belief is correct, for compared to the old pagans our material living standards are remarkably high – but so is the level of misery in our civilization. The richnesses of the quality of life, the dignity and wisdom that are such a characteristic of the great pagan cultures,[1]* are conspicuously lacking in ours. Despite our centuries of mocking and despising them, the pagans still have much to teach us about living with the reality of the forces of nature.

This is hardly news: the cry of 'Back to the land!' has been a recurrent one throughout the centuries, and its present forms can be seen in the increasing number of 'weekend country cottages' and 'self-sufficiency communes', and the increasing use of the 'fresh from the country' theme in advertising. This idyllic view of nature and the countryside is a false one: it's a civilized image far removed from reality. The 'country cottage' boom has pushed the prices of country properties way above the level that those who have to work in the country can afford: the country idyll meets with the 'market forces' of civilized greed. The average life of a 'self-sufficient commune' is apparently now around six weeks: few civilized people appreciate the sheer hard work needed to survive in the country at all, let alone to pay off the bank-loan and taxes as well. Few would-be communards appreciate the reality of human nature and those communes

* These numbers refer to notes which start on page 249.

that do survive do so either through strict self-discipline, through falling back on the civilized safety-net of Social Security payments, or both. The food advertised as 'fresh from the country' is, more often than not, just another variety of factory-processed pap, carelessly grown to produce maximum profit regardless of real quality, and carefully selected and scrubbed to remove any uncivilized irregularities and dirt. In looking to the countryside to provide the quality of life that our civilization lacks, we take our civilized ideas along with us, and are then surprised that the miracles which we expect, don't happen. If we are to 'go back to nature' in a realistic way, we have to deal with nature as it is, not how we assume it to be.

The trap is our belief that we can be 'above' nature, for we can only understand nature if we accept that we understand it, 'stand-under' it. That is what the pagans did. It's clear that people in pagan cultures never saw themselves merely as being 'close to the land', but as an inseparable part of it: they accepted they were part of nature, and could live best by working with it instead of trying to fight against it. They realized that to fight nature was to fight human nature too. For all its irrationality, paganism was a way of working with nature, a way that worked so well that even in Britain it flourished in most country areas until well into this century, and still continues as the basis of most local traditions and religious festivals.[2] Paganism was a way of working with nature to provide quality, meaning and hope in life.

But if we are to look to paganism to help us balance out some of the excesses of civilization, and to restore some quality, meaning and hope into civilized life, we have a real difficulty in knowing where to start. The old pagan gods just seem ridiculous in a city context, and the 'country bumpkin' and 'ignorant peasant' images of paganism that civilization has so carefully nurtured don't help. Without a pagan awareness of nature, the old techniques of paganism can be terrifyingly destructive, particularly on an emotional level, as many civilized fools who have played with witchcraft have found out: the civilized Church, which still denies the existence of many aspects of nature, was right at least in that respect. The whole pagan world-view is different from our civilized one. It has a totally different definition of reality, one that makes little or no sense in terms of our religion of 'science'. If we are to make use of the pagan world-view to help us understand nature, and thus understand ourselves, we have to find some key point around which the pagan world-view and our civilized one can be made to make sense.

That key point seems to be the pagan view of the 'spirit' of a place, the *genius loci*. To our civilized view, places are just commodities, to be bought and sold like any other commodity; but in the pagan view, probably best typified by that of the American Indians,[3] places can have a sacredness, a spiritual importance, that seems to bear no relation to the more physical characteristics of the place. We normally look to the past to study paganism, since civilization has made sure that very few pagan cultures survive intact; but the procedures of conventional archaeology are of little use for studying 'sacredness', for they are only suited to finding and studying objects, not beliefs or forces. As far as conventional archaeology is concerned, our knowledge of why sacred sites and structures are where they are has progressed little further than Defoe's comment about Boscawen-un stone circle in the seventeenth century: 'that all that can be learn'd of them is, That *here they are*'.[4] But if conventional archaeology cannot help us in our search for a new understanding of nature, the work of researchers like Guy Underwood, Alfred Watkins, Tom Lethbridge and Alexander Thom, on the less conventional fringes of archaeology, can. Looking at their work, it becomes clear that the pagan sacred sites are not as randomly placed as they at first appear to be: there are definite if subtle characteristics, apparently natural characteristics in some cases, that go together to make up the 'sacredness' of a site.

In looking at the past in this study, we have to remember why we're doing so. We're not looking at the past for its own sake: the past is gone. Our aim should be to learn from the past, to put our studies to practical use, to understand the pagan world-view in terms of its practical relationship with nature. We have to remember that paganism *worked*, in areas where our civilization so obviously does not. So a good starting point for our study, our search for a new understanding of nature, would be an aspect of old pagan practice that still produces real and measurable results, but which clashes with our assumptions about reality. The dowser's art provides us with such a starting point, and if we combine dowsing with archaeology, some interesting things start to happen – not just to our view of the past, but to our view of reality as well.

2

Dowsing and Archaeology

New motorways, factories, quarries, housing estates, all demand huge tracts of land each year; and as the ground is cleared to make way for a questionable future, all traces of the past are destroyed. Archaeologists, if they want to rescue anything from this mass destruction, are faced with the monumental task of surveying the land in as much detail as possible, and as early as possible, to select the sites with the highest priority for 'rescue' excavation. Traditional archaeological tools and techniques were designed only for small-scale detail work, and are too slow for survey work: the five-summer dig at Cadbury-Camelot was enormous by conventional archaeological standards, but it uncovered little more than a couple of acres of the site. So in recent years a number of new techniques have had to be developed, so as to cover large areas in some detail: hence aerial archaeology, and the development of sophisticated electronic tools like the 'banjo' and the induction locator. Another tool, too, is beginning to be used more and more for this kind of 'rapid search' work: the dowser's rod.

The acceptance of dowsing into the realms of archaeology has been something of a quiet revolution, one that is rarely acknowledged in public. The only text-book I know that discusses the use of dowsing to locate trenches and ditches is John Coles' *Field Archaeology in Britain.* Two examples from the recent Cadbury-Camelot dig are fairly typical of the kind of dowsing work that now goes on: the dowser involved, who was one of the administrators for the dig, told me that he used a strip of flexible curtain rod as a kind of dowsing pendulum to find the outline of the cruciform trench (subsequently confirmed by excavation, and tentatively identified as the foundations for an unbuilt church) and to show that the Arthurian-period hall was not, as had been assumed, set into trenches but mounted on large and very shallow post-holes (the only trench was for an internal partition). Dowsing is a skill, the basics of which anyone can learn with a little practice and awareness; but the problem is that the reliability of the results depends on the skill and experience of the dowser, among many other factors. There are plenty of inexperienced and over-confident amateur dowsers about, so perhaps the archaeologists are not being too evasive when they conceal the use of dowsing, as was the case at Cadbury-Camelot, under vague phrases in their reports, such as 'probing with metal rods'.[1]

In the meantime, many dowsers are discovering the full scope of their skill for the first time, finding that dowsing can be used not only to find water, but virtually anything, anywhere, even from maps.[2] Again, this requires practice and experience before it can be reliable, but dowsers working for archaeologists have located specified objects of any given period, have dated objects and even the periods of occupation of sites accurately, and have identified sites of which little or nothing immediately recognizable remains.[3] Dowser Bill Lewis gave me an example of the latter: he has located burial sites when all that remains of the body – as in some acid soils – is a pale brown smudge and a hollow where the stomach used to be, both signs easily missed by an inexperienced excavator.

Barrows and trackways seem to have been particular concerns of recent archaeological dowsers, judging by articles published in the *Journal of British Society of Dowsers* – a mine of odd information and clues for the archaeologist. James Plummer, for example, describes how he used angle rods and pendulum on site and from maps to locate, track, measure and analyse six Roman stone roads, a junction and possibly a Roman temple, all in the South Fylde area of Lancashire. All were confirmed in some degree by excavation and library research.[4] Captain F. L. M. Boothby noted traces of salt in the foundations of many pre-Roman tracks, particularly in the Winchester area, and suggested that the salt was used as a primitive weed-killer to clear the tracks of nettles and brambles.[5] In the same vein, Helmuth Hesserl, commenting on the way that some Roman roads on the Continent twist about instead of following straight courses, noted that these roads tended to follow 'water-lines', apparent underground water-courses. These latter tend to inhibit plant growth directly above them; so Hesserl suggested that the reason for the roads' lack of straightness was that the Roman engineers had simply taken the 'line of least resistance' through the undergrowth of virgin forest.[6] It's only through the use of dowsing in archaeological research that clues like these can arise.

It is with underground water-courses, and with the traditional role of dowser as water-diviner, that we find our first clues about the placing of ancient sacred sites. Dowsers have discovered, often independently of one another, that water-lines, the underground water-bearing courses or fissures, intersect beneath many types of sacred site: not just the obvious ones, like the holy wells, but barrows, standing stones, stone circles and dolmens. The first reports on this that I know of, in 1933 and 1935, were both French;[7] the first report in English seems to be Captain Boothby's article *The Religion of the Stone Age* in 1935.[8] Boothby described how he found that water-bearing fissures – or 'springs', as he called them – ran underneath a tumulus that an archaeologist he was visiting was working on. After finding that the same applied to every barrow he visited, including long barrows, he decided that 'it would appear that the whole layout of these ancient monuments is based on subterranean water; but', he added, 'until the whole has been tested it is impossible to be certain about this', and he called for other dowsers to test his results for themselves.

Other dowsers did test his results, and confirmed them. Perhaps the most important of these dowsers was Reginald Allender Smith, who gave a lecture on the subject to the British Society of Dowsers in February 1939.[9] He was a well-known and respected archaeologist of the inter-war period, a specialist in prehistoric implements. His lecture was based on a year's research that followed his retirement from a senior post in the British Museum in 1938. He explained in it that Merle and Diot (the two French re-

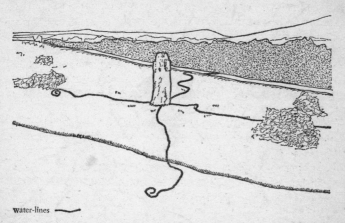

water-lines ────

1 Water-lines under standing stones: a christianized stone near Dartmeet, Devon.

searchers) had found that erect standing stones stood directly above the intersections of two or more underground 'streams'; tilted stones are not directly above such intersections, but lean towards them from a few feet away; and some dolmens and tumuli fit into the angles between converging streams, or are surrounded by them. Both Boothby and Smith slightly disagreed with Merle and Diot, for according to the British results barrows and tumuli were centred on 'knots' of these water-lines (or 'blind springs', as Smith called them) rather than being surrounded by them; but both sides agreed that there seemed to be a definite connection between prehistoric sacred sites and underground water. Both sides also agreed on their interpretation, which was that some pre-Druidic priesthood had used a form of dowsing to locate underground water in prehistoric times, and had marked these 'emergency water supplies', as part of their routine religious observances, with their stones and barrows.

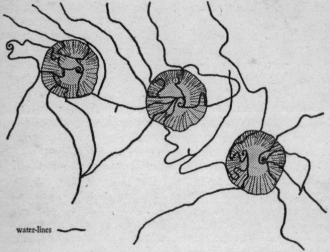

water-lines ━━

2 Water-lines under barrows: the easternmost three of the Priddy Nine Barrows, Somerset.

With that conclusion the research came to an end for nearly ten years, for Smith died only a year later, and Boothby had already moved on to other work. It's interesting to speculate what would have happened if Smith had lived a little longer, for the report on his lecture is fascinating; but it gives frustratingly little detail of what had evidently been an enormous amount of work. He stated, for instance, that according to his results the present stone circle at Rollright in Oxfordshire was only the second in a set of four concentric stone circles around the same blind spring; the present King Stone outlier, about three hundred feet from the centre of the present circle, was, he said, originally one of eleven stones on the outermost circle of that set of four.

A comment he makes about Avebury is also interesting: according to Stukeley, writing in the eighteenth century, there used to be another stone avenue, similar to the present Kennett Avenue, but running south-west towards Beckhampton. Archaeologists usually dismiss this as 'a flight of fancy' by Stukeley, even though the latter had produced accurate plans of Avebury and many other sites at a time when most of the stones were still there to be seen. Smith claimed to have rediscovered the sites of all the stones in this 'lost' Beckhampton Avenue – or rather an Avenue in the right direction in which 'the very twists of the Kennett line are reproduced', and which ended in an oval enclosure, similar to the Kennett Sanctuary, on the downs to the south-west of Beckhampton. Silbury Hill was, he said, exactly equidistant between the two sanctuaries.

There is plenty more information in the same vein in the published version of his lecture; sadly, that report is now the only record of that work. As so often happens, all his notes, diagrams, and the 'series of lantern slides made for the occasion and exhibited for the first time' seem to have been thrown away after his death: at any rate, no one seems to know where they are, or even if they still exist.

Smith's work may have been lost, but it wasn't forgotten. After the War another member of the Society, Guy Underwood, followed up the clues given in that lecture, and spent several years of his retirement visiting sites in various parts of the country – particularly in Gloucestershire, Wiltshire and his native Somerset. Underwood wrote up his research in a long series of articles, which were published in various issues of the Journal of the British Society of Dowsers between 1947 and 1951.[10] During the 1950s he extended, revised and reformed these articles into his important book *Pattern of the Past*, which was not published until 1969, five years after his death.[11] In it he refined the work of the previous researchers (some would say over-refined, as we shall see) and extended it to apply to several other types of sites, including crosses, crossroads and junctions, 'heel-stones' in roadways, boundaries and field-divisions, stocks, gallows and pre-Reformation churches. Underwood's research has formed the basis of much modern research on dowsing and ancient sites, and we need to look at it in some detail.

Underwood was not the only one to discover the apparent connection between churches and underground water: a dowser by the name of W. H. Lamb commented, in a note to the Journal in 1965, on his (or her) discovery that two or more 'streams' cross over each other at different depths directly beneath the high altar of every church visited.[12] In

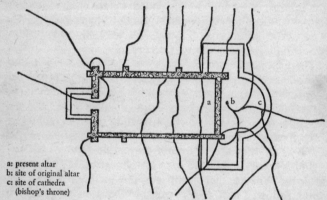

a: present altar
b: site of original altar
c: site of cathedra
   (bishop's throne)

3 Water-lines under churches: Othona/St Peter-at-the-Wall, Bradwell, Essex, a seventh-century cathedral.

the next issue of the Journal there was a reply by Muriel Langdon, who had made a similar discovery, finding what she called 'domes' of rising water beneath church altars, fonts, chancel steps and doors.[13] Judging by the tone of the articles and the terms each writer used, both 'discoveries' would seem to be independent of each other, of Underwood and of the earlier researchers. So many of the dowsers I've talked to recently have 'discovered' and confirmed for themselves the 'blind spring'/sacred-site connection, especially since Underwood's book was published, that it seems something *must* be there.

This was certainly Underwood's feeling. Throughout his research, he seems to have been convinced that the various types of sacred and not-so-sacred sites were water-marks, or markers of and for 'geophysical anomalies': the forms of the sites and the structures upon them were, he believed, determined by the positions of underground fissures and waterflows. The pattern formed by the fine web of lines below the surface determined the shapes and forms of the sites and their structures above; the pattern of the lines was the 'pattern of the past'. This was much the same as Boothby's and Smith's view, as we have seen; and Underwood, in his articles and his book, produced an enormous amount of evidence to back it.

But it's important to realize, in looking at his work, that he was the major exponent of only one school of thought of the time. Many of his contemporaries believed that the 'streams', according to their results, only *appeared* to cross beneath the stones and the like, since the stones themselves distorted the 'image' of the 'stream' below, producing the apparent intersections that Underwood and the others had found. Colonel Bell, then the editor of the Society's Journal, went so far as to add 'Editor's Comments' to the end of Underwood's last two articles, saying that the patterns Underwood described were more likely to be the effects rather than the causes of the siting of roads, tracks, standing stones and the like.[14] He said, rather caustically, that there was 'no reason to suppose that our Neolithic or Bronze Age ancestors knew anything of dowsing as now practised', that Underwood's whole idea of this 'pattern of the past' was 'far-fetched, if not fantastic,' and that the whole of his theorizing was probably based on 'entirely subjective observation'. Given this kind of criticism, it's not all that surprising that Underwood's writing became progressively more and more dogmatic as time went on; but that dogmatism doesn't help us in trying to assess the value of his work and his ideas.

Going through the literature on the subject, we can see that most of Underwood's contemporaries were as certain as he was about the existence of a connection between standing stones and underground water; most, though, were less certain about any likely interpretation. Underwood's dogmatism didn't help to clarify matters: and when he went on to discover (or to invent, as his critics suggested) two new types of 'dowsing influence line' – which he called 'tracklines' and 'aquastats' – most of his contemporaries just gave up and moved on to other studies. That is probably the reason why Underwood's work on standing stones and the like is the only well-known work on the subject. It is important to realize that it isn't the only work that has been done.

Few dowsers have exactly repeated Underwood's experiments, because few have been able to use his favourite dowsing tool, the 'sensitive geodetic rod' that he invented. It's one of the most awkward and cantankerous tools that I've ever come across, but there seems to be little doubt that Underwood himself could use it accurately and with ease. The version that one of my dowsing students made for me consists of a file handle and a short stub of metal rod, an unfolded paper-clip, a piece of motor-bike brake cable and four soldered cable clips. The handle is held in one hand, the loop of the brake cable is held in the other: the idea is that the unwound paper-clip holds the rod and the cable apart when you try to push them together, and the springiness makes the whole thing unstable, tending to make the cable rotate around the rod as a dowsing reaction. This sounds a little awkward, but the illustration should make it clear. As I say, few dowsers bother with Underwood's rod, since the type of dowsing tool makes little difference to the accuracy of the results as far as a skilled dowser is concerned. In my own work I've mostly used 'angle rods', the L-shaped rods described in the 'rescue-dig' image at the beginning of this chapter.

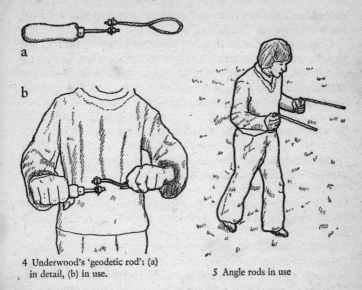

4 Underwood's 'geodetic rod': (a) in detail, (b) in use.

5 Angle rods in use

Underwood's earliest experiments produced results very similar to those of Boothby and Smith. He found that water-lines intersected beneath sacred sites such as barrows, standing stones and henges. He also found, though, that water-lines formed large spirals round stones, several spirals converging on the same stone or stone circle in some cases, as at the Sanctuary near Avebury. As far as he was

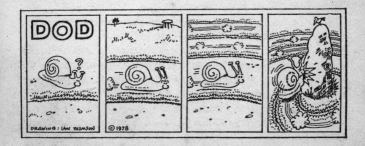

DOD

DRAWING: IAN THOMSON   ©1978

concerned, the water-line was triple, three close and near-parallel lines making up each water-line; and he felt that this triplicity of the lines had been deliberately used in the past to determine the shapes of – for example – henge ditches, as the outer influence lines seemed to move outward from the central line following the centre of the ditch, to coincide with the often erratic outer edges of the ditch. But there are other interpretations, and his critics maintained that this was proof that the influence lines he plotted out were the result of the shape of the ditch rather than the cause of it. Underwood denied this, of course, but the key question of 'cause or effect' remained open, despite his efforts to resolve it in his favour.

The question of 'cause or effect' opened still further with Underwood's 'discovery' of his second type of 'influence line', the 'trackline'.[15] Track-lines, said Underwood, are slightly weaker than water-lines, and are formed of three close, near-parallel groups of three still-closer 'hair-lines'. These nine-fold lines often run in pairs, from ten to sixty or more feet apart; and when they do they coincide closely with the hedges or ditches of old roads. The width of single track-lines – from four to ten feet – tallies closely with the width of the tracks with which they coincide. Underwood claimed that the winding courses of many old roads and tracks was 'controlled entirely' by track-lines and track-line pairs, and suggested, as his results seemed to show, that any alterations from the original prehistoric courses of the road would be shown up by deviations from the unchangeable courses of the track-lines.

Once again, his critics suggested that the lines themselves were 'due to some electrical phenomenon consequent upon disturbance of the earth's surface by man'; and once again Underwood denied this, saying that he had found track-lines across the thin turf of chalk downs, where no man-made disturbance could be seen. But he could not say for certain what track-lines were: he suggested that they were connected in some way with regular fissuring in rocky sub-soils, but he admitted that he wasn't sure. One of the reasons for his uncertainty was that, unlike water-lines, the track-lines were not always continuous. They seemed to be interrupted at times, each hair-line of the nine-fold group forming a twisted loop on either side of the interruption. Where a track-line came to a dead stop, all nine of its hair-lines converged on the same point, often forming a spiral in the process.

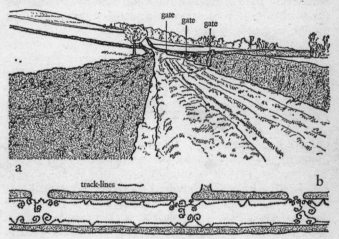

6 A 'green lane' to Lollover Hill, Dundon, Somerset: (a) seen from the east, (b) in plan view, showing track-lines.

The distinctions between water-lines, track-lines and Underwood's third type of 'dowsing influence line', the aquastats, have always seemed very minor to me – but Underwood evidently felt that the differences were crucial. Water-lines gave strong reactions, and they usually ran as single three-fold lines. Track-lines were weaker, were nine-fold and usually ran in pairs. Aquastats, like track-lines, were weaker than water-lines and always ran in pairs; but like the water-lines the lines of the aquastats were three-fold, not nine-fold like track-lines. It's interesting that aquastats seem to coincide even more closely with the courses of tracks than did the track-lines: Underwood even temporarily re-named the latter 'geostats' to avoid confusion – or so he thought! The aquastat pairs coincided with the edges of the roads themselves, and were always continuous; track-line pairs coincided with the outer edges of the roads' verges, and were often 'broken' or distorted at field gates, junctions and wide points of the verges. Aquastats seemed to be more 'important' than track-lines for some reason, for wherever the two types of line crossed each other it was always the track-lines that gave way.[16]

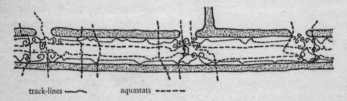

track-lines ━━━━━   aquastats ━ ━ ━ ━

7 Track-lines and aquastats in the lane at Lollover.

Underwood always assumed that all three types of line were 'lines of electrical equipotential' arising from 'geophysical anomalies' – sub-surface rock-fissuring and the like – and were thus permanently and immutably fixed in relation to the surface. The only exceptions to this general rule were one or two cyclical variations in the patterns that the lines formed, the cycles apparently being linked to those of the sun and the moon.[17] Therefore, suggested Underwood, the lines coincide with tracks and the like because some prehistoric priesthood had used them deliberately in laying out boundaries and marking emergency water supplies, and generally as 'good magic to impress the populace'. Almost all the works of man, from the pre-historic period right through until the practice faded out during the Reformation and the European Renaissance, were directed towards this end, he suggested. All sacred and secular structures in the landscape were designed to mark and define the various patterns formed by the three types of line and their inter- actions, patterns like the spirals mentioned earlier, and others called 'feathers', 'arcs', 'parallels', 'haloes', 'trivia', and so on. The underground patterns thus became the patterns on which structures were designed; they were the 'pattern of the past'.[18]

So, according to Underwood, this 'pattern of the past' *determined* the positions of all sacred and some secular sites, and all the major and some minor details of any structures upon them. Thus a water-line can be found under every altar in pre-Reformation churches, and two or more water- lines mark where a barrow was permitted to be built. Multiple water-lines (several water-lines running parallel, not necessarily at the same apparent depth) are indicated at ground level by marks on stones;[19] single water-lines are marked by ditches and the lower parts of lynchets (old agricultural terraces), among other features. Aquastats mark the main courses of old roads, and are also indicated by linear mounds, by terraces and the upper edges of lynchets, by stone rows and stone circles. They can also be found to be coincident with the central axes of all old Christian sites, and appear always to meet a door, window or other gap wherever they go through walls at sacred sites – Underwood suggested that it was 'forbidden' for them to be blocked. Track-lines define where the edges of lanes and old roads should be; they also define animals' tracks and field- divisions, and solifluction or 'soil-creep' lines on the sides of steep hills.[20]

8 Knowlton church and henge, Hampshire, seen from the south. The church is Norman, the henge Neolithic; they stand over a mile from the nearest village.

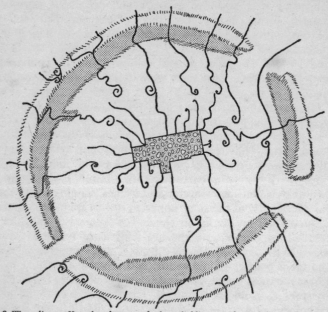

9 Water-lines at Knowlton henge: only the radial lines are shown. The small spirals may mark the sites of former standing stones in the henge.

Like many other dowsers, my own work tends to agree with Underwood's *observations*, as the illustrations show; but I've never been happy with the theories he derived from them. They seem somehow too rigid, too exclusive to match either the information we can collect from other disciplines, or the overall 'feel' that we can get from the sites themselves. I tend to side with Underwood's critics, who suggested that the patterns were 'the pattern of the present' rather than 'the pattern of the past'; but even that view doesn't match the 'feel' of the sites, for there seems to be something else there as well. Both Underwood and his critics are right, but both parties are too limited. If we may combine their views, how-

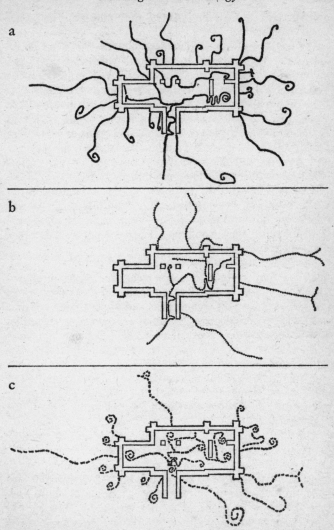

10 Knowlton church, showing (a) water-lines, (b) track-lines and (c) aquastats.

ever, and study their limitations, they may take us somewhere worthwhile.

We could say that Underwood and his critics set us an
interesting 'hen-and-egg' conundrum: which came first, the
patterns or the structures? Underwood was certain that the
patterns came first; his critics were equally certain that
the structures – the altars and the stones, for example – were
themselves the 'cause' behind Underwood's patterns. Both
parties were agreed that from a dowsing point of view there
was definitely some kind of connection between the patterns
and the sites and their structures: but then all the parties
concerned in this particular conundrum were dowsers. Many
other people, both then and now, would maintain that the
whole question was pointless and meaningless, for it was
based on nothing more than 'unscientific superstition':
dowsing itself, they would say, has no basis in fact other
than 'mere coincidence'.

Now from my own experience I would dispute this view;
but in a way these critics are right, for dowsing *is* unscientific, and it *is* based on coincidence. But that doesn't
prove that dowsing is meaningless and useless: much of that
supposed 'proof' depends on what is meant by 'scientific'
and 'coincidence'. As usual, everything depends on your
point of view. Most of these critics, I've found, have a very
limited and distorted view both of what science is and what
it does, and of what coincidence is. The misunderstanding of
coincidence stems mainly from the misunderstanding of
science, so I had better deal with the 'scientific' side of the
argument first.[21]

The first point here is that we have to draw a distinction
between science and technology. Their aims and principles
are very different. The aim of science, crudely speaking, is
to assemble the whole of knowledge into one consistent and
coherent system; while technology is – or should be – concerned only with practical results. Science's main tool is
logic, while technology assesses knowledge more in terms of
its practical value rather than its logical 'truth'. For example,

no scientist *knows* how even a simple thing like a light-bulb works: he has a range of models which explain how some aspects seem to work, but since they are not logically compatible – as in the wave and particle theories of light – they cannot be said to be scientifically 'true', in the classic and socially accepted sense of the word 'science'. But a technologist is quite happy to use these 'unscientific' theories in order to design light-bulbs: the theories don't explain how bulbs work, but they do explain how the bulbs can be worked.

The same can be said of oddities like dowsing. We don't understand how dowsing works, but we do understand that it can be worked to produce usable results,[22] and we also understand how it can be worked.[23] In that sense dowsing can be said to be a technology, though it can't be scientific. There are in fact good reasons for suggesting that technologies are more closely related to traditional magic than they are to science – but that's something I'll have to leave for another book.

The other catch is 'coincidence'. Coincidence is simply coincidence: things coincide. The whole of our observation of life is built up through observation of coincidences; some of them are meaningful, some are not. The only form of meaningful coincidence that classic science recognizes is a particular form of repeatable coincidence called 'causality': when one action repeatedly precedes another the first action is said to 'cause' the second one. Any other kind of connection between two incidents cannot be handled in a 'scientific' manner, which is why in our culture, with its 'scientific' bias, all other kinds of connection are dismissed as 'mere coincidence'. But that does *not* mean that these other coincidences are meaningless: it simply means that they can't be studied scientifically. Instead of being assessed for their causal and logical 'truth', they have to be assessed for their value – 'what use is this coincidence?' – which brings us back into the realm of technology, as 'play it by ear', or the famous 'rule of thumb'. It isn't scientific, but it works, and that's what really matters.

Perceptual systems, like seeing and hearing and 'sensing', are interesting in this respect, because they compare the information coming in from a number of sources in order to decide the overall 'value' of a given situation. Imagine if someone suddenly clapped their hands in front of your face – NOW – what would happen? You'd blink, and jump back, probably. The scientist would ask 'what was the cause of this?', but you can't give a definite scientific answer, because in that situation there are at least three causes, and science has to pin the answer down to just one in order to come to any logical conclusions. You would have heard the sound of the clapping, which is one cause; you would have seen the hands closing rapidly towards your face; and you would have felt the change in air pressure as the hands passed by. Any one of these can trigger off the blink-and-jump reflex.

Even imagining the blow can trigger off the same reflex, so you can't pin down the 'real cause', you can't tell 'how it really works'; the relevant 'signal' comes through, all the same.

This is important when we look at dowsing, for dowsing works as a perceptual system.[24] The dowser's rod works because the dowser's hands give a reflex twitch to some signal; apart from certain rare cases the rod doesn't move entirely of its own accord. But this does cause problems if we try to study dowsing 'scientifically', for we can never be sure what the 'real cause' of any given reaction is. It could be a reaction to some 'magnetic' or 'electrical' stimulus; it could be a 'hypersensitive sense of smell'; it could be 'an unconscious knowledge of the terrain'; it could be some equivalent of 'sonar' scanning; it could be something magical, like clairvoyancy or 'astral travelling' or whatever. An enormous number of models have been proposed and they do all make some degree of sense in practice. But the real problem is that all perceptual systems involve a certain amount of filtering in the mind, to separate 'signal' information from 'noise', so the cause of any dowsing reaction – or lack of it – could equally be prejudice, preconceptions, wishful thinking, inattention, clumsiness, lack of physical or mental discrimination. The ability to limit and control these faults is the basis of a dowser's skill; but in studying the work of any dowser, or of anyone working in similar fields, we do have to decide how much of their observation is 'real', and how much 'imaginary'. The judgements I've made and will be making as we go along are based on my own experience and practical work, but you must judge for yourself.

So to return to our earlier conundrum, the various dowsers' results were 'real' as far as I am concerned, at least in the sense that they observed *something*. But before we can interpret their results, we have first to decide *what* they observed – and that's not easy, because so many kinds of stimuli, at several levels, could have triggered off their dowsing reactions. Dowsing is a perceptual system, and all our ways of perceiving things, are limited by the paradox 'Things have not only to be seen to be believed, but also have to be believed to be seen'. (If this isn't obvious, compare the propaganda of the various political parties at election time: it's the clearest example of people seeing what they want or expect to see.) So a dowser's beliefs about dowsing, the theories and assumptions on which he or she operates, limit not only what they see but also how they see it.

For Underwood, and for most of his contemporaries, dowsing was 'the sensation of electromagnetic radiations'; Underwood in particular felt that it was *solely* the sensation of perception of some kind of 'radiations'. He thought that the lines that he perceived – the water-lines, track-lines and aquastats – were 'lines of electromagnetic equipotential' resulting from the interruption of some force, emanating from the core of the earth, by 'geophysical anomalies' like faults and rock-fissures. His idea was that these fissures interrupted the 'earth force' in much the same way as a spider's web interrupts a beam of light and casts a shadow on a wall. The different types of line were, he thought, probably different 'electromagnetic frequencies'; the patterns formed by and between them were the result of interactions between the different 'frequencies'.

The lines and patterns originated from faults and fissures deep in the body of the earth: therefore, reasoned Underwood, the patterns thus formed on the surface must be permanent and immutable. Because the patterns coincided with sacred sites and structures to a remarkable degree, the sites and structures *must* therefore have been deliberately chosen and designed to mark those patterns: hence the 'pattern of the past'. His critics held much the same beliefs about the causes of dowsing reactions: dowsing was the result of the perception of 'electromagnetic radiations', and water-lines were the 'shadows', on the earth's surface, of water-bearing fissures below. (This idea that water-lines are in fact 'images' is important, and I'll return to it shortly.) They also agreed that the track-lines and aquastats, and the patterns they formed, were aspects of this 'earth force': but they felt that they were not so much interruptions of this 'earth force', as with water-lines, but surface diffractions of the force by the structures on the sites themselves. Underwood's patterns, they therefore suggested, were the 'pattern of the present' rather than the 'pattern of the past'.

All this theorizing assumes that the sole cause of dowsing reactions is electromagnetic in origin. But as we have seen, this is not necessarily the only cause of Underwood's results. As one of his critics put it, it's possible that most of his results came from his imagination rather than the 'real' world. I don't think that is so, but we have to bear the possibility in mind. All of Underwood's theories are based on the assumption that the patterns he observed are permanent and immutable; if they are not, then his observations take on some new meanings. Underwood also assumed that the builders of the sites and structures deliberately incorporated the 'earth-force' patterns into their work: but there is no reason why they should not have done it unconsciously, because it 'felt right' to them. If we remember that Underwood's theories are based not on fact but on assumptions, then we can go beyond his limiting 'pattern of the past' to something more directly relevant to today.

First, though, I'd like to return to that idea of the waterline as an image or 'shadow'. This is important for a number of reasons: not least because it defuses the geologists' 'scientific' objection to the dowser's concept of 'underground streams'. Geologists say that, apart from limestone and chalk, no rock structure will carry the literal kind of 'stream' that dowsers seem to talk about. Dowsers agree with this: the idea of an underground 'stream' cannot normally make sense in terms of geological theory; but the dowsers point out that that is how they *perceive* underground water, and they realize that it may not be like that underground. In retaliation the dowsers also point out that geological theory is limited by the way *it* perceives things, viewing the world underground solely in terms of overall structure rather than local detail: hydrogeology is useful for predicting the level of the water-table in any given area, but cannot explain why dowsers can find water in areas with 'bad' geology (like Somerset, where dowsers have always been active), on hill-tops and at other places that geologists had decided were 'impossible'. Geology sees the large structure, but not the detail; dowsing sees the detail, but not the overall structure: they're just different ways of seeing things.

So when Underwood described the water-lines as interruptions of some 'earth force', that was simply the way he saw them; that may not be what they are in reality. Waterlines, blind springs and the like aren't 'real' at all, they are ways of defining and describing the *apparent* lines and points on the surface that coincide with certain kinds of definable water-flows below. You could call them a 'constructed reality', an imaginary reality, in the same way that the image on a radar screen or television screen is a reconstruction of reality.

To continue that analogy, the image on a radar or television screen can be distorted, or modified so as to add further information: wind-speed and direction, aircraft speed, alignment to the runway, and so on, in the case of an air-traffic controller's radar set. In the same way, the 'images' of water in dowsing can be distorted to show further information, particularly of depth and the direction and rate

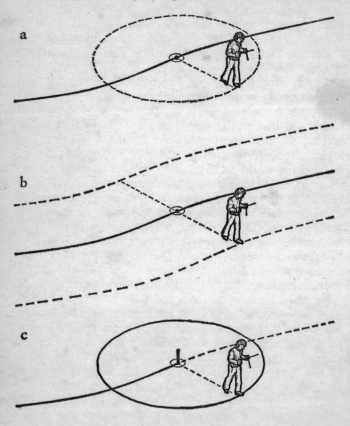

11 Three depth-images from a water-line: (a) the Bishop's Rule, (b) Underwood's 'parallels', and (c) Creyke's system. In each case the distance out to the secondary reaction is the depth of the water-flow at the original point on the water-line.

of flow. In Underwood's system of dowsing these are shown by what he calls 'parallels' and 'flow-lines'. Underwood uses the term 'parallel' for an image version of the so-called 'Bishop's Rule', a depth-finding technique that has been used by dowsers for centuries. Underwood's 'parallels' run parallel to the water-line and separated from the centre of the apparent line by a distance approximately equal to the depth of the water-flow at that point; while the Bishop's Rule states that if you walk outward from directly above the centre of the water-line, you will get a second reaction of your dowsing-rod at a distance out that coincides with the depth of the stream at the point which you started from. In both cases the rule is that 'the distance out equals the distance down'; Underwood's 'parallels' can be seen as the loci derived from measuring the Bishop's Rule outward from an infinite number of points on the water-line. Underwood's 'flow-lines' are small feathery lines, usually S-shaped, formed on both sides of the water-line; they 'follow' the apparent strength and direction of flow, rather like the eddy-currents formed in still air by the passing of a car.

Underwood maintained that these patterns, like all his others, were fixed and immutable (apart from a regular oscillation on a daily cycle), and thus formed part of his 'pattern of the past'. But we can see these patterns as Underwood's way of collecting information about depth and flow, for many other dowsers had other ways of collecting the same information, and never 'saw' Underwood's patterns at all. To them, Underwood's lines simply did not exist. One of the popular contemporary systems for finding depth was Creyke's 'staking' method, which is important to our study because it challenges Underwood's assumption that all the patterns *must* have been fixed. Underwood said that the water-line parallels were parallel lines which expanded and contracted in relation to the centre of the water-line by about ten per cent on a daily cycle; but Creyke's 'staking' system produced an unmoving circular 'parallel' around the point on the water-line which had been staked with a metal bar – a 'parallel' which vanished once the stake was removed.[25]

A lot of dowsers still use Creyke's method. The procedure is that you first have to find the exact centre of the water-line, and then, at a point exactly on that centre-line, hammer a large metal stake into the ground. Immediately, as far as the dowser is concerned, the water-line 'disappears', to be replaced by a circle around the point. According to the original system the radius of that circle is the depth of the stream at that point. There are variations: for some dowsers the radius of this circle is only a half or a third of the actual depth – which can cause embarrassment at times – and other dowsers don't actually stake the water-line, but rather place large lumps of metal or, in one case I know of, a small amethyst crystal, on the ground at the centre of the water-line. Underwood's and Creyke's systems can be reconciled by saying that Creyke's system produces an artificial version of the Bishop's Rule, which leads us back to the relation between the 'parallels' and the Rule. But, more important, Creyke's system does imply that Underwood's apparently permanent patterns can be changed by inserting a 'needle' into the ground – and that, as we shall see, is a key point in a new understanding of sacred sites.

Water-lines may not in themselves be 'real', but they do at least tally with something 'real' underground. We can't so easily say the same of Underwood's track-lines and aquastats. In practical dowsing work, water-lines seem reassuringly solid, and have a definite 'feel' of depth to them; but the track-lines and aquastats seem only to be surface phenomena, and to be far more ephemeral. Underwood never actually defined what track-lines and aquastats were, and it seems he only *assumed* that they were 'lines of electromagnetic equipotential'. We've seen that if we agree with his assumption, we get trapped by the conundrum of 'Which came first, the patterns or the structures?'. The way out of that trap is to look elsewhere for the 'cause' of at least some of those patterns: and one 'cause' which seems to make a great deal of sense, particularly in relation to tracks, boundaries and the like, is some kind of interaction between certain qualities of a place and aspects of the minds of people passing by. If this is so, then what Underwood observed as aquastats and track-lines could in some cases be 'memories' of the meeting of people and place: and Underwood's results do tally more closely with that interpretation than they do with his rigid theory of the 'pattern of the past'.

This idea of track-lines and aquastats as 'memories' is not as strange as it may seem at first. Even a physical track is a 'memory', in a sense, of people and animals that have passed along it. Imagine a bare heath, with no tracks on it at all: to cross it you would have to push a pathway through the bracken and gorse. But next time you pass that way, would you make a new path? Probably not: it's much easier to follow an existing path than to make a new one. Each time you pass that way, you wear down the track still further, reinforcing it as a 'memory' of your passing. You leave the district, and the path falls into disuse: but it is still there as a memory of you and your passing that way – a 'memory' at first as a bare line across the heath, then later (as it silts up, and conserves moisture better than elsewhere) as a line of denser undergrowth. You retain memories of your walking that path: it retains memories of you.

It seems that it retains those memories in more than just the sense of a worn pathway. Underwood's critics, with their idea of the 'pattern of the present', suggested that some of the patterns were 'electrical phenomena consequent upon disturbance of the earth's surface by man', and this is probably true in many cases.[26] But we can go beyond this, to suggest that it retains 'memories' outside of a purely physical sense: we can say that such a trackway retains a ghost of you, to be seen or felt by other people passing by.

By 'ghost' I don't mean some 'spirit of the dead', since obviously you're still alive. Rather, I mean the specific sense of the term as developed by the late Tom Lethbridge in the series of delightful books that he wrote in the 1960s.[27] He suggested that most of the so-called 'ghosts' and 'ghouls' that people come across are 'memories' of emotions or images 'projected' into and stored by certain characteristics of some places by people at those places – and these 'memories' could be reconstructed, and thus 'seen', by other people passing those places later or, as seems to occur in some cases, earlier. This theory does work in practice, and seems to have gained a wide acceptance in recent years. In Church writings, such ghosts and ghouls are referred to as 'place-memories', and a recent official report on exorcism (of which more later) suggested that they account for some nine-tenths of all reported 'hauntings'. If a track or boundary can retain 'place-memories' of passers-by, Underwood's track-lines and aquastats could be a side-effect of the storage of these 'place-memories' as much as, or rather than, 'lines of electro-magnetic equipotential'.

The apparent conditions under which images and emotions can be stored in and retrieved from a place as 'place-memories' are complex, and I'll have to leave a detailed discussion of them for later; but one of the conditions is known to be that state of mind of both 'transmitter' and 'receiver', and this gives us a clue as to what the difference between aquastats and track-lines, as 'place-memories', might be. Underwood said that both track-lines and aquastats coincided with roads and tracks, but aquastats seemed to be the 'holier' of the two types of line. So if we take the lines to be interactive 'place-memories', this would suggest that the aquastats are 'projected' into the place by a 'holier' state of mind than that required for track-lines. This does explain a number of loose ends in Underwood's theories: it suggests, for example, that track-lines 'give way' to the continuous aquastats because the 'holier' state of mind is a more powerful one, giving an effect like a strong radio signal swamping out a weaker one; it also suggests, as another example, that the coincidence between aquastats and boundaries that Underwood describes may be connected and caused by semi-religious ceremonies like 'beating the bounds'.

This also suggests that to look for track-lines and aqua-stats and the like may be to miss the point, for they may only be side-effects of something more important. To study them alone may put us in the same position as the hi-fi fanatic who studies the technical quality of each recording so closely that he forgets to listen to the music. Important though studies of Underwood's patterns may be, we must remember to keep them in context with a wider view of the sacred sites, and of nature as a whole.

3

As Below, So Above

Stand at a stone circle, and see with different eyes. At your feet, as you know, are Underwood's patterns, a network of lines weaving and interweaving across the surface of the grass; but now you see them, as glowing wires, as twisted cables gleaming in their own light, the different types of line distinguished by different colours, different hues.

But this is not all. The stones themselves glow with light, their colours and intensities changing and pulsing as you watch. The ground itself is glowing, concentric rings of muted colours spreading out from the centre of the circle. Above the ground there is activity too: sparks of coloured light jump from stone to stone around the circle, travelling along taut wires of light, like messages chattering from stone to stone. Occasionally, all this activity comes to a climax: the top of one stone gleams brightly for a moment as a huge pulse of energy emerges from it and disappears into the distance, like a firework rocket travelling horizontally on an almost invisible wire. A message of some kind, travelling from one site to another – or a pulse in a nerve of the body of the earth itself.

As you can see in the image above, Underwood's patterns are only a part of the picture of sacred sites that can be constructed from recent research. (The image is more than an analogy, by the way: several dowser-psychometrists have described the sites to me in these terms; and I remember how a friend of mine, working with me at Stonehenge, suddenly discovered he could 'see' the lines as bright silver 'wires' winding and twisting just below the surface.) A lot has been going on since Underwood's time, and very little has been published – which is not all that surprising, since until recently most archaeologists dismissed this kind of work as the furthest extreme of the 'lunatic fringe'. But attitudes are changing even within the narrow confines of academic archaeology; and this new research is of still more value when seen in the wider context of the relationships between places and the forces of nature.

Underwood found his patterns below ground, or just at the surface. Like many of his contemporaries, that seems to be the only level at which he looked for anything. However, even in his time it was known that points or places could be polarized or 'charged', in a dowsing sense, in relation to others; and this includes a variety of types of polarization at sacred sites. Some of these 'charges' are, like Underwood's patterns, on points at or below the surface: others, though, are above.

It seems, from what little published evidence there is, that the first above-ground 'charges' to be found were on standing stones. I've tested this for myself, both on my own and with my students: it does seem that standing stones are polarized in relation to the ground around them and, in stone circles, polarized in relation to each other. It's easiest to describe this polarization in terms of 'charge', but that isn't quite accurate in a physical sense, and we don't actually know what it is. There does seem to be a physical component involved in it somewhere, for John Taylor and Eduardo

Balanovski, working with the dowser Bill Lewis in 1975, found a 'significant' distortion in the local geomagnetic field around a standing stone near Crickhowell in South Wales. The normal strength of the geomagnetic field in that area has a value of about half a gauss; the maximum deviation expected was no more than a few hundredths of a gauss, but immediately around the stone the local field had more than doubled in strength – 'significant' indeed![1] According to recent correspondence with one of my colleagues, Taylor has since claimed that the results were 'inconclusive'; and this seems to be because he, like Underwood, assumed that the strength of any pattern would be fixed, and it was not. But Lewis told me that he had warned Taylor from the start that the field-strength rose and fell on a regular cycle. 'Scientific' research in these fields has to be truly scientific if it is to be of any use, and preconceptions of any kind, particularly in this area, are likely to make such research unscientific.

Taylor's work was also limited in that, again like Underwood, he assumed that any polarity around the stone must be solely electromagnetic. This is an assumption which forty-year's-worth of their own research into the physical factors of dowsing has taught dowsers to beware.[2] Most dowsers would agree that an electromagnetic component is involved, but many of those I've discussed the matter with have suggested that this may only be a side-effect of something, some energy, on what they would call another 'level'. Each time someone tries to pin down any 'cause' in dowsing to one specific physical mechanism, it suddenly stops and reappears as some other apparently physical mechanism. This effect is well-known in other research on the mechanisms behind 'psychic' phenomena, particularly psychokinesis: it's sometimes called the 'bloody-mindedness' of those phenomena.[3]

The polarities seem to represent something more complex and less tangible than purely physical energies, though the physical level does come into it somewhere. But though we don't know what they are, we can at least distinguish be-

tween the various types and the relative polarities of each
type. The most common form of polarity seems to be related to the Chinese duality of 'Yin' (or 'female-principle')
and 'Yang' (or 'male-principle'). For practical purposes
these are usually referred to as 'negative' and 'positive'
respectively: but note that this does not mean that Yang is
'better' than Yin, it's just a useful way of labelling them for
practical dowsing work. The usual way of picking up these
relative polarities or 'charges' in dowsing practice is to use
a pendulum in one hand, and rest the other hand on top
of the standing stone (or whatever else it is that is being
tested). The pendulum's 'neutral', for me at least, is when it
is swinging backwards and forwards in an even oscillation;
as the dowser touches the top of the stone with his (or her)
other hand the pendulum gyrates, and the direction of the
gyration is used to imply the polarity of the stone at that
time. In my case, a clockwise gyration of the pendulum is
'positive', and anti-clockwise 'negative', but this does vary
from one dowser to another.

Few of the polarities on standing stones stay the same for
long, particularly at stone circles. I did a week-long study of
the morning, afternoon and evening polarities of the stones
at Rollright in the summer of 1973, and only about a dozen
of the seventy or so stones there maintained the same charge
for the whole week. Most of them changed from hour to
hour, and many of them had minor changes occurring on
a twenty- to twenty-four-second cycle. But churches, and
Christian sites in general, are different: the altars of those
that I've tested are almost invariably 'positive', and stay
that way. The exception to this is that many Lady Chapel
altars are equally fixed at 'negative'. Church buttresses –
particularly at the east ends, for some reason – are more like
standing stones, as their 'charges' wander somewhat; and
other points within churches that tend to be strongly polarized are fonts and piscinas.

Whole areas can also be polarized in relation to others,
mainly at ground level, but possibly above or below.

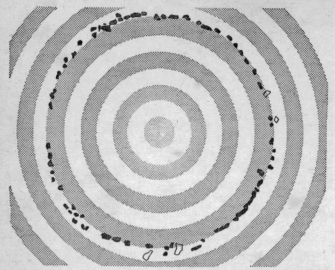

12 Rollright stone circle, Oxfordshire: rings of 'charge' spreading out from the centre of the circle.

During that survey at Rollright, using angle rods, I discovered a set of concentric rings of alternating 'charge': the rods crossed on passing through the line of the stones, opened out again further towards the centre of the circle, and repeated this 'opening and closing' to give seven concentric rings around the centre. It would seem that the polarities here are relative rather than the more absolute 'positive' and 'negative', for I found that if I started with rods crossed, they opened out as I passed through the line of the stones, and so on in reverse to the centre of the circle. The effective pattern is similar to what Underwood called a 'halo', a set of concentric rings around a major point, such as the intersection of nave, chancel and transepts in a cathedral; it's also like a multiple version of the pattern produced in the Creyke system of depthing described earlier.

This alternation of 'charge' at Rollright continued outward from the circle for at least three more alternations; it is likely, from the 'feel' of it, to have gone further, but obstructions like hedges and the fast-moving traffic on the road hard by the circle made it difficult to trace more of the pattern. I have since found a similar, though weaker, pattern at Gors Fawr stone circle in Pembrokeshire; I haven't yet been able to test for it at other circles, but other dowsers I've talked to have reported similar effects at some of them. I haven't yet studied area polarization in churches either, partly because most of the significant old churches are still in daily use: but it would be interesting to see what patterns are to be found there.

In the same way that there tend to be concentrations of 'charge' at various points on a site, there tend also to be concentrations at specific points on the structures of those sites – such as church buttresses and, particularly, standing stones. These concentrations showed up in Taylor's research on that stone at Crickhowell, as narrow bands of double-strength geomagnetic field running horizontally across the stone at various heights upon it. These bands move up and down a little on the surface of the stone, following what appears to be a lunar cycle: and because Taylor was apparently expecting these bands, once he found them, to stay still, that may be another reason why he said his results were 'inconclusive'. There are seven of these bands on most large standing stones; smaller stones, below about four or five feet, may only have the first five, though there are a number of exceptions to this general 'rule' – the smallish wall-stones in the chambers at Belas Knap long barrow in the Cotswolds, for example, have all seven bands. Two of the bands are usually below ground level, and the third just above or below the surface; the top band will be at or very close to the top of the stone, and the remaining one or three bands (or however many the stone has) are usually spaced irregularly over the rest of the height of the stone.

All seven bands, according to several researchers I've talked to, are tapping points into a spiral release of some

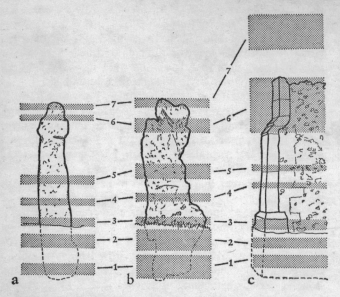

13 Energy bands on stones and buttresses: (a) christianized stone near Postbridge, Devon, (b) stone 3 at Rollright, and (c) the north-east buttress of Knowlton church. All are shown to the same scale.

kind of energy that moves up and down the stone, following that lunar cycle. The cycle appears to control the release of this energy in a sine-wave form, the zero-points of the cycle occurring on the sixth day after New and Full Moon.

Underwood noticed a similar, if not identical, cycle guiding regular changes in some of his secondary patterns; and, as he pointed out in *Pattern of the Past*, this coincides precisely with the structure of the Celtic calendar, at least as described by their first-century bronze 'tablet' found at Coligny in France at the end of the last century.[4] According to the tablet, the months started on the sixth day after New Moon, and were divided into two fortnightly periods (hence the English 'fortnight', a fourteen-night); the New Year started on the sixth day after the first New Moon after the spring equinox. (The West-European Easter is a Christian takeover of the old pagan New Year festival, which is why Easter is a 'movable feast'.) Underwood stated that the cycle in his secondary patterns repeated its zero-points almost to the second each fortnight; and another researcher, Andrew Davidson, timed the zero-points of the cycle of the spiral energy-release round a set of standing stones in Scotland to within seven minutes.[5] Either way, a measurable cycle of that accuracy – better than most clocks until well into this century – would seem to be a useful guide for any pagan calendar: so the parallel with the Celtic calendar may be more than 'mere coincidence'.

The spiral feeds energy from the ground to the sky during one half of the cycle, and feeds from the sky to the ground during the other half. The bands on the stone seem to connect the stone into this flow of energy, apparently to control it: they seem to 'plug' the stone into energies both above and below ground, while the stone itself both marks and is the right point through which the interchange of energies can take place. The bottom three bands connect the stone into the energies below ground; among other things, they seem – from my research results at least – to connect up in some way with Underwood's patterns, but I've not been able to work out what the connection is. The remaining bands connect up with other energies, or networks of energies, *above* ground; and in the case of the fifth and seventh bands this connection, as far as many dowsers are concerned, produces some interesting side-effects.

The effect of the fifth band on the dowser may have given a standing stone in Gloucestershire its name: the Twizzle Stone. When a dowser leans against the level of the fifth band on a stone or buttress, the band somehow affects the dowser's balance, producing an effect which feels like a slow and gentle push to one side or the other. According to the skill of the dowser (and, it must be admitted, more subjective factors like a sense of showmanship), this sense of 'being pushed' can be increased until it looks as if the dowser has been thrown to one side by the stone. The same lunar cycle controls the strength of this effect: the thrust waxes and wanes, and reverses, in the same way as the spiral release of energy around the stone. Around First and Last Quarter the response tends to be weak and unclear, while on the day before New and Full Moon there is often no doubt at all that the effect is there.

The usual procedure is to use a pendulum to find the position of the band, using the free hand as a pointer to move up the surface of the stone. Then place both palms flat on the surface of the stone at this point; lean against the stone, resting your weight on your palms, and *relax*. By 'relax' I don't mean 'go floppy': rather, I mean that you should allow the tension in your muscles to ease evenly, and – perhaps more important – to relax and clear your mind of 'doing', analysing, thinking. If you've done this right, and if the conditions are right, 'upright', in a subjective sense, suddenly ceases to be upright, and you'll roll to one side or the other. The direction of this 'thrust' will remain the same, for you at least, until the end of that lunar cycle; for the next fortnight it will reverse; and so on. Different people are 'pushed' different ways, for some reason, and different stones may induce different apparent 'thrusts', so don't assume that if it works for you in one way at one place it must therefore be the same for everyone everywhere.

I once showed Paul Devereux, editor of *The Ley Hunter* magazine, how to find this fifth band effect, working on one of the main stones at Avebury and on the tower on top of Glastonbury Tor. Since he hadn't been able to dowse before this time, his comments are interesting. He said that the immediate effect of the fifth band was 'like when you've had just one drink too many': it was a feeling that hit him as soon as he made contact, and this sense of a loss of balance developed, in a couple of seconds, into a definite 'push' to one side. It's interesting to see how specific this effect is: on the west-end buttresses of the tower on Glastonbury Tor it could only be felt from a narrow band about six inches

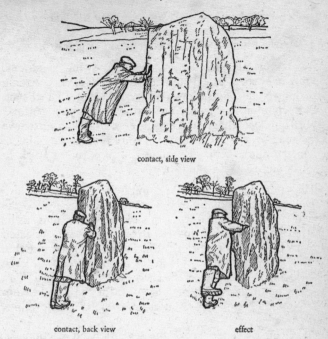

contact, side view

contact, back view   effect

14 The fifth-band's effect on a dowser.

high and around four feet off the ground, while it couldn't be found at any height on the east-end buttresses. Since the latter were only put up to support the tower after its church had collapsed in an earthquake, and were thus not part of the original layout of the church, that perhaps isn't so surprising.

Another often-reported effect at the stones, probably from contact with this band, or the seventh, is the feeling that the stone is rocking or moving or, as one of my students put it, 'jumping about'. Again this is a subjective feeling, since the stones are usually firmly rooted in the ground; but a lot of people, dowsers and non-dowsers, have felt it. The late

Tom Lethbridge, in his book *The Legend of the Sons of God*, described how this effect occurred when he tried to date the stones of the Merry Maidens circle at Lamorna in Cornwall:

> As soon as the pendulum started to swing, a strange thing happened. The hand resting on the stone received a strong tingling sensation like a mild electric shock and the pendulum itself shot out until it was circling nearly horizontally to the ground. The stone itself, which must have weighed over a ton, felt as if it were rocking and almost dancing about. This was quite alarming, but I stuck to my counting . . .[6]

This 'tingling sensation like a mild electric shock' is also one of the characteristics of the seventh band's effect on the dowser. With a skilled dowser this can be spectacular: as he touches the band with his fingertips, the energy released triggers off a violent reflex contraction of the back muscles, throwing him backward as much as ten or fifteen feet. Even non-dowsers can often feel the energy at this point as a slight warmth or tingle, which may account for the name of another standing stone in Gloucestershire, the Tingle Stone, near Avening.

My strongest experience of this seventh band reaction was at Avebury, when a friend and I were trying to find the former height, by dowsing, of the Obelisk Stone, which once stood in an inner part of the southern circle there. The stone isn't there now – it was pulled down and destroyed in the seventeenth century – and all that remains is a large concrete marker. Because of this, we thought we would have to work at maximum sensitivity if we were going to find the 'memory' of the stone. We used a 'booster' technique, in which a second dowser – to use a radio analogy – acts as a series amplifier on the 'signal' that the first dowser receives: we thought that the 'signal' would be too weak to be noticed if we didn't do this. We were wrong, of course. Using a pendulum in one hand, I used my other arm as a pointer, to find the former height of the tip of the stone. We did, at

contact effect

recovery

15 The seventh-band's effect on a dowser.

about seventeen feet: but at the same time we found the 'memory' of the stone's seventh band. It was quite a reaction. I'm not quite sure what happened then, since all I remember is jumping back with the shock, but my wife, who was watching at the time, tells me that my arms went out wide, and I only just managed to keep upright. My friend went sprawling on the ground about ten feet back from where he started, for, being 'booster', he'd caught the brunt of what I'd managed to dodge. It was several minutes before either of us recovered enough to start work again.

Many dowsers have had experiences in a similar vein, so

it's not surprising to find them wary of working at stone circles and other sacred sites. I remember a student of mine overtired herself working on one of the stones at Rollright: she suddenly found herself having a giggling fit after tripping over a tiny piece of chervil, which she swears wrapped itself round her ankle; she only sobered up – and instantly at that – when we helped her out of the circle. Another dowser reported finding her pendulum doing a miniature version of the Indian Rope Trick when she dropped it after working at the same circle too long. One medical dowser I talked to warned me that the energies involved are capable of damaging human metabolism: so it is important to know what you're doing when you're working at these sites, and to treat the energies with some caution. As in other fields, casual dabbling may be dangerous.

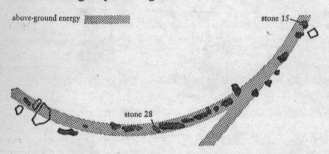

16 Rollright stone circle: spin-energy at the eastern 'gate', stones 15 to 28.

This was brought home to me in the early days of my experiments, when I 'borrowed' a teenager as a helper at Rollright. We had been noticing for some time that each time we crossed the line of the stones with angle rods, the rods reacted in a way that implied there was some kind of energy jumping from stone to stone around the perimeter of the circle, moving in a sun-wise direction about three feet off the ground. Basically, this energy was just 'spinning' round the perimeter of the circle; but there are two points at Rollright which seem to be 'gates', in the sense that the line of the stones breaks so that as you walk round the circle just inside the line, you will find yourself going outside the line at these points. The interesting thing was that the line of the energy became double at these two points, one moving round the circle as usual, but the other part apparently moving off at a tangent to the circle. We thought that one of the stones close to the eastern 'gate' might be the 'gate-latch', so to speak; so my helper stood in the 'gateway', pendulum in hand, and I tested the 'gate-latch' stone with my pendulum. The result, for both of us, was instant migraine.

It wasn't until quarter of an hour later that the headaches began to clear: intangible and immaterial though it might have been, the massive pulse of energy we'd released through the 'gate' had been real enough to us. Since that experience, I've been careful to learn basic protection techniques and, as far as possible, to work only with people who have also learnt them. I've also learnt the value and importance of 'feeling' when something is wrong, or about to go wrong: but unfortunately these things can only be learnt through practice, and through sometimes bitter experience. If you don't already know what I mean by this, you'll have to find out for yourself – there's no other way that I can show you.

I'm still not sure what happened then, for by the time that we had recovered enough to start work again the energy pattern around the circle was exactly the same as before our experience – pretending, as it seemed, that nothing had happened. As far as I can work out, though, this aspect of the circle resembles a cyclotron: some kind of energy, possibly derived from the blind spring at the centre of the circle, and implied by the concentric 'haloes' round the centre that I described earlier, spread outward from the centre, and was collected at the perimeter of the circle, to be stored there by 'spinning' the energy from stone to stone. By inserting a small amount of energy into any of the 'gate-latch' stones – which is what I had done, in testing the stone – the relevant 'gate' was opened, releasing all the stored energy in one go: and that was what had flattened us in its passing. I've never been able to work out what happened to the other energy patterns of the circle during this momentary convulsion; and since, for obvious reasons, I'm unwilling to repeat the experiment, I probably never will.

The interesting thing here was that the pulse of energy, whatever it was, seemed to leave the circle at a tangent to the line of the stones, travelling in a dead straight line. I think it went about six miles to the south-west, to a stone called the Hawk Stone, and then split off in two different directions from there – or rather, that's what the dowsing results implied, because it doesn't quite make sense according to the map. The important point was that not only did this pulse travel straight across country, but a faint continuous line marked out its course, in a dowsing sense, above the ground. This line was the continuation of the tangential line coming off the 'spin' at the 'gate', the line which we had found before we had accidentally released the energy pulse. It started, like the 'spin', at about three feet off the ground, and shortly after leaving the circle had widened from is original two feet width to about six feet, which seemed to be its 'normal' width for what I could track of its course across country.

As I found more of these lines travelling above ground to and from various stones at Rollright and at other sites, I called them 'overgrounds' in order to distinguish them from Underwood's patterns underground. The dowsing techniques to find them are exactly the same as for Underwood's patterns, except that you have to remember to keep in mind that you're looking for patterns above ground, not at the surface or below. Soon after I had found these 'overgrounds', I discovered that other dowsers had known of them for some time because of their effects in a different field of dowsing research; but they referred to them by another term – 'leys' – which, as we shall see shortly, is a particularly important one in the history of the study of sacred sites.

Mirroring Underwood's patterns, these overground lines connect in some way with those bands or 'tapping points' above ground on the stones; though again, as with Underwood's patterns, they don't seem to connect directly, but rather relate to them by some complicated linkage or relationship that I don't yet understand. The different bands also seem to have different functions: all of them deal with these overground 'communications', but the fifth and seventh bands seem to 'hold' or diffuse the pulses in some way, while the sixth band tends to deal with long-distance communications from site to site, and the fourth band to deal with 'local' communications within the site of the local area. These are tendencies rather than rules, though: from my results at least it seems that every band can perform every function.

The local communications, the pulses jumping from stone to stone on a site, show up in other ways that we've come across already. At stone circles, one set of pulses jumps from stone to stone either clockwise or anti-clockwise round the circle, forming the apparent 'spin'; and other pulses, jumping around in a less obvious sequence, change the polarities of the stones on their regular and irregular cycles. From a dowser's point of view, watching these pulses move around on a complex site like Rollright, it is no exaggeration to describe the site as 'living, breathing, pulsing'.

But to me it is the long-distance overgrounds, or rather their 'carriers', which are particularly interesting. There are a lot of them: the main outlier at Rollright, the King Stone, had more than a dozen linked to it the last time I checked, and there may well be more. There are probably more than a hundred of them linking in to the whole Rollright complex, if we include all the minor and irregular links; there are so many of them that an image of stone circles and standing stones as stone 'telephone exchanges' springs to mind.

That image may not be as fanciful as it seems, for a striking analogy can be drawn between the overgrounds and present-day microwave telecommunications. Much of Britain's telephone traffic is carried on microwave links between various towers dotted around the country: the best-known of these are the concrete Post Office towers in the centres of London and Birmingham, but there are about a hundred other towers and steel pylons in the chains that run from end to end and side to side of the country. If you look at these towers, you can see ten-foot-high 'horns' mounted high up on them: these are the main microwave aerials. Each horn can transmit several thousand telephone conversations at the same time, which is why the towers were built in the first place; and it transmits these as modulations of a single narrow beam that jumps from one tower to another along the chains. The beam from each horn is a cone with less than one-third-degree spread (the smaller 'dishes' on the towers aren't quite so accurate), and because the horns are placed high up on the towers, that are themselves usually built on high ground, the beams rarely touch the earth.

This is the really ingenious part of the design of the British microwave network, for it is something of an open secret that the 'secret' Government centres are built on or under those hills that the beams just touch. For example, the only hill that the beam between the towers at Stokenchurch (where the M40 crosses the Chiltern ridge) and Bagshot Heath touches has an ex-World-War-II arms factory hidden underground beneath its summit, now converted to one of the government's semi-secret 'Sub-Regional Controls'. The same beam passes directly over the RAF Staff College at Bracknell and the defence communications headquarters (again underground) at Medmenham. This hidden aspect of the towers' function was discovered by a pacifist group called 'Spies for Peace' during the 1950s.[7]

Political implications apart, the interesting point here is that the major sites of the network, the towers, were placed on carefully selected hills so that minor sites on other hills could tap into the beams: all the hills align. Hence the analogy with the overgrounds and the sacred sites, since they too form alignments of major and minor sites along the same straight overgrounds. Major sites such as stone circles

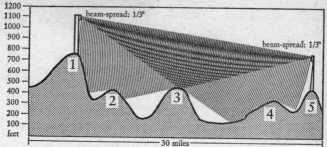

1: Stokenchurch microwave tower
2: RAF Medmenham, underground Defence Communications headquarters
3: Sub-Regional Control 61, Warren Row, formerly a wartime underground arms factory.
4: RAF Staff College, Bracknell
5: Bagshot microwave tower
Warren Row is the only point where both beams touch the ground.

17 The microwave towers and their alignments: a cross-section between Stokenchurch and Bagshot towers.
(*after Peter Laurie*, Beneath the City Streets, Granada, 1979)

and large standing stones are terminal points for each over-ground, analogous to the microwave towers; and spaced irregularly along the overgrounds are the minor 'tapping points', like the small mark-stones that you can see in many places set into the side of the road.[8] Like the small micro-wave dishes on the hills, they aren't placed as randomly as they seem; and like the dishes, they are there for a reason, though not, I think, the same one.

This matter of alignment, or apparent alignment, is well known in the study of sacred sites. In recent years a lot of research has been done on inter-relationships of certain types of sites along astronomically significant alignments,[9] but much of this was pre-dated by the work of Alfred Watkins and the members of the Old Straight Track Club in the 1920s and 1930s.[10] It was actually my interest in Watkins' 'leys' that started me dowsing in the first place, because I had wondered if it was possible to find and check them by dowsing. Since I couldn't find any dowsers to help me at the time, I taught myself to dowse; but I couldn't find

any leys by dowsing then, and anyway my interest was soon
caught by Underwood's work. It wasn't until I had done
some work on overgrounds that I realized there was a
possible connection between dowsing and leys – but that's
something I'll come back to shortly. For the moment, we need
to look at Watkins' leys and the concept of the alignment of
sacred sites.

Watkins' first essay on leys, *Early British Trackways,
Moats, Mounds, Camps and Sites*, was written with obvious
excitement in the short period between 30 June 1921,
when he had his first clue (or 'vision', as some later writers
have put it) of the ley system, and the September lecture on
which the essay, published the next year, was based. His
thesis was that the pre-Roman trackways of Britain were
constructed in straight lines marked out by sighting from
major intervisible points: mountain peaks in high districts,
and hills, knolls or artificial mounds in lower ones. The
trackway itself was marked by a variety of secondary points,
also intervisible, and deliberately designed to be 'picked out'
from the surrounding countryside. In addition to using
standing stones and the smaller mark-stones (which are
natural boulders 'foreign' to the area) as markers, the
ancient surveyors – according to Watkins – constructed
mounds on intermediate ground, cut away notches where
the tracks crossed ridges, and made cuttings and causeways
where the tracks crossed rivers. These water-points on the
tracks were sometimes visually 'assisted' by being banked up
into a 'flash', so as to glint in the sunshine when seen from a
point higher up on the track. The tracks didn't necessarily
run the whole length of the sighting line from mountain
peak to mountain peak, they just used those parts which were
practical for trading purposes.

The mark-points must also have had some religious signi-
ficance, for sacred wells, stone circles and known sacred
groves are also primary or secondary mark-points on the
'old straight track'; and when the Church took over, it also
took over the old sites as sites for their new churches. The

Romans before them took over parts of the old track for their own purposes, using them as foundations on which to base some of their own not-so-straight roads; we have to realize, said Watkins, that the old straight track was as old to the Romans as their roads are to us. Watkins derived his term 'ley', which he used to describe the old straight track, from its frequent appearance in the names of places along the tracks.

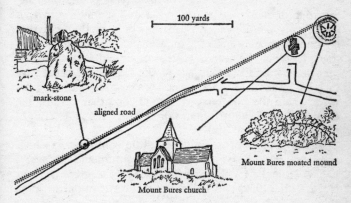

18 A classic ley-type alignment at Mount Bures, Suffolk.

Over the next few years, Watkins' thesis changed a little, becoming more complex and sophisticated. In his most important book, *The Old Straight Track*, published in 1925, the different traders' tracks are identified by different groups of place-names – 'white' or 'wick' for salt, for example, and 'knap' or 'chip' for flint – and the Beacon Hills are added to the list of mark-points. By 1927, when he published his *Ley Hunter's Manual*, the list of mark-points had grown, in their order of reliability, to the following: prehistoric mounds (except where closely clustered together), moated mounds, wayside mark-stones (where distinguishable from casual 'erratic' stones), circular moats, castle keeps (usually on old mounds), Beacon Hills and similarly named mounds (like One-Tree Hills), wells with traditional names, old churches (especially if on a mound or other evidence of prehistoric use of the site, or with certain types of related folklore), ancient crosses, alignments of road or trackway, fords, traditionally-named tree-groups or single trees (especially if Scots Pine), hillside notches, and cross-roads, zigzags and other road junctions.

A map will only show some of these types of site aligning, say four or five good mark-points in ten miles, and that might only be 'coincidence'. It was only in the field that ley-hunting made sense, for on a chance alignment no further sites would be found, whereas on a 'real' ley you would find un-recorded mark-stones in the hedgerow, causeways through ponds that blocked the ley's course,[11] paired gate-ways where the line crossed a road, or other details like confirmatory folklore about tunnels or 'the old straight road'.

The possibility of finding these little confirmatory clues, combined with the whole sense of adventure and discovery, helped to make ley-hunting into one of the great popular crazes of the 1920s and 1930s. But if it was popular with the ramblers who walked the leys, it was not at all popular with the archaeologists of the time. The Diffusionist theory, which maintained that all culture and civilization came out of the 'fertile crescent' of the Tigris and Euphrates, had just been nicely established as 'fact'; it 'proved' that the life of early man in Britain had been, to use Hobbes' famous description, 'solitary, poor, nasty, brutish and short'. In this view, the first properly surveyed and engineered roads in Britain were those of the Romans; the only roads prior to that had been mere trackways, the old and winding ridge-ways and drove-roads. Watkins' leys had to be absurd, to the archaeologists, for they implied the need for a complex culture and technical ability in at least one section of the population in prehistoric times – and this concept could in no way be made to fit into the orthodox archaeology of the time. The archaeologist O. G. S. Crawford said then that Watkins' work was 'valueless', 'based on a misconception of primitive society and supported by no evidence'; and this statement is still quoted, fifty years later, by writers like Glyn Daniel and W. G. Hoskins, as 'proof' that Watkins' work was and is 'valueless'. And that, they say, is final.[12]

But archaeology itself has undergone some revolutionary changes in the last ten years, and Watkins' work, while not without its flaws, fits more closely into the framework of the new archaeology than can the old Diffusionist ideas. It turns out, ironically, that it was Crawford who had the 'misconception of primitive society': the new dates given by the improved radio-carbon dating, the fieldwork on archaeo-astronomy and the geometry of stone circles by Thom and others, and the new syntheses by archaeologists like Colin Renfrew and Euan MacKie all point towards a technical ability in Neolithic and Bronze Age man in Britain – particularly of surveying and selecting sites for their topographic properties – that is way beyond the conception of the archaeologists of Crawford's time.[13]

Crawford's statement that Watkins' work was 'supported by no evidence' is interesting, for as far as I can discover no serious study of Watkins' concept of the ley system has ever been undertaken, by Crawford or by any professional archaeologist. Crawford's comments are still quoted as 'proof' that the ley-system is 'chimerical'; yet Crawford, to my knowledge, never studied the evidence in the field; he dismissed the whole idea *a priori* because it could not and would not fit his view of archaeology. The archaeological 'proof', in fact, is a comfortable myth.

Archaeology is rather fond of myths like these: another one concerns the 'vitrified forts' of Scotland and Ireland. A number of forts there have at some time been subjected to such an intense heat that the rocks of which they were built have 'vitrified' and melted. In every archaeological textbook that I've seen which mentions the subject, it is stated as fact that the forts were vitrified because wooden structures inside

and beside them were set on fire by raiding parties. But this is
not a fact, this is an assumption: an assumption that is
denied by a closer study of the forts. In many cases the
structures are more heavily melted at the top, which suggests
that the heat came from the top *downwards*, not upward
from the bottom as would occur with a more ordinary fire;
and one case in Scotland is simply too big for the orthodox
explanation to work, for a half-mile length of the hillside
beside the fort was vitrified at the same time. Recent research shows that the vitrified rocks are mildly but un-
naturally radioactive; and the few studies that have been
done on the temperatures involved – which I've never seen
quoted by the archaeologists – all state conclusively that no
wood-fire can reach anything like the temperature required
to turn stone into glass, as happens in the vitrification process.[14]

We just do not know what melted and fused the rocks of
those forts. But as with the non-'study' of the ley-system, the
archaeologists have, for decades, quoted as 'fact' an untested
assumption which turns out to have little or no basis in
reality. It's sometimes useful to remember that while professional archaeological research is usually scholarly and
well-disciplined, it is every bit as speculative and fallible as
that of the 'lunatic fringe' the archaeologists despise.
Certainly no archaeologist has the right to say, as Professor
Stuart Piggott once did on a television programme, that
'only professional archaeologists can put forward ideas
about prehistory'.

So, to return to Crawford's claim that the ley-hypothesis
was 'supported by no evidence', there is in fact a great deal
of evidence for the ley-system from both map-work and
fieldwork; but most of it has been collected in such a
haphazard way and, in many cases, with so little care and
discrimination that Crawford did have a point. I know of
only one systematic ley-hunting study of a defined area that
has been done to date, and that is John Michell's study of
the megalithic sites of the West Penwith peninsula in Corn-

wall in 1974, published as his *The Old Stones of Land's End*. Michell was careful to use only those sites which were known to be prehistoric; several stones modified into Christian roadside crosses did fall into the pattern, but he regarded them as secondary evidence only, on the grounds that they might have been moved from their original sites during the early part of the Christian period.

During the survey he found twenty-two alignments between the fifty-three 'valid' sites in the area, eight of these sites being unmarked on any map. These alignments were, he said, 'of rifle-barrel accuracy', the sites being aligned precisely centre-to-centre over a distance of up to six or seven miles, an accuracy checked both in the field and with a horse-hair stretched over air-photographs of the area. By walking these alignments, Michell found not only the eight previously unrecorded sites, but also found that the sites were precisely intervisible, being placed exactly on the skyline between one site and the next. Both of these aspects of leys had been described by Watkins some fifty years before. The first systematic study of ley-type alignments was, predictably, ignored by the professional archaeologists: their evasive correspondence with Michell on the subject was subsequently published in *The Ley Hunter* magazine under the ironic heading of *The View Over Ivory Towers*.[15]

Two years later Michell's Lands End work was subjected to a detailed computer analysis by Chris Hutton-Squire and Pat Gadsby, who published their results in the alternative-technology-magazine *Undercurrents*.[16] Working mostly from maps, and working to a maximum allowed width of ten metres (but not more than one metre per kilometre), they confirmed all bar two of Michell's original alignments, and added twenty-nine more. (The two that 'failed' did so because of the difficulty of choosing where they both met the Merry Maidens stone circle: the analysis assumed that all lines went to the centre of each site, but Gadsby and Hutton-Squire suggested later that there was a better 'fit' if the lines struck the circle at the tangent.) The most striking result was that a rather insignificant stone at Sennen, near Land's End itself (Michell's 'stone 17'), had no less than seven alignments running through it, while on a randomized simulation (to give a figure for 'chance' alignment) that Gadsby and Hutton-Squire also ran through the computer the 'dummy' stone 17 had only one alignment through it: as they said in their article, 'this appears to be good evidence of deliberate alignment'.

Their randomized simulation used 'dummy' sites matched to each of the 'real' sites, but placed randomly within the same kilometre square as each of the 'real' sites, so as to produce roughly the same clustering that the 'real' sites showed. This gave a statistically acceptable figure for 'chance' alignment. The real sites produced a number of alignments that was well above the 'chance' figure – statistically, 160 to 1 in the case of the three-point alignments and 250 to 1 in the case of the one five-point alignment – and some of the 'real' lines were indeed of 'rifle-barrel accuracy',

the sites being exactly aligned with each other, with no appreciable deviation, over several miles. The other interesting point which the random simulation picked out was that, using the 'chance' figures that it gave, not only are many of the real sites aligned with each other to a greater degree than chance, but other real sites are *non*-aligned with each other: they have *fewer* alignments between them than chance would predict. This is an important point in a new understanding of leys, as I'll explain shortly. Gadsby and Hutton-Squire's statistical study is the only one to date which, to my knowledge, has handled the data available in anything resembling a scientific manner: there have been other studies, but they have been based on assumptions (particularly about ley-width, length and type of alignment) that no serious student of leys could accept.[17]

The other problem which statistical studies present is that while they show that many of the apparent alignments must be due to chance, they can't tell us which alignments are 'real', and which are not. So we're presented with another conundrum: when is an alignment a ley? For that matter, given the apparent *non*-alignment mentioned a moment ago, when is a ley an alignment? There's no easy answer. So here we come back to the whole question of what a ley is in the first place. In Watkins' original thesis it was a trackway formed between sighted intervisible points of so many incongruous types and of such different periods that it's not surprising that the archaeologists at least queried the idea.

It's true that the sites do seem incongruous, but if we compare Watkins' mark-points with Underwood's sites we find that the two lists are almost identical: a significant coincidence, I think. There's also the question of whether leys really are trackways in essence, for while sections of road and track do align with other sites, it seems from comments by several recent researchers that the ley – if it is 'real' – tends to run down the side of the track rather than down the middle of it. This suggests that the 'trackway' aspect of leys was a sort of side-effect or after-thought rather than part of the original design. Many leys make no sense at all as tracks anyway, for they do strange things like dropping over precipices, taking the longest line over marshes, and recrossing the same river many times. Apparently Watkins himself realized the limitations of the trackway hypothesis towards the end of his life, and is said to have been unhappy about the more mystical or magical interpretation of the

lines that this implied. Nevertheless, the more mystical or
magical interpretation of leys seems to be the one which is
preferred by most ley-hunters at the present time; and that
brings us back to dowsing and the overgrounds, for it seems
that the overgrounds are the semi-physical or non-physical
reality behind leys.

If the overgrounds are the reality behind leys, then it
suggests a rather different model and function for the ley-
system. The classic Watkins model states that an alignment
is a ley if a given number of sites align precisely centre-to-
centre within a given distance – typically, four sites within
ten miles – with the exception of camps and the larger 'area'
sites like big stone circles, which leys tend to meet at the
tangent rather than centre-to-centre. A true ley will be confirmed by the discovery of minor details like unrecorded
mark-stones or aligned gateways, and also by folklore
evidence; a chance alignment won't have this back-up, and
will simply feel 'wrong'. The model implied by the overgrounds agrees with this classic model in many respects,
but takes it further in a number of directions.

The first is that both the major and minor sites on a true
ley will also coincide with concentrations of Underwood's
patterns, thus apparently using the sites as connection-points
between two separate energy-systems, one below and one
above the ground. The connection between Underwood's
patterns and the 'reeling road that rambles round the shire',
to use Chesterton's phrase, is recognizable even if the cause-
effect relationship between them is not; but the connection
between the overgrounds and the occasional stretches of
ancient straight track aligned on them is anything but clear.
Some dowsers have put forward very complicated models to
explain it, involving 'colour-coding' of the energy in the
different overgrounds to mark out sections of track, but I
think the simplest and most likely answer is that, as with
Underwood's track-lines, the lines and the roads are where
they are because that's where they felt they ought to be. And
I'll leave you to decide which 'they' is the road-makers, and
which the tracks themselves . . .

Another difference between the classic model and that implied by the overgrounds is that a ley can still be real and 'active' even if one or more of its sites has been moved. The overground doesn't actually divert from its original straight course, but on reaching the original site of the mark-stone (or whatever) sends out what some dowsers have termed a 'ray of union' to connect the stone to the original line. There is an example of one of these in St Stephen's churchyard in St Albans in Hertfordshire: the three-foot-high mark-stone just inside the churchyard wall, according to Bill Lewis's and my dowsing results, was originally in the middle of the

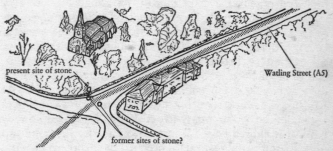

present site of stone

Watling Street (A5)

former sites of stone?

19 Path of an overground at St Stephen's church, St Albans, Hertfordshire.

ancient Watling street, which comes to a crossroads just by the church. The stone was moved at some time from the middle of the road to the footpath, and then again from the footpath into the churchyard, for the overground that runs (unusually) up the middle of the road does an apparent sharp double bend to 'talk to' the stone before carrying on on its way north. So far the maximum distance found between a moved structure and its original site, where the structure is still 'talking' in this way to the original site, is about half a mile.

In the same way there appear to be two-point overgrounds, or two-point leys, depending on how you look at them. Except in the cases of the moved sites I've just mentioned, these appear to be deliberate non-alignment so that the energy from some outlying point can be channelled exclusively to one point on the main overground: all of the two-point leys I've heard of so far have been connected to a major ley at one end. This doesn't seem to be the only aspect of non-alignment, for, as we shall see shortly, non-alignment in the sense of deliberate non-connection also seems to be important for a rather different reason.

It's also important to realize that, as Watkins did in fact imply, centre-to-centre alignment is by no means the only type of alignment, particularly on large and complex sites, or sites that have, like churches and castles, been re-used for other purposes at a later date. Overgrounds, as we saw earlier with Rollright, leave stone circles at any angle between the perpendicular and the tangent; the same seems to be true of camps, though, as Watkins noticed with his leys, camps seem to 'prefer' tangential alignment. It's more difficult to predict contact-points at re-used sites, since the later use often placed the emphasis elsewhere on the site. At Rudston in Yorkshire, for example, the church-builders couldn't destroy the twenty-five-foot high Rudstone, so they built their church beside it instead of, as elsewhere, on top of it. At some other sites I've been at, the main overground has missed the church completely, and contacted to some uninspiring little hummock on the edge of the churchyard instead. These details are very difficult to pick out in mapwork: in practice, whether by dowsing or more conventional ley-hunting, they can only be appreciated in the field.

The most important aspect of the new model is that it implies that the leys, or overgrounds, or whatever you care to call them, are mainly concerned with present-day energy rather than prehistoric commerce. This came over most clearly when, after I had done my original research on overgrounds and their relationship with leys, I found that others had been that way before me, and were talking of leys as conductors of energies of a number of different types and levels. One dowser who specialized in what might be called a form of environmental medicine told me that she often had to 'neutralize bad energy down ley-lines' in order to improve the environmental health of some farm or community. I'm told that one of the Church's great present-day exorcists started his career at an exorcism of a stone circle, working as assistant to a man who believed that the Russians were using the site as a focus for energies 'transmitted down ley-lines', energies which they were using to stir up industrial unrest. This was fifty years ago, when Watkins had only just formulated the concept of leys! Leys, as they say, ain't quite what they used to be.

If we suggest that the leys or overgrounds carry energies of various types, then since the overgrounds 'plug into' Underwood's patterns at the sites, we can also suggest that Underwood's patterns are, in much the same way, also carriers or markers of some kind of energy-flow or interaction. As above, so below. But what, you may ask, is the point or reason for all these energies to be moving about the countryside, assuming that they do exist? For a clue towards an answer we have to move to yet another area of study, Chinese geomancy or Feng-shui, which deals with the practical use of natural energies flowing both below and above the ground, in channels both sinuous and straight.

4

Sinuous and Straight

We stand on the slope of a small hillock, facing south. To our left the mountains start, sharp against the sky-line; the foothills roll gently away to our right. The blue dragon of the mountain and the white tiger of the foot-hills meet in harmony. Below us, a stream winds its way through grass and quiet trees, and beyond it is un-dulating pasture: no straight lines can be seen in the landscape. At the meeting point of Heaven and Earth, Yang and Yin are joined in perfect proportion. For Feng-shui, this is an ideal site for a dwelling place for the living or for the dead.

Feng-shui, to the Westerner, is one of those typically Chinese puzzles. The word itself, although literally it means 'wind-water', is meaningless as a description of anything. It is, say the Chinese themselves, 'a thing like wind, which you cannot comprehend, and like water, which you cannot grasp'. At one end of the scale it seems little more than an inchoate mass of superstitions to do with luck and ancestor worship; but at the same time it is a highly complex system of town and country planning whose results are in close accord with Western principles of aesthetics and environ-mental hygiene. The manipulation of Feng-shui, and the selection of sites with the most favourable Feng-shui for a client and his purposes, formed a major current in Chinese thought and practice for many centuries, and probably still continues (though in a covert fashion) under the new more materialistic dynasty. The strangest and most important thing is that, as a system of geomantic planning, it worked: for the Chinese landscape is said to be one of the most – if

not *the* most – consistently beautiful and harmonious landscapes in the world.

A large part of the landscape was made more harmonious
in the distant past – certainly before 1000 BC – by subtle
modification with earthworks and other structures. In some
cases a pointed hill has had its tip sliced off, to form a small
dome or plane; on others, originally flat-topped, pointed
mounds (later replaced by pagodas) were added to change the
outline. Water-courses were eased into gentle curves, trees
and forests planted, earthworks and embankments raised –
and all this not just for the sake of some abstract idea of
'beauty', but in the belief that to do so would definitely
improve the health and fortunes of the people living there.
The forms of nature, they believed, had been improved so as
to improve the 'breath of nature'.

We can see that in one sense at least they were right, if we
take Feng-shui in its literal sense of 'wind-water'. A south-
facing slope, well-drained and with plenty of sun, and
sheltered by mountains to ensure a good circulation of air,
would be regarded as ideal by any Western architect; it
would certainly encourage good health in anyone and anything living there. As far as people were concerned, it
could quite possibly improve their fortunes and 'luck', for
a large part of what is often called 'luck' is not only being
in the right place at the right time, but the ability to *recognize*
that you're there at the right time. That, to some extent at
least, requires a mental alertness that can only come with
good physical health. Health and fortunes *do* go together.

But the Chinese did not arrive at their definition of a
'good' site by observation, as the Westerner would have
done; instead, they reached it by a complex system of alle-
gory, analogy, astrology, numerology, geometry and heaven
only knows what else. It was, and is, far too complex a
system to memorize: in practice the Chinese geomancers
relied on a tool called the 'geomantic compass', which
was an ordinary compass surrounded by anything from
sixteen to thirty-eight rings of symbols for the various

aspects of Feng-shui, to pick out the harmonies and dis-
cordances in the landscape as predicted by Feng-shui. The
complete system is fascinating, and its analogies and correspondences have many parallels with the medieval
alchemy and astrology of Europe; but for the purposes
of our study, and our search for a new understanding of
nature, we only need look at some of its aspects.[1] The two
which I think are particularly relevant to our study are,
first, the way in which forms in the landscape are given
specific attributes and functions; and second, the underlying
and central concept of the 'breath of nature'.

Forms in the landscape are given both symbolic and allegorical attributes. At the first level, different 'elements' are
assigned to different shapes of hill, and the inter-relationship
of these elements is deemed to be one of the factors that
determines the health and fortune of the areas around and
beneath those hills. The Chinese elements are not quite the
same as their Western counterparts: they are earth, fire,
water, wood and metal, as opposed to Western earth, air,
fire, and water. The Chinese elements, as in Europe, have a
vast number of 'correspondences': for example, a pointed
hill has not just the attributes of the element fire, but also,
through correspondence, the attributes of the planet Mars,
the season of summer, the southern cardinal point, hot
weather, and all manner of other things, including its
allegorical representation as the red bird, or phoenix.

A flattened-off peak is wood, or Jupiter, and should
ideally be to the east of the chosen site; a wavy ridge is
water, or Mercury, and should be to the north; a rounded
dome is metal, or Venus, and should be to the west; and the
element earth, or Saturn, is represented by a steep-sided
plateau, which should be near the centre of the area. Some
relationships of hills are mutually constructive, others are
destructive, and others have no great effect one way or the
other. For example: to build a house by a flattened-off peak
standing close to and above a sharp peak – fire below wood,
in Feng-shui's terms – is to invite trouble from fire. The

▲	Fire	Mars	South
⌂	Wood	Jupiter	East
∿	Water	Mercury	North
⌒	Metal	Venus	West
⊓	Earth	Saturn	Centre

20 Feng-shui: hill-shapes and their elemental attributes.

geomancer would suggest that you abandon the site unless you don't mind your house being burnt down repeatedly; but if you can't abandon it, you could reduce the risk by rounding off the fire-peak to a wavy ridge to change its attribution to water, or else by building a wavy-topped tower – a water-tower in several senses – between your house and the fire-peak.

This interaction is made still more complex by the planetary and seasonal attributes of the elements, for they cause the relative strengths of the various hills to wax and wane with the seasons and the positions of the planets. This is where astrology and numerology come into Feng-shui, but we don't need to deal with them here. If all the combinations are bad at a particular time, Feng-shui predicts that they will coincide with a particular misfortune at that time – the interactions of the attributes don't so much cause misfortune as occur in exact parallel with it. For example, fire is at its weakest in winter, while water is at its strongest: so while, in summer, all will seem well with the combination of a sharp fire-peak next to a ridged water-peak, in winter the water-peak will become dominant, damping the fire of your children's lives and leading to their death in youth. Fire over metal leads to natural disasters; metal over wood leads to wasting away and injury; and so on. But if you know this beforehand, you do have a choice about what may happen to you. 'It is the boast of the Feng-shui system', wrote Reverend Eitel, 'that it teaches man how to rule nature and his own destiny by showing him how heaven and earth rule him. ... It is left in great measure to man's foresight and energy to turn his fortunes into any channel he pleases, to modify and regulate the influences which heaven and earth bring to bear upon him.'

This freedom to choose the best possible site for your own purposes, combined with the traditional Chinese belief in the ability of one's ancestors to guide one's fortunes as they pleased, led to some interesting lawsuits in the later more decadent phase of Feng-shui practice. Brothers often hired different geomancers to choose sites for their father's tomb so as best to suit the aspirations and ambitions of that brother; where the geomancers picked out different sites – which they often did – the father would remain unburied, sometimes for years, while the brothers fought over which site should be used. This is not, however, the aspect of Feng-shui which concerns us here: it is the energy aspect which is more relevant to the model of nature that we seem to be developing from our earlier study of dowsing-patterns in Britain.

This is where the allegorical form of the landscape and the 'breath of nature' come in. The five elements are seen as by-products of the interplay of the two great forces – opposed by complementary – known as Yin and Yang, and symbolized by the white tiger and blue dragon respectively. In addition to being seen in terms of the elements, the hills are also seen in terms of these two animals. Dragons are everywhere: a long ridge may be a dragon, and so may a cluster of small hills with a high mountain. Wherever there is a true dragon, there must also be a tiger: they are inseparable. There are also other allegorical descriptions of hills, such as a tortoise, or a bear, or an up-turned boat, and these all have meanings of their own; but these are tertiary influences, coming after the interplay of Yin and Yang and the five elements.[2]

The two forces are also known as the 'two breaths' or, in Chinese, *Ch'i*. (The five elements are secondary varieties of *ch'i*.) Yang is the masculine aspect, the creative inbreath; Yin is feminine, the dissolvent outbreath. Which is interesting, since I've always thought that it's the males who do the destroying, and the females the creating: but it does make sense if you think of Yang as a force which tends towards a system of order, and Yin, as a force which dissolves, under control, so that re-creation may take place. These two forces flow in currents around the countryside; the paths along which they travel may or may not have physical counterparts, but they definitely travel in winding paths, often following the contours. These paths are sometimes called '*lung mei*' or 'dragon's veins'. In ordinary countryside, a 'good' site is one just beside a point where two *mei*, one of Yin, the other of Yang, cross each other; but the geomancer would prefer to follow these veins like a dowser following a water-line, 'riding the *ch'i*' as it is called, in the hope of finding a point where several *mei* carrying the *ch'i* gather together. Such a point, I think, is what we could call a sacred site.

At a concentration of *mei*, it's also important that the two forces should be in balance with each other, and that they should both gather at and disperse from that point evenly. Again, this is where the form of the landscape came into the system, for the *ch'i* was deemed to collect and disperse according to the form of the area. Sharp mountainous land was predominantly Yang, and undulating countryside Yin: a preferred site in each area would be a Yin plateau in a mountainous area, or a steep Yang hill in undulating pasture. An example of the former in Britain would be Castlerigg stone circle, on a flat clearing amidst mountains in Cumbria in northern England; while the classic example of the latter is Glastonbury Tor, rising steeply above the fenland and the Abbey below.

If the landscape is monotonously either Yin or Yang, all

undulation or all mountains, it will have difficulty in 'breathing'; and flat country and hollows, says Eitel, 'do not breathe at all'. An unsheltered plateau is no use as a site, for the wind will blow the *ch'i* away; and fast-flowing water or steep ragged ridges will allow it to drain away too quickly to be of any use. In particular, straight lines of any kind in the landscape – whether natural or man-made – are an anathema, for they drain the *ch'i* away fastest of all.

This last may seem a little odd, if we are trying to compare Feng-shui with the energy system we seem to have in Britain, which consists of both sinuous underground energy courses and straight overground ones. The Chinese seem to have regarded sinuous as 'good', and straight as 'bad' or malefic: because of this some British writers have suggested that there is a sort of 'mirroring' between East and West as far as energy systems are concerned. This seems to be based on the assumption that the straight lines of the ley-system must be 'good', since they connect sacred sites to each other.[3] The answer to this, as we shall see, is that the energy system in Britain is more complex than just 'straight is good, bent is bad' – and so is Feng-shui. They're just not that simple.

Another important aspect of this concept of the 'breath of nature' is that it can be weakened in various ways, and even 'poisoned'. The two *ch'i*, as long as they are in balance, will tend to produce health and fertility at the sites where they meet; but they are, like the secondary *ch'i* of the five elements, subject to cyclical changes in relative strengths, which can throw them off balance at times. The geomancer would aim to predict those times by the way the currents seem to be moving, and by the direction in which the associated dragon- and tiger-hills are facing. The geomancer also has to beware of certain types of countryside, such as marshland, stagnant water, scree and other 'rotten' rocks, for they can change the whole character of the *ch'i* as it passes through them, 'poisoning' it so that it becomes *sha* or, literally, 'noxious exhalations' – a fair description of the smell of stagnant water. But *sha* goes further than just a bad smell, for it operates destructively at every level that *ch'i* operates, killing people and livestock, ruining their health and their fortunes, causing premature decay. And as we shall see, there is an exact parallel of *sha* to be found in aspects of the energy-patterns in Britain.

But Feng-shui, as a system of geomancy, is not directly comparable with those hints of an ancient system of geomancy that we've seen in Britain. For a start, Feng-shui deals essentially with the shape and form of the countryside, with little concern for stones or sacred sites: China never seems to have had a megalithic culture like that which produced the British standing stones and henges, and its use of mounds and pagodas, in a geomantic sense, seems to have been limited to modifying the elemental attributes of hills. But if we scale up another Chinese system – acupuncture – to landscape dimensions, and combine it with Feng-shui, we would have a system of geomancy that closely resembles what we can see of the megalithic geomancy in Britain. In a system of earth-acupuncture, there could hardly be a more obvious 'needle' than a standing stone.

In acupuncture theory, the body's physical and physiological processes – blood circulation, absorption of oxygen in breathing, digestion of food, information-transmission in the nerves, and so on – are all controlled and directed by the interplay of Yin and Yang and the five elements, operating in a semi-physical or non-physical way in the body. Yin and Yang and the five elements are deemed to be 'above' the ordinary processes of the body. The interplay takes place throughout the body, but it is particularly accessible on or just beneath the surface of the body – so it is on the surface, or just beneath it, that all acupuncture operations take place.

This surface movement of Yin and Yang shows itself as some kind of energy flowing through 'veins' or 'meridians' which can be plotted out on the surface of the body. (These 'veins' are not blood-veins, by the way: in Chinese the term for them is '*mei*', the same term as in Feng-shui, and these acupuncture-*mei* are deemed to work in much the same way

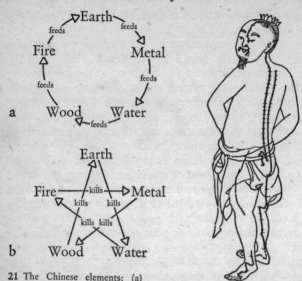

21 The Chinese elements: (a) mutual support and (b) mutual destruction.

22 A small acupuncture chart, showing two of the twelve *mei*.

as the *mei* of Feng-shui.) Different schools of acupuncture define different numbers of meridians in the body, but there seems to be some agreement that there are twelve major meridians, and any number of minor ones from thirty upwards. Each major meridian is associated with a major organ in the body, and is said to control the function of that organ.[4]

In addition to the twelve organ meridians there are a number of other meridians of varying importance, which control the remaining body processes and the interaction of each meridian with the body as a whole. So far as Chinese medicine is concerned, the body is a network of energies interacting at a number of levels. While these energies permeate every cell of the body, they appear to concentrate in these *mei* or meridians at the body's surface. As we have seen in our brief look at Feng-shui, this can be said as much of the body of the earth as of a human body.

As long as the energy-flow through the meridians remains in balance, or at least close to balance, the body will function 'normally'; but any disruption of the energy-flow, producing an excess or shortage of energy at some point, will lead to ill-health. Some imbalances occur cyclically, a sort of astronomically-linked tide-like surging: this too is normal, but it can lead to problems in the diagnosis of which part of which meridian is disrupting the normal pattern of balance during ill-health. Each meridian has a number of nodal points along its course – less than ten in some meridians, more than forty in others – which seem to act, to give an analogy, like valves or sluice-gates to control the energy-flow. It is on these nodal points – the 'acupuncture-points' – that most acupuncture therapy takes place.

Although by tradition acupuncture points are more symbolic than physically real, they have recently been found to coincide with abnormally large skin cells that happen also to have a much lower electrical skin resistance than the surrounding cells.[5] In a Kirlian-type electrophotograph of the skin they flare out like flaming torches by comparison with the rest of the skin. Some Western theorists have assumed from this that acupuncture therapy is solely electrical or electrostatic in nature,[6] but I'm certain that there's far more to it than just electrostatics. Western medicine is based on Western science, and our science is highly prone to what one writer has dubbed the 'nothing-but' mistake:[7] one example that we met earlier was John Taylor's assumption that any energy field around standing stones could be 'nothing but' electromagnetism. Electromagnetism comes into it, as does electrostatics into acupuncture: but there's more to the energies of standing stones and acupuncture than that.

Through practical experience, the Chinese discovered not just the acupuncture-points, but also the particular area or problem to which each point relates. Few of them relate in any obvious way with the area which they are supposed to control, but some do tally with Western observations: for example, the common observation that a pain running from the middle of the chest to the little finger coincides with a particular heart disease, angina pectoris, tallies with the acupuncture statement that the heart meridian runs from the little finger to the top of the arm, and there connects with the middle of the chest. There are, however, a large number of acupuncture points which can be worked on to relieve various types of heart complaint; only five of these are on the Heart Meridian, and none is at its end, the little finger. Acupuncture therapy is not simple, by any means.

As far as acupuncture is concerned, problems arise from disruptions of the energy-flow, either through blockage or leakage, or for some other reason. One type of blockage comes from bruising or scarring, and one example that one text-book I read gave should illustrate the difficulty of diagnosis in acupuncture. Westerners tend to assume that the site of any pain is also the site of the trouble that causes it: but even in Western medicine it's recognized that this is only sometimes true. The example in the text-book was of a woman who came to the acupuncturist complaining of nausea and headaches, inflammation of the eyes and pains under the rib-cage – as you can see, there's no obvious connection between her symptoms. But after careful questioning it transpired that she had broken her ankle a short time before; this had been treated, and didn't hurt, so it hadn't seemed relevant to her when she was describing her symptoms. According to acupuncture theory, this was highly relevant, for scar tissue round such a break would block the energy-flow of a meridian that led through the rib-cage, round the back and the side of the head, and ended under the eyes. Blockage at the base of this meridian would lead directly to the symptoms the woman described. Careful massage around the ankle reduced the scar tissue and the energy blockage, and everything returned to normal.

Massage is only one of the three main acupuncture

techniques. The other two are the use of the well-known needles, inserted into selected acupuncture points; and the application of heat at selected points, either by heating an already-inserted needle, or by burning a cone of *moxa* (dried leaves of Mugwort) on the surface of the skin, removing the cone as soon as the heat is only just bearable. According to the type of manipulation and the relationship between the point of action and the patient's problem, these techniques can be used to reduce blockage of energy-flow, to supplement the energy or to drain away an excess: the same technique is used with only slight variation in each case.

Any technique can be used on almost any of the many acupuncture points, but certain points are 'forbidden' to needle techniques, others to the use of moxa; a few are forbidden to either needle or moxa, and one or two that are forbidden to any technique at all. Sometimes there is an obvious physical reason – as in forbidding the use of moxa on one or two points directly below the eyes – while in other cases there seems to be no reason at all. This forbidding of the use of certain techniques at certain points has an interesting parallel, as we shall see, in what appears to be a system of earth-acupuncture in Britain.

Another major concern of the acupuncturist is with diet – and here again there is a correlation with Feng-shui, for the acupuncturist's approach to diet is based on the same concept of the interplay of the five elements, seen in diet as the five flavours. In acupuncture the element Wood is sour, Fire is bitter, Earth is sweet, Water is salty, and Metal hot, pungent or aromatic. As with the inter-relationships of the elemental shapes in Feng-shui, the inter-relationship of these elemental flavours is complex, and as before I can only give a brief summary here. Each flavour is said to enter the body through one of the five organs – liver, heart, spleen, lungs and kidneys – and to be the proper food for another; each has a particular overall effect on the body, is counteracted (if in excess) by one of the other flavours, and itself counteracts an excess of another. Sweet things, for example, are said to enter the body through the spleen, and are the proper food for the liver; they have a harmonizing effect; in excess they are counteracted by sour things, and themselves counteract an excess of salt. Whether this is true or not in terms of Western medicine is beside the point, for when used with the rest of the Chinese system of medicine it does work. I ought also to point out that the 'organs' are seen more as labels for functions rather than solely the physical organs that Western medicine recognizes; the labels 'spleen' and the like are the only practical Western translations for what were probably more generalized labels in the original Chinese.

So we can summarize the principles of acupuncture as the manipulation of energy-flow – whatever that energy might be – by means of the insertion of a needle, or the application of heat or massage, at selected points on lines of concentration of that energy. This is combined with precise control of diet, seen in terms of the balanced interplay of the five elements. The energy-flow and the balance of the elements are both in a constant state of flux, partly due to their interaction with each other, and partly due to 'outside' influences. The 'outside' influences include the inter-relationship of the two modes of the primal energy, Yin and Yang, in their various aspects as positive/negative, creative/dissolvent, masculine/feminine, Sun/Moon and the like; and also the interplay and the varying strengths of the elemental attributes of the five planets.

The parallels with Feng-shui are, I think, obvious: but the differences are important too. If we were to combine Feng-shui with a landscape-scale acupuncture, the energy-flow in the landscape could be controlled not just by shape – as in Feng-shui – but also by landscape-scale 'needles', landscape-scale heat, landscape-scale massage to reduce scars on the landscape. It's likely that a system of geomancy based more on acupuncture techniques than on shape would tend to show up the *lung mei*, the concentrations of the energy into lines or channels, more in terms of the nodes or points on those lines rather than the lines themselves; and it's also likely that there would be far more of these meridians or energy-lines on the body of the earth than on the body of a human, and that they would be laid out in far less obvious a way than in human acupuncture, for the simple reason that the landscape has no obvious organs and no obvious arms or legs or head. As you will probably have recognized, this matches the picture of the landscape implied by our study of dowsing-patterns in Britain.

A system of geomancy that combined Feng-shui with acupuncture in this way would not be 'better' than Feng-shui: it would simply be different. After all, it's still the same earth in each case, still the same energies, and even still the same concentrations of those energies: the techniques of operating upon those energies may vary, but then the techniques of building bridges – for example – may vary, though the results are still bridges, built to the same physical rules. The techniques may be different in the two approaches to geomancy, but they still operate through the same physical and not-so-physical rules.

From what I've read of Chinese geomancy, it seems unlikely that a combined system of this type was ever used in China. But it does seem likely that something close to it was used in the megalithic period and earlier in Britain, and possibly as late as the Middle Ages. Whether it was used deliberately or not, consciously or not, I do not know, and – some would say 'heresy!' – I do not particularly care: but the evidence for its existence and use seems to be there, and the parallels are certainly there. British geomancy, if it did exist, would seem to have been a system of earth-acupuncture, with the sacred sites as acupuncture points on energy-channels both sinuous and straight, and with the standing stones and the like as massive needles of stone.

5

Needles of Stone

Return to that stone circle that we saw before, glowing
and pulsing with points and lines and zones of coloured
light. As you watch, the battered and timeworn stones
seem to dislimn, becoming smoother, finer, sharper:
needles of stone set in the body of the earth, to match
the needles of bone the ancient Chinese set in the body
of man. Stone or bone, the needles controlled, and still
control, the flow of energy through each body.

But stand back – you stand too close to see. Rise up into
the air, higher, higher, like a hawk: the stone circle
recedes to a glowing dot in a landscape that rolls away
into the distance below you, a patchwork quilt of light.
Around the circle the glowing lines spread out to connect every cell of that body: you see a fine filigree of
threads just below the surface, weaving their way outward from the centre that glows; you see harsh beams of
light connecting centre to centre across the country in
straight lines. These centres are dotted along every line,
but here and there you can see major intersections of
the straight lines and the filigree, like focal points in a
vast multi-layered cobweb. In some ways the whole
scene is reminiscent of a micrograph of nerve cells and
their ganglia, but on a much larger and brightly-
coloured scale: in a sense, that is what the centres are, for
in a sense what we see here is the circulation and
nervous system of the body of the earth.

The focal points, the node-points in this matrix of
energies, are the equivalent of acupuncture-points on a
landscape scale. And set into these points are 'needles'
not just of stone, but of all the five elements: a lone Scots
Pine on a One-Tree Hill for wood, a sacred well for
water, a barrow-mound for earth, and an ancient beacon
for fire. For metal, a modern steel microwave mast, or

the postbox that replaced the mark-stone on a lonely crossroad. The pattern of the past repeats itself in the present.

It is a mistake to think of ley-lines and the like solely in terms of the past. It's true that evidence for some kind of geomancy in Britain can be found most easily by studying the placing of ancient and historical sites: but the same pattern can be seen in the siting of much more modern structures. Sometimes, as with the towers and the post-boxes, there are obvious geographical and socio-geographical reasons why this should be so; but with others, particularly the extraordinary frequency with which railway stations fall on ley-alignments, there is no sensible reason.[1]

This leads us back to the same questions that Underwood avoided: Are the patterns, the matrix of energies, the patterns of the past or present, or both? If there was a system of geomancy in the past, was it applied with or without conscious knowledge? And if it was applied consciously and deliberately in the past, as Underwood and most of the recent writers on the 'earth mysteries' have maintained, do we have to credit the Victorian railway-builders and the present-day Post Office and Ministry of Defence with conscious knowledge of the same system of geomancy? The more we look into it, the more confusing and improbable the whole field becomes.

There is one solution to this set of conundrums which every writer seems to have avoided, and that is the pagan solution: that the earth is not only alive, but intelligent, and capable of a crucial if limited range of actions on a number of levels. The aim of any system of geomancy, in pagan terms, is to locate and identify sites where human actions of one kind or another would – to put it in anthropomorphic terms – please or displease the earth: as Eitel put it, 'it is the boast of the (geomantic) system that it teaches man how to rule nature and his own destiny by showing him how heaven and earth rule him'. It is indeed 'left in great measure to man's foresight and energy . . . to modify and regulate the influences which heaven and earth bring to bear upon him', but not all the choices are due to man: something else has choices too. That 'something else', or at least part of it, is the earth itself.

This probably sounds insane, when seen from a 'common-sense' viewpoint; and in those terms I suppose it is. But it's only in the past few centuries that 'common-sense' has become so blinkered that it denies the very existence of vast areas of human experience. It is only when you realize the full scope of geomancy – stretching far into the distant past, and including as it does many areas of experience that modern 'common-sense' ignores – that you realize the inevitability of the pagan solution. It is the pivot around which all of the 'earth mysteries' begin to make sense.

But we haven't got there yet: and I don't think it can make sense until we have a clearer idea of what this geomantic 'earth-acupuncture' is, and what the energy – or energies – that it is supposed to control are, so we'd better return to those first. To talk of an earth-acupuncture presupposes the existence of something equivalent to both acupuncture meridians and acupuncture-points. The leys or overgrounds and Underwood's water-lines (and possibly also his track-lines and aquastats) would seem to be equivalent to meridians, while sacred sites would seem to be the equivalent of acupuncture-points. If we can assume – for the moment at least – that this is so, then we do have at least the basics of a system of earth-acupuncture.

It's not just the obvious sacred sites, like churches and standing stones, that form the 'acupuncture-points' of this earth-acupuncture: the pre-Christian pagans in Britain recognized a wide range of types of site to have special characteristics that set them apart from the rest of the land-scape. These include not only those sites whose use was forbidden by later pro-Christian law – 'we strictly forbid . . . the worship of . . . sun or moon, fire or flood, water wells or stones, or any kind of wood-trees', as Canute's

'Laws' of 1030 AD put it[2] – but also those picked out and
emphasized by local folklore: particular cross-roads,[3]
bridges, fords, castles, forts and barrows. Note, though,
that it's only particular cross-roads, particular barrows:
some visually impressive examples have no folklore and no
local importance attached to them, while others have plenty
of folklore and seem, in the case of barrows, to be concealing
more than just an ancient burial. If we combine both law and
lore, we can see that all the types of site that Watkins and
Underwood and their followers researched are represented;
and we already know from their work that such sites are
interconnected both above and below ground. Watkins' and
Underwood's work, when viewed from an 'earth-energies'
angle, does fit in with an 'earth-acupuncture' model of
nature.

The system of geomancy I'm suggesting would be a
combination of acupuncture and Feng-shui: from what we
can see of the sites it seems likely that any structure at the
site will act as a 'needle' in an acupuncture sense. We can
suggest, then, that different characteristics of the site and its
structure – elemental attribution, shape, astronomy, number,
colour and so on – will select the effect the site has on the
flow and interchange of energies at and through the site.
We can see in Canute's list, for instance, the elements Fire,
Wood and Water; barrows and earthworks are obviously
Earth in terms of their elemental attribution; but it seems
that in the past the elemental Metal was not used or represented. It may be that in the early period hard stone was
equivalent to Metal; but we can see that in the present time
there is far too much Metal, and it seems that the only
element 'worshipped' is Metal, combined with the lifeless-
ness of concrete. But that is something for later.

The element Water can be seen in Watkins' ley-ponds and
other water mark-points, and in Underwood's 'holy wells'.
It seems odd to think of water at a sacred site as a 'needle',
and it may be that it is more a needle in reverse, a needle of
nothing connecting the energies of the water to the outside

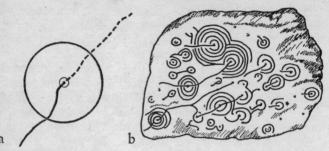

23 Cup-and-ring-marked stones as possible maps: (a) simple Creyke depthing pattern in dowsing, and (b) cup-and-ring marks on a stone at Old Bewick, Northumberland. *(after WH Matthews, Mazes and Labyrinths, Longmans 1922)*

air. There may be a needle connected to the water, as in Creyke's system of depthing which we met earlier; if so, it's possible that one interpretation of the mysterious 'cup-and-ring' marks to be seen on stones in various parts of Britain would be that they are maps of local water and energy networks, shown up by the circles and dots to which the Creyke system converts the water-lines, as far as the dowser is concerned. There are other interpretations of the cup-and-ring marks, of course, but this one has a certain degree of elegance from a dowser's point of view. But to return to the element Water, it may be that 'holy wells' and the other Water points are not so much controllers of the energies as tapping points from which to withdraw energies as needed. The adjective 'holy' does seem to imply this: linguistically the word has many links and meanings, and these include 'whole', 'hale', 'healthy' and 'healing' as well as the obvious sense of 'sacred'.

The element Fire should be obvious, as the fires of the old pagan festivals of Beltane and Hallowe'en; as the Beacon fires on the old beacon hills (the real 'needles of fire', perhaps); and as the wend-fires or need-fires that were lit by peasants during times of livestock disease until well into the last century. These latter fires were lit at particular points on

local trackways; the entire livestock of the area were then
driven through the flames in the hope of curing and protect-
ing them of the murrain. It seems to have worked, or the
peasants would never have done it.[4] It could have worked
partly by a crude high-temperature sterilization of the skin,
to kill off infective bacteria on the surface; but I think there
is probably an element of 'needles of fire' or moxibustion
there as well. The Beacon fires may also have had a double
function, agents of moxibustion as well as 'needles of fire'.

It's interesting to note, thinking of the Beacons, that very
few of the Beacon hills had any structure on them. It seems
as though they were 'forbidden to structure', analogous to
'forbidden to needle' in acupuncture, although there is also
the point that any structure high up on the hill might have
obscured the flame and reduced the Beacon's effectiveness as
part of a communications chain. The reverse is true of some
sites, in that they seem to be 'forbidden to Fire'. The owner
of Rollright stone circle often held a firework party there
around Hallowe'en each year, until recently. She had candles
placed, in jam-jars, on almost every stone, so that the circle
glowed with points of coloured light; but she had no bonfires. 'The very idea of having a bonfire here seems wrong,
my dear', she said, 'the stones wouldn't like it'. She was
probably right: and the 'feel' of a site can tell us a great
deal about it.

The element Earth is represented by earthworks in general,
whose functions are more complex than those of the
Beacons. All the varieties of earthworks seem to act as
energy stores or reservoirs that stabilize the energy-flow
passing through them: but the way they store the energy
depends on their shape. Round barrows, and possibly long
barrows, store their energy statically, like water in a tank;
where barrows are closely linked to standing stones they
may have a special storage function which I'll come back to
shortly. But the other earthworks store their energy in a
different way: for the energy trapped within them is constantly on the move.

I first discovered this during some work on Gors Fawr stone circle in Pembrokeshire. I'd just been studying the 'spin' energy moving round the perimeter of the circle, and was surprised to find an energy-flow almost identical to the 'spin' crossing a gateway that had been cut through a nearby stone-and-earth 'hedge'. The flow crossed the gateway at about waist-height, almost exactly level with the middle of the 'hedge's' cross-section. If I remember correctly, the energy was moving in both directions across the gap at that height. But this was only one aspect of a maze of energies moving very fast backwards and forwards inside the stone 'hedges' surrounding Gors Fawr; I had only found the energy in the gateway because it was jumping the gap between the two sections of that hedge. Further along the same hedge, part of the structure of the hedge had been broken down to make room for a road-widening scheme: the stored energy came ripping out of the broken edge, hung around for a moment, apparently trying to find something to hold on to, and then shot back inside the 'hedge'. The broken edge seemed to be 'boiling' with loose energy in this way. When we look at practical earth-acupuncture, we shall see that 'loose' energy of this sort can cause some serious problems.

Circular structures, like henges and ring-ditches, store their energy by moving it round the circle, jumping any gaps as necessary, like the 'spin' of stone circles; more complex earthworks, like some of the so-called 'hill-forts', hold the energy locked in each section. There is a visual analogy between this energy storage and the 'trapping' of high-energy physical particles by the earth's magnetic field in the two Van Allen belts about two and ten thousand miles above the earth's surface. Loose electrons are caught in the higher of the two belts; the heavier protons are trapped in the lower belt. The amount of energy involved is very high, and poses serious problems for space-flights: to give an idea of the level of energy, on average it only takes the electrons in the upper belt two seconds each way in their endless travelling from one magnetic pole to the other, and back again.

We can use this as an analogy for one of the functions of the 'hill-forts'. The complex 'hornwork' of forts like Maiden Castle, which was undoubtedly a fort in later days, may

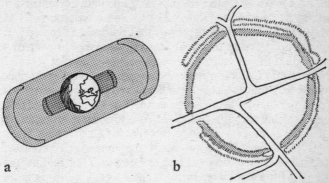

a   b

24 Shape and energy-storage: (a) the earth's Van Allen radiation belts, and (b) the earthworks at Avebury, Wiltshire.

originally or incidentally have been designed as an energy-store, being derived from a barrow-complex already existing on the site. It's generally admitted by archaeologists that many of the hill-forts are derived from the linking together of very early hill-mounds, and that some of the fort-like earthworks are too poorly sited or simply too big to have been much good as defensive structures.[5] Many hill-structures only became true hill-forts – defensive forts, in other words – during the Bronze and Iron Ages; there doesn't seem to have been much need for them before then, as the relative rarity of weapon-burials in the Neolithic period appears to confirm.

The shape of the structure seems to control some of the energy aspects of certain other types of site, particularly standing stones, stone circles and churches in Britain, and temples in general elsewhere. Alexander Thom has shown the complex geometry of stone circles in Britain: and that geometry seems, from my own experience, to play an important part in the site's control of energy, particularly energy coming in to the site on astronomically-linked pulses. Of churches, we know for a fact that the Gothic cathedrals at least were designed to precise geometric formulae for more than just structural reasons.[6] Some writers, such as Keith Critchlow, have demonstrated the use of geometry in sacred architecture to reveal – and presumably to control – 'the descent of spiritual energy into material form'.[7] Michell and Critchlow have also shown the complex number symbolism that seems to have been used in sacred structures from the time of Stonehenge to the late Gothic cathedrals, and possibly through to the sacred and secular architecture of seventeenth-century architects like Sir Christopher Wren and Inigo Jones.[8] This geometry and numerology controls the shape of the structure; and as Feng-shui has told us, the shape of the structure, in geomantic terms, controls more than just its visual appearance.

We can also see that some of the standing stones and mark-stones dotted around Britain would appear to have been chosen and sited according to their shapes. The most obvious example of this is at Avebury, where the stones of the Kennett Avenue are alternate pillar and diamond or lozenge shape; but in other districts it seems that shapes were chosen for something other than or additional to the 'male and female' interpretation that Professor Piggott gave to the Avenue stones. Watkins, in some of his beautiful photographs, showed how the shapes of mark-stones seemed to echo the shapes of the hills on which they were aligned.[9] Stones like the Devil's Arrows at Boroughbridge in Yorkshire, the nearby and similar Rudstone at Rudston, and the Fish Stone at Cwmddu in Gwent, seem literally to be 'needles' or 'nails' driven into the ground. Watkins pointed out that the common coincidence of mark-stones with markets, and thus the placing of money on the stone, may have led to the phrase 'paying on the nail'.[10]

Recent research in various countries suggests that particular shapes enable objects to give off or store energy, or convert it to some other form of energy. Sometimes the energies involved are clearly physical, as with the ball-shape that enables a Van der Graff electrostatic generator to store enormous electrostatic charges; but sometimes the energies are not so obviously physical. Pavlita in Czechoslovakia is generally credited with the discovery (or rediscovery) of many 'multi-energy' shapes, including a range of 'psychotronic generators' that revolve when you think at them in a particular state of mind, a toroid shape which appears to kill flies within its space, and another which purifies polluted water, allegedly changing the molecular structure of the water in the process.[11] Another recent discovery has been the way in which food stored in particular geometric shapes seems to keep fresher and longer than otherwise.[12]

But there are hidden catches to this that we ought to beware of. I ought to give a warning here: the energies involved are real, even if they are 'imaginary' in some cases – so if you just play about with the shapes in the hope of attracting energies, without knowledge of what you're doing, you may find yourself in trouble or danger. A friend of mine, whom I'll call Peter, had an experiment of this type go wrong at Stonehenge, when he was using an *ankh*-shape as an aerial. The ankh was a big one, nearly two feet high, made out of cooker wire in outline form, to resemble a dipole aerial. The aim of the experiment was to see if the ankh could be used to pick up energy from the circle – and it succeeded rather too well.

He climbed onto the roof of a car in the Stonehenge car park (he's not very tall) and, holding the ankh by the loop at the top, and pointing the open end away from him, he moved the ankh like a scanning radar aerial. The moment this 'aerial' came into line with the stones he felt an enormous surge that seemed to burn his arm, and he lost consciousness for a moment. When he recovered from that, he found that he had been – as another friend put it – 'thrown bodily off the car', and his arm seemed to be paralysed. It took six months before he was able to use the arm fully again. Whether the paralysis was objective or subjective, it was still 'real' from a practical point of view. So please *don't* play around with these energies: we don't yet know enough about them to know in detail what is safe and what is not.

Even the well-researched pyramid-shape springs surprises. My friend Peter, and another friend, Richard, were doing some experiments with a hollow wooden pyramid which had a quartz crystal at its tip. Both said they could feel some kind of energy coming off the tip as a stream of upward-moving heat. Peter warned Richard to take his watch off, as 'the energy might damage it'; the watch was a new quartz-controlled digital type, and Richard, thinking vaguely of the stray magnetic fields he dealt with all the day in his job as a recording engineer, ignored the comment, as those magnetic fields don't affect the kind of quartz oscillator used in the watch. Unfortunately, the energy from the pyramid did affect it. A few minutes after the comment, Richard noticed that the display on the watch was visibly flickering; then it slowed, stopped and faded away.

Richard checked the battery, but the watch's back-light was working normally, showing that the battery was still 'live'. Frantically pressing every button on the watch, he managed to restart it – but he found, on checking with the telephone 'speaking clock', that it was losing one second in ten. Half an hour later the display faded out again, and no amount of button-pressing would restart it. Since the watch was still under guarantee, Richard took it back to the importers to be repaired. They were somewhat surprised, for it was the only watch of that type that they'd ever had returned. I don't know if Richard ever told them how he broke it, but I'm not sure that they would have believed him anyway.

The importers didn't repair the watch, they simply replaced it, but it's interesting to speculate on what had happened to it. There are only four parts to a digital watch: the quartz oscillator, the electronic 'chip', the display unit and, of course, the battery. The battery was 'live', for they had checked that; the display unit seemed to be working normally, and anyway wouldn't affect the time-keeping ability of the watch. This leaves only the 'chip' and the oscillator. The circuitry in the 'chip' – which is itself mostly 'doped' quartz – drives the oscillator and counts and converts the oscillator's pulses into a form suitable for display. There's not much that can go wrong with it, and if it does go wrong it tends just to stop, not slow down. The only way in which the oscillator can slow down is if its shape is changed, for its oscillation frequency depends on its shape. So for the watch to go wrong in the way that it did, it would seem that the energy from the pyramid either overloaded the 'chip' electronically, or physically distorted either the 'chip', the oscillator, or both – which isn't bad going for a force which many so-called scientists claim doesn't exist.

Quartz is interesting to us in this study for a number of reasons, not least of which is that it is one of the few common factors among standing stones. To my knowledge, it is found in some form or another in every type of rock used for standing stones. Its traditional use in magical and initiatory rites around the world suggests that it has values on more than one level,[13] while its strange mechano-electrical properties may provide an explanation on at least one level both for the magnetic fields reported by Taylor to be round a standing stone, and for the 'tingling' or 'charged' feeling that many dowsers and non-dowsers have experienced from the stones.

Silica, the basic compound from which all the quartzes are derived, is the most abundant mineral in the earth's crust, so it's not so surprising that it is a common factor in standing stones. Sandstones and conglomerates are chiefly composed of small quartz crystals, and it is found in veins in some rocks, like the veins of milky quartz crystals that can often be seen in granite. On some standing stones you can even see large chunks of the milky quartz standing out from

D

the surface of the stone. The milky form is the one which most people recognize as quartz; but with the addition of various impurities a whole family of quartzes are formed, a surprising variety of semi-precious crystals and stones: amethyst, citrine, cairngorm, chalcedony, carnelian, agate, flint, onyx and jasper are all members of the quartz family, and all are basically silica. The magical use of these gems and semi-precious stones goes back for millennia; but I've also seen modern dowsers use some of them to manipulate the effective energy-flows in water-lines and overgrounds. For the moment, though, it is the mechano-electric (or 'piezo-electric') aspects of the quartzes which is the most interesting to us, for it provides us with one way of understanding the basis of that elusive 'natural energy' that we have supposed is carried by the water-lines and overgrounds.

The principle of the mechano-electric effect is simple, and it is used a lot in modern technology. In a 'once-only' form it's used in 'electronic' gas lighters and similar tools that produce a single electrical spark; and in a 'resonant' form, it's used in radios, electrical clocks and watches, and any other electronic bits and pieces that need stable oscillators. The idea is that if you apply an electrical charge to a quartz crystal it will change shape or, in some thin crystals, its curvature; and conversely, if you change the crystal's shape, particularly by compression, it will produce a relative electrical charge across its faces. The quartz family aren't the only crystals that will do this, by the way: the tourmaline family will do it as well.

If you apply pressure to one of these crystals fast enough and hard enough – as with the spring driven 'hammer' used in some gas lighters – charges of several thousand volts can be produced across the crystal, enough for a spark strong enough to light a gas jet. If you apply a charge to a crystal that is already under some tension, the crystal will initially expand or curve, but then spring back (producing a momentary opposite charge) and then expand again if the original charge is maintained. This leads to a resonance, both mechanically and electronically, with the crystal alternately expanding and springing back like an electronic tuning fork. This precisely regular oscillation can be used in a number of ways: controlling an electronic frequency in a radio transmitter, for example; for providing a regular flow of electronic pulses for a quartz digital watch; or a regular flow of mechanical pulses for a quartz analogue watch.

The frequency of the crystal's resonance depends on its size, shape and cut; and here we return to the quartzes in standing stones. We know from dowsing work that standing stones are placed over underground water-flows, which might well produce regular mechanical vibration under some stones; we also know from dowsing research that some of the energies are linked to a lunar cycle, so gravitational links could produce another regular change of the mechanical forces acting on some stones. We could thus expect that the stones might 'resonate' in some way. Certainly some stones do feel as though they rock slowly backward and forward when you lean on them, and others seem to 'buzz'.

This difference in what is admittedly a subjective oscillation could be explained, perhaps, in terms of the different sizes and shapes of natural crystals in each stone applying oscillating charges or deformations when people 'earth' them to the ground around the stone. Many standing stones are not so much poor conductors as semi-conductors, according to the initial results of some experiments some friends and I are doing: their electrical conductivity seems to change according to a variety of conditions, and one of them is whether various points on the stone are 'earthed' either by wires or by people. I don't know of any 'official' scientific research on this, other than Taylor's search for magnetic anomalies around the Crickhowell stone, but I wouldn't be surprised if this is at least the physical reason why the Tingle Stone at Avening got its name. It may also have been behind the magnetic anomaly that Taylor found at Crickhowell, but I don't yet know enough about the interaction between oscillating electrical fields inside the semi-conducting substance of a stone and the apparently stable magnetic field around it.

Quartz crystals can also be 'excited' electronically to produce extremely high-frequency radio waves, called microwaves. If this is done in a particular way to crystals of a particular shape the waves so formed come off the crystal at such precisely regular intervals that they form a very narrow beam. This is called 'microwave amplification by stimulated emission of radiation'; the abbreviation of the term, 'maser', is usually applied to the assembly that does this. The visible-light version, which works in much the same way but at a still-higher frequency, is the well-known laser.

There are various types of laser, but the original type used a ruby crystal which had a small proportion of chrome impurity in it. It's the chrome in a natural ruby that colours it red: pure ruby is colourless. The crystal used was a short rod which was fully silvered at one end, but only thinly silvered at the other. Light was 'pumped' into the crystal by repeated flashes from a flash-tube – usually a spiral flash-tube in the early versions. The energy was stored by altering the atomic structure of the chrome atoms in the ruby crystal, until a kind of saturation point was reached. Then one chrome atom, then another, then another, would release the stored energy in the form of red light: there was a kind of chain reaction, in which each atom released its energy when triggered by any other, but only when the distance between the first and second atom was an exact multiple of the wave-length of the light produced. By bouncing the light backwards and forwards inside the crystal, by means of the silvered ends, all the stored energy could be retrieved in one chain-reaction, and finally released from the half-silvered end of the crystal as a very brief pulse of precisely regular light.

All the energy of the light is concentrated into one brief moment, and can be made to do physical work: laser pulses are now used to compress particles to start fusion reactions in nuclear fusion reactors for power plants, and even the early lasers were rated in 'gillette power', the number of razor blades they could punch through in one go. And the pulses of a powerful ruby laser can be very short: the laser used in the moon-ranging experiments after the Apollo landings produced a pulse so brief that the beam was better described as a rod of light only thirty yards long, and the beam's spread was so slight that it was little more than three hundred yards wide when it reached the moon. But what is interesting to us here is that the presence of certain types of quartz in some standing stones may lead to a kind of 'stone maser' or, as one punning friend put it, a 'leyser'.

The closest parallel here comes between ruby lasers and the oolitic limestone used for some standing stones: the Tingle Stone is one example. Oolitic limestone is composed of 'eggs' of limestone formed round a central core of quartz or, occasionally, sea-shell, by much the same process as the formation of a pearl. The parallel here is between the quartz 'seeds' in the limestone and the chrome atoms in the ruby. It seems possible that mechanical vibration from the stream below, or the spiral energy-flow round the stone (note the analogy with the old lasers' spiral flash-tube), or both, could provide energy to be stored by the quartz 'seeds': electro-mechanical charge from the ground, and possibly some not-so-physical energy from the spiral round the stone. As with the ruby laser, this energy storage should reach a critical or super-critical state, at which any suitable stimulus would set the whole thing off. A 'suitable stimulus' might be a gravitational alignment, perhaps, or the tiny electrical and non-physical charges produced in the finger-tips of a dowser spinning a pendulum next to the stone. If this were to be so, the result would be the same kind of 'massive pulse of energy travelling in a straight line' that I noticed when I accidentally released the 'spin' energy at Rollright.

One point where this analogy appears to break down is

that, given the shape of the typical standing stone, its base in the ground would be the equivalent of the 'fully-silvered' end of the laser crystal, and the tip as the 'half-silvered' end; so we would expect the pulse to go skyward, not horizontally across country in a straight line. This puzzled me for some time, for the analogy seemed to be so close; and it was not until I found a reference to quartz in an old dowsing journal that I found anything resembling a solution. The reference was unfortunately only an abstract of an article from a German dowsing magazine, but it stated that it was important to beware of quartzes and flints in buildings, when dealing with 'earth energies', for they 'changed the plane of the radiations from the vertical plane to the horizontal'.[14] If quartz can turn its own 'radiations' from the vertical to the horizontal plane, we would appear to have our 'leyser'.

Unfortunately that change of plane doesn't make sense in physical terms, so I think we'll have to say that the energies which this 'leyser' transmits are at the most only semi-physical. But there is another aspect of British geomancy in which physical energies play a large part, and that is to do with lightning and a possible system of weather-control.

The correlation between lightning, certain types of trees, and underground water is important here. If you walk around forests you will have noticed that certain types of trees – oaks in particular – are often blasted by lightning, while other types – beeches, for example – are rarely struck. Some dowsers researching this found that every tree which was struck was sited on or very close to an intersection of two or more water-lines;[15] so the apparent reason why only certain types of trees are struck is related to the way in which those types of tree collect their water. According to dowsing work, it would seem that the oaks prefer to collect their water direct from underground water-courses, while the beeches and similar trees collect theirs from the percolation of water from the surface. Dowsers use these differences sometimes to pick out possible water supplies: I remember one farm I went to had two willow trees growing in place of two cherry trees in a cherry avenue, because the water-line underground at that point had made the conditions below the ground too wet for the cherry trees to survive.

The dowsers also noticed that in open country, wherever it was possible to plot the exact position of the strike, lightning invariably struck directly above the intersection of two or more water-lines. There are good physical reasons for this, of course. A lightning bolt is a massive electrical charge trying to find the quickest route to discharge itself, and that means that it has to find the quickest route of highest conductivity within its immediate area. The jagged path of the strike through the air is known to be due to its following slight variations of conductivity: but no-one seems to have thought in similar terms about its landing point.

The charge has to dissipate very fast, and in electrical terms a damp area of ground would be its best bet. Something as damp and that spreads over such a long distance as a water-line would be a very fast pathway for dissipating a charge, and a point where two or more water-lines meet would be better still, from the lightning's point of view. Whether the water-line represents a true underground stream or just a trickle of water in a water-bearing fissure matters not a whit in this respect, since it is still a damp 'cable' for the lightning. Neither does it matter that the water the water-line represents is some way underground, for at an intersection of water-lines in particular the conductivity between that intersection and the surface will still be somewhat higher than that of the surrounding ground. Even if the conductivity is only marginally higher, the lightning will probably still take that route in preference to any other. If this is so, it means more than that the old adage of 'lightning never strikes the same place twice' is wrong: it means that we can use the connection between the water-lines and lightning to build up a limited but effective system of weather-control.

The key to this is the function of the lightning conductor. We tend always to think of these solely as conductors, leading any lightning-strike to earth: but this is only the 'passive' part of their function. A lightning-conductor can also have an 'active' mode of operation, counteracting the charge of a thunderstorm before any lightning occurs; this isn't so obvious as the 'passive' mode, because its effectiveness depends on the siting of the conductor. A conductor *is* simply a conductor: we should remember that it can conduct *both* ways, not just from the sky to earth, but from the earth to the sky as well. The conductor *connects* earth and sky.

Because it connects the two, it tries all the time to stabilize their charges in relation to each other. If a positively-charged cloud passes overhead, the conductor will collect a negative charge from the surrounding area, and try to push it up to the sky to eradicate the difference between earth and sky. With most conductors, sited on 'ordinary' sites, the charge that the conductor will be able to collect will be minute, even in wet conditions; but even so, because the charge has to come from somewhere, and because that somewhere is the ground in which the conductor is set, the ground around the conductor will have a net shortage of negative charge (in this case), and will, effectively, be positively charged in relation to other points on the surface. Any lightning strike from a positively-charged cloud will be

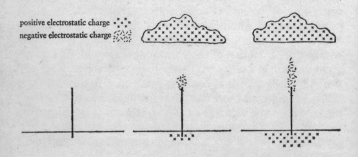

25 Lightning conductor collecting charge from an 'ordinary' area.

looking for somewhere that is negatively charged in relation to the surrounding ground; so by inducing an effective positive charge in the ground beneath itself, the conductor makes the ground less liable to a lightning strike.

The area that the conductor protects varies according to the type of conductor: probably the least efficient is the flat-strip type fitted to factory roofs, but even these will protect an area swept by an angle of about 50° downward from their run.[16] The most effective kind is the old-fashioned 'spike' type, and this, once again, is due to its shape. The distribution of charge on a surface is dependent on the radius of curvature at each point – the sharper the point, the higher the relative density of charge. On a stormy night you can sometimes see the charge coming off one of these old-fashioned conductors as a faint glow, or even as the strange 'St Elmo's Fire.'

Because of the high density of charge on the tip of a spike, a spike-type conductor can literally 'spray' charge upward into the sky – and it is this 'spraying' of charge that we see as St Elmo's Fire. With a conductor sited in ordinary ground this 'spraying' can't last long, because the relatively low conductivity of ordinary ground limits the amount of charge

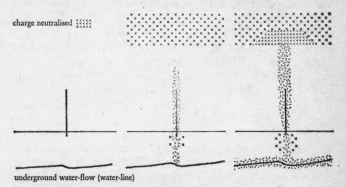

charge neutralised

underground water-flow (water-line)

26 Lightning-conductor sited on a water-line, collecting charge from an underground water-flow to produce an 'electric wind'.

that the conductor can collect from the surrounding area. But a conductor placed directly over – or even close to – a water-line or, better, an intersection of water-lines, should be able to collect charge from the whole area the stream under-lies. In some circumstances a conductor sited over water-lines could put up enough charge to neutralize the charge of the cloud. It would be rather more liable to lightning strikes than an ordinarily sited conductor, because the charge it induces in the ground is relatively low; but if it can put up enough charge as the charged cloud comes into the area, there wouldn't be any lightning to strike it anyway.

A side-effect of this is that since a high charge moves off a point as an 'electric wind' – a vertical 'wind' in this case – a conductor 'spraying' a high charge into the sky would send up a charged air-stream as well. This air-stream will carry up with it a fair amount of dust, grit, bits of leaves and so on, all of them becoming charged by the 'wind' in the process. It is around charged dust particles and the like that rain-drops form: so the effect of a lightning conductor connected to water-lines would be to change a potentially violent thunder-storm into an ordinary rainstorm.

This only applies, though, to a lightning conductor in the unusual position of being close to a network of water-lines, and preferably major water-lines at that, if the collection of charge is going to be fast enough to deal with a large area of charged cloud. But we already know from dowsing work that most if not all types of sacred sites are so placed, so we can suggest that the structures upon those sites could be made to 'control' the weather in the same way.

Frazer, in the *Golden Bough*, commented that in Europe at least, the points where lightning struck were regarded as sacred, and suggested that the frequency with which the oak was struck by lightning was the reason why it came to be regarded as a sacred tree: the lightning, he suggested, gave the tree 'a nimbus of glory'.[17] We now have another way in which certain types of structures and sites – par-ticularly church spires, standing stones and 'sacred groves' –

could gain a 'nimbus of glory', a visible nimbus of glory, and that is from the visible glow of the charge around them, collected from the streams below during a thunderstorm. Under those circumstances they would literally be 'glowing points in the landscape'.

We can go further than this, and say that the standing stones and circles not only might have controlled thunder-storms in the past, but that they still do to some extent. Megalithic sites are in the right places, and their shapes and semi-conductor properties would help the production of an 'electric wind'. This is not just speculation, for there is statistical evidence for it from another quarter, or at least evidence which could be interpreted in this way. If you look at a distribution map of the surviving megalithic sites in Britain, you'll find that they are mostly sited in the west of the land-mass, particularly in the south-west and north of England, and a very large number up the Atlantic coast of Scotland. There are so many sites on the Island of Jura, for example, that Alexander Thom said he couldn't understand why they were there: some of them, he suggested, could have been used as lunar observatories, to calculate and predict the complex tides of the area, but even so there was simply no need for that many sites.[18]

But if you compare this with the weather distribution maps of Britain, there is a correlation between megalithic sites and weather-patterns – particularly of rainfall and thunderstorm activity. Admittedly there are some geographical reasons for the higher rainfall in the west of Britain, but they could be expanded to include the distribution of the old megalithic sites. The coincidence between the distribution of the sites and thunderstorm activity – or rather the lack of thunder-storm activity – is even more striking. The Electrical Research Association publishes maps of the distribution of thunderstorm-days in each year. The largest number of thunderstorm-days shown on the last map I saw was shared by London and Yarmouth, in East Anglia; the area of East Anglia generally was heaviest hit by lightning, and shortest on megalithic sites. The number of thunderstorm-days fell off fairly steadily to the west, except for a 'high' area that coincided almost exactly with the big conurbations of the Midlands; and the area with the smallest number of thunderstorm-days – none at all, in fact – was the Island of Jura. A 'mere coincidence'? I don't think so.

The coincidence becomes more striking still when you realize that the distribution map shows thunderstorm-*days*, not the amount of energy involved in each storm. Thunderstorms in Cornwall, for example, may not come very often, but when they do come they can be of staggering ferocity; London and the east of the country may have many days with thunderstorms, but the storms themselves are rarely more than a few feeble flickers and bangs. If we take the eastern storms to be 'normal', it looks as though storms in the west and north are somehow stored until a sort of saturation point is reached: for while the west may have fewer days of thunderstorms, the overall amount of energy expended in each area is probably much the same.

This idea that the energy of thunderstorms might somehow be locked up or stored until some kind of reservoir reaches bursting point brings us back to the idea of barrows as energy-stores, and to an interesting piece of archaeological folklore. There's always been a folk-superstition that some kind of 'divine retribution' follows the 'desecration' of ancient sites, particularly barrows. If you look back through the records, you'll find that this superstition has a basis in fact, for in the case of some barrows a thunderstorm followed within hours or minutes of the opening of the barrow.[19] The same coincidence still occurs from time to time, as happened when a barrow on Parliament Hill in north London was opened recently; and I've heard that it is apparently a respectable piece of professional lore among present-day archaeologists. What is not respectable is to suggest that there might be a causal link between the breaching of the barrow and the thunderstorm that followed.

But it does make sense, even if not in archaeological terms.

It seems only to have occurred with a few of the thousands of barrows that have been plundered over the centuries, but the effect on breaching them was exactly like short-circuiting some kind of 'thunderstorm capacitor'. Henges seem to be 'capacitors' too, as a friend of mine found out: he and a group of fellow-researchers were doing a ley-line survey of a stone circle and were soaked through by an 'instant rain-storm', which only lasted two minutes, when they accident-ally triggered something in or around the circle. What is interesting, from the point of view of our hypothetical 'earth-acupuncture', is that the downpour started the moment they rammed a stake into the ground at the circle exactly on line with the ley they were plotting.

We've seen that it makes some degree of sense to suggest that standing stones and the like have the same 'thunder-storm-control' ability as lightning conductors. We know from archaeological evidence, or from simple observation, that barrows and henges are often associated with standing stones and circles. And we know from dowsing evidence that barrows and henges and the associated stones and stone circles are on the same water-lines, and are thus connected in an electrical-cum-electrostatic sense at least. From this we can build up a picture of a more complex system of weather control, based on standing stones, with the barrows or henges as energy-stores, in which the stones have two modes of operation.

The first is the counteracting mode that we saw before, where the stone 'sprayed' charge into the cloud, and received rain in return. The second mode would need to be employed if the area the charged cloud covered was too big to allow the stone to collect 'spare' charge from outside its area – as can often happen, for the whole country is sometimes covered by one cloud-mass. This would be a 'draining and storing' mode, in which the charge of the cloud was drawn off by the stones and stored in the associated barrow or barrow-complex (such as a henge), to be dispersed slowly at a later stage. Given this, we could expect that 'short-circuiting' a barrow by breaching it would release all the stored energy through the associated stones, producing an immediate thunderstorm. Hence the folk-superstition, for the immediacy of the thunderstorm would certainly seem like 'divine retribution'.

The only trouble with this more complex form of weather-control is that it can't work – at least not in electrical terms. It's just possible that the necessary electrostatic switching could be done automatically by the stone itself, using the natural semi-conductor properties of the quartzes in the stone to select current-flow according to the relative polarities and strengths of the charges involved; but there is no way in which a barrow can be made out to be an electro-static capacitor. It might be able to store a small charge, perhaps, but nothing like the levels of energy involved in the weather-control system I've been describing. But even if barrows and the like cannot be electrostatic capacitors, they do resemble them, and they do seem to be capacitors for some kind of energy.

At first sight a typical barrow would appear to be just a mound of earth: but they are in fact complex layered structures, a point which was first noted by Leslie Grinsell or O. G. S. Crawford during the 1920s or '30s.[20] A barrow may or may not have a burial at its centre; but its structure is almost invariably built up of alternating layers of organic and inorganic materials. Typically, it may start with a wooden

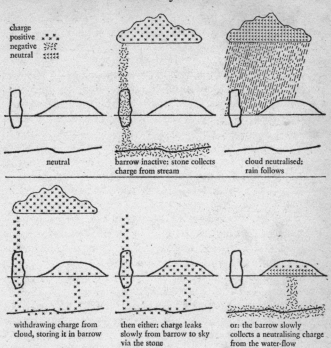

charge
positive
negative
neutral

neutral

barrow inactive: stone collects
charge from stream

cloud neutralised;
rain follows

withdrawing charge from
cloud, storing it in barrow

then either: charge leaks
slowly from barrow to sky
via the stone

or: the barrow slowly
collects a neutralising charge
from the water-flow

27 Two modes of thunderstorm control with the stone-and-barrow system.

structure of some kind in the centre, surrounded by a stone
cist; then a layer of brushwood, a layer of earth or stones, a
layer of rolled turves, a layer of fine gravel – and so on,
alternating layers of organic and inorganic, ending with the
turves on the surface, or in some cases a peristalith, a ring of
small stones surrounding the barrow. A structure of this
kind, made up of layers of natural organic and inorganic
materials, may not work as a store for electrostatic energy;
but it does exactly fit the description of a store for another
kind of energy, described variously as 'od', 'odyle', 'orgone',
'prana' and many other names. A typical barrow, in effect, is

more like an 'orgone accumulator' than an electrostatic accumulator. And that means that our complete 'stone-and-barrow' weather-control system – assuming that it does exist – cannot be entirely physical.

But if we describe the weather-control system in terms of 'orgone', we can find an almost exact replica of it designed, built and, sadly, destroyed, within the last thirty years: Wilhelm Reich's 'cloud-buster'. Before we can describe the weather-control system in terms of 'orgone', we have first to define or at least describe what this 'orgone' is – and that's not easy. About the closest I can come to a definition is to say that it is an energy that is mainly seen as an aspect or mode of the atmosphere; an energy that operates most noticeably on the emotions but has physical and physiological side-effects; an energy that exists in two forms, defined by Reich as 'orgone radiation' (OR) and 'deadly orgone radiation' (DOR).[21] In some ways these appear to be identical to the *ch'i* and *sha* of Feng-shui respectively.

OR can be sensed as a feeling of 'life' and brightness in the atmosphere, and can be seen (or, more correctly, 'seen') as bright fast-moving dots of light; while DOR, according to Reich, is responsible for 'dullness' and bleakness in the atmosphere, most easily sensed as the oppressive 'weight' of the atmosphere that builds up in the days before a big storm. The concept of orgone is more complex than this, though, and has a number of ramifications and side-issues which I haven't the space to go into here: for our purposes I'm only concerned with the concept of orgone as the theory behind Reich's 'cloudbuster'.

The cloudbuster itself was an assembly of ten-foot-long steel pipes mounted as a block on an old anti-aircraft-gun carriage, so that the whole assembly could be aimed at any point in the sky. It looked rather like the truck-mounted 'Moaning Minnie' multiple rocket launcher that the Russian Army used towards the end of the Second World War. The pipes were hollow, and the back end of each was wired onto a large cable, which was itself earthed into underground running water at the bottom of a well. And that was all: no power supply, no chemicals, no missiles, no 'secret ingredients'. Yet from the evidence there is little doubt that with this device Reich was able to manipulate the weather in the area immediately around his base, both forming and dispersing rain clouds.[22]

The principles and practice of the operation of the cloudbuster are both obvious and simple once you accept certain basic assumptions. One is that orgone exists; another is that it is absorbed by water; another is that the *ch'i* aspect of orgone assists in the formation of ordinary rain-clouds; yet another is that a water-laden cloud is an area of higher orgone energy potential; and there are various other assumptions which needn't concern us here. The next part of the theory of the cloudbuster was derived from an early observation of Reich's, that not only does looking through a long metal tube make it easier to 'see' orgone energy, but the tube will push or pull – so to speak – the energy in direct line with it. Reich originally noticed this when casual pointing of a long tube appeared to cause the wind-ripples on the surface of a lake to change their direction of travel. Given this ability of a tube to 'draw' orgone from a place, it is then necessary to put the collected energy somewhere: hence, in the final version of the cloudbuster, the connection of the tubes to running water, which absorbs the energy that the cloudbuster collects, and carries it away.

Given this as a theoretical and practical basis, the bank of tubes on the cloudbuster are assumed to be able to 'draw' orgone energy from whatever part of the sky they are aimed at. By pointing it at the centre of a cloud, the amount of orgone is reduced, and thus also its ability to hold water in vapour form: the cloud therefore dissipates and disperses. By pointing the cloudbuster to one side of the cloud, the local atmospheric distribution of orgone is upset, and the cloud expands into the drawn area. By some inversion which Reich never explains, this gives the cloud a higher orgone potential, allowing it to carry more water in vapour form.

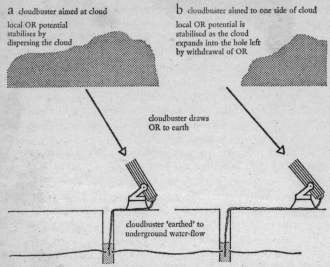

a cloudbuster aimed at cloud

local OR potential
stabilises by
dispersing the cloud

b cloudbuster aimed to one side of cloud

local OR potential is
stabilised as the cloud
expands into the hole left
by withdrawal of OR

cloudbuster draws
OR to earth

cloudbuster 'earthed' to
underground water-flow

28 Reich's cloudbuster: (a) destruction of clouds, and (b) creation or expansion of clouds.   *(after Wilhelm Reich, Selected Writings, Noonday (USA) 1960)*

If the process is carried on long enough, the amount of water vapour held by the cloud becomes too much for the cloud to hold, and so falls as rain.

In 'flat' or 'dull' weather conditions cloud-forming tended to produce DOR clouds, but these could, like the ordinary clouds, be 'drawn' into the well by pointing the cloudbuster directly at them. Most of these experiments took place in 1952. During his later experiments (between '53 and '55, I believe) he also pointed the cloudbuster at UFOs which were apparently frequently to be seen 'snooping' round the Reich Institute in Maine in the USA. He found that, as with the clouds, the UFOs faded away if the cloudbuster was aimed directly at them. This was the era when all UFOs were believed to be 'nuts and bolts' space machines piloted by aliens from other planets; and Reich became convinced that his 'space-gun', as he began to call the cloudbuster, was the only defence that the United States had against these invaders.[23] The United States Government was not impressed.

His rejection and then persecution by the American authorities led to his death in prison in 1957, following a questionable legal action against Reich by the Federal Food and Drugs Administration. The Administration destroyed most of Reich's equipment and research records on the unproven and largely untested ground that his work was fraudulent, and many of his works are still banned in the United States today.[24] But the Reich Institute was allowed to survive – though strictly limited in what it was allowed to do or research – and so was the original cloudbuster. I'm told that at that time the only one who really understood how to use it was Reich himself, though others are now starting to work on his cloudbusting techniques again. For many years it stood forlorn on its pedestal, the open end of the bank of pipes pointing at the ground because, although no-one wanted to dismantle it, no-one knew how to turn it off either. A sad end to an interesting experiment, and to a great if eccentric man.

But Reich may not have been as crazy as he seemed when he claimed he had 'dispersed' those UFOs. I'm certain that he was wrong to describe the cloudbuster as a 'space-gun', but he was still right in a sense, because if the barrows in that 'stone-and-barrow' weather-control system are indeed orgone accumulators, a definite link is beginning to emerge between orgone and UFOs – but a link that only makes sense if we abandon the idea that UFOs are 'spacecraft from Outer Space'. The way things are going, 'craft from *Inner* Space' seems more likely.

The link comes in some recent and as yet unpublished research by Paul Devereux, the present editor of *The Ley Hunter* magazine, and a fellow-researcher, Andrew York, on geographical correlations between geological structure, megalithic sites and folklore – particularly folklore about supposed paranormal and other 'Fortean' phenomena. These last, named after Charles Fort, the great collector of information 'damned' as non-existent and ignored by so-called scientists, include anything which doesn't fit the 'normal' pattern of life: reports of hauntings, crazy weather phenomena like fireballs, ice-falls and even a case of rain falling from a cloudless sky, meteorite landings and, of course, UFO sightings. The survey was restricted to Leicestershire, but even so it took three years of their spare time to do.[25]

But the results do seem worthwhile: for a start, working from clues given them by local folklore, they located and identified about forty standing stones (or their recent sites – several were destroyed in recent road 'improvements') in a county where the archaeologists knew only of one and the former site of another. The most striking part of their results was the geographical correlation: almost all the standing stones were sited in definite zones which coincided with the major geological faults of the county – and the majority of the Fortean phenomena, including UFO sightings and 'landings', fell in exactly the same zones. The correlation was so precise that an apparently anomalous area, which had the right folklore and some Fortean phenomena but apparently no geological faults, turned out in a later geological survey to be heavily faulted, and is due to become the Belvoir Vale colliery as a result.

Dowsers already knew about the link between underground fissuring – forming water-lines – and standing stones, but the link with hauntings and the like was not so well-established. Some other people, working in a different field of research for different reasons, were only too well aware of the connection: 'the proximity of ancient sites may . . . be the only explanation of places of disturbance which are not centred on a home', as one of them put it. The disturbance this writer, John Richards, described is an imbalance of many levels of energies at a particular place; and if our geomancy, our earth-acupuncture, is to have any value, it must be able to balance energies of every level within the landscape. That means that we have to broaden the scope of what we are asking it to handle. John Richards continues:

> 'The activities of occultists and magicians often centre on Celtic sites such as tumuli, circles and snake-paths, and such places, which, with or without the encouragement of ritual, may suffer a psychic 'hangover' from previous usage. This is particularly true of sites that have been desecrated. One theory is that some circles, for instance, were constructed to attract energy. Whether this is so remains a matter of opinion, but it does seem that such centres act as distribution points for occult forces, however created or whatever their nature, forces which appear to run on power lines or 'leys' between each centre. The assessment by young people of a place by its good or bad 'vibes' (vibrations) and their willingness to spend hours at such sites as Glastonbury Tor, stems probably from an instinctive awareness of such things.'[26]

I think you'll see what I mean by 'broadening the scope of our geomancy'. One of John Richards' colleagues stated their problem, and ours, in rather more detail:

'Places – churches, houses, towns, countryside – may be strained or influenced by a variety of causes, and frequently by more than one of them at a time. Among these causes may be listed:

(*a*) Souls of the departed (ghosts proper): most often of those who have recently died.

(*b*) Magicians claim to be able to instigate and operate 'haunts', and this can be in some measure substantiated.

(*c*) Human sin: a house or site used for sexual misbehaviour (in the countryside often the ancient fertility-cult site), but equally the office of an organization devoted to greed or domination, can often incur trouble or act as a dispersal centre. Human sin also opens the door for other forces to enter in.

(*d*) Place memories: these account for some nine-tenths of what are popularly called 'haunts'. They are impersonal traces of earlier personal action, and seem to be caused either by habitual actions or by actions accompanied by violent emotion . . . (The tone of family life in a house is one factor producing place memories; hence the blessing of a new home is a not irrelevant activity.)

(*e*) Poltergeists, and the accompanying asportations, levitations and other phenomena: these remain a mystery. It is exceedingly hard to arrive at adequate facts about them. There is the possibility of psychic action similar to table-turning, and possibly planchette, due to some uncontrolled human subconscious in the house, to the interference of magicians, or even perhaps to some form of non-human mischievous sprite.

(*f*) Demonic interference: this is common on desecrated sites such as ruined sanctuaries, as well as in connection with seances. This kind of activity and that of magicians (as in (*b*)) frequently revivifies ancient celtic sites such as tumuli, circles and snake-path shrines, and so causes a general sense of 'buzz' or strain which can be disturbing, if rarely dangerous.

There are therefore at least three quite different types of forces which may possibly be operating on any given place: those which are purely human (*a*, *b* and *c*); those which are impersonal (*d* and perhaps *e*); those which are demonic (*f*). Only in cases of demonic interference with a place can exorcism be regarded as the major cure.'[27]

From the tone of this passage it is obviously Christian; in fact it is part of the *Report* of a commission on exorcism convened by the Bishop of Exeter. What may surprise you is the recent date of the *Report*: it was first published in 1972. The problems it describes aren't superstitions of the distant past, they are realities of the present: and as such they form a necessary part of our new model of nature.

6

Ghosts and Ghouls

'From ghosties and ghoulies and long-leggit beasties
and things that go bump in the night, may the good
lord protect us.'
(An old Scottish prayer)

'Ghosties and ghoulies' and their equally strange allies are
more than a medieval nightmare: for imaginary as they are
in many ways, they still exist both in imagination and outside of it, and they are aspects of human experience that we
can no longer afford to ignore. If we ignore them, we cannot
control the effects they have on us; and whether those
effects are 'objective' or 'subjective', they are still real to
anyone who experiences them.

I ought to mention that I've never seen anything that I
could recognize as a 'ghost' in the traditional sense; but over
the past few years I have become acquainted with a number
of magicians and exorcists, and have learnt to respect their
knowledge and experience of this field. One aspect of their
work that has come over most clearly is the close link
between certain types of hauntings and the special characteristics of certain types of place – and in this they agree closely
with our 'lunatic fringe of archaeology'. Independently, they
too saw sacred sites (and some others) as centres for some
kind of 'occult forces'; they too saw that energies of some
kind travelled down the leys; and they too saw – much
though it went against the 'common-sense' of Victorian
science and theology – that the earth had and has a life and
mind of its own.

The link between sacred sites and hauntings is important
to us because, as far as I can tell from my own experience
and from my discussions with magician friends, many of the

hauntings are manifestations or side-effects of the concentration and movement of energies at those places. By studying the various categories of hauntings and their relationship with places, we can use them to tell us what the energies involved in our 'earth-acupuncture' might be.

But before doing so there are two important obstacles to be moved out of the way. The first of these is the still-asked question of 'Do ghosts *really* exist?', usually accompanied by a demand for 'proof' one way or the other. The answer to this depends on what the questioner means by 'existence', and what he or she will accept as 'proof'. So, to deal with the 'existence' part first, we can see from the categories of hauntings in the *Exorcism Report* that very few of these would produce directly measurable effects on a physical level: this would apply almost solely to the poltergeist group. Of the rest, it is true that they have little or no *physical* existence, but that does not mean that they do not exist at all, for it is clear that they have enough existence and reality to create the experience people recognize as 'haunting'. To take the *Exorcism Report*'s categories, place-memories, for example, can be said to 'exist' on an emotional level, operating on human emotions, and existing either as stored emotions or something stored by emotions. The other categories operate on or through other levels of existence, including those of the imagination, which can't so easily be described with a simple label. Poltergeists, as an example, seem to operate through a whole range of levels at once, from the most abstruse levels recognized only by occultists, right down to recordable and measurable physical effects.

As for 'proof', there is only one kind of unambiguous proof of the existence of ghosts or ghouls, and that is direct first-hand experience. Most of the people who demand proof are unable to get any true proof of this kind because, as we shall see, to recognize a haunting for what it is requires an openness and flexibility of mind which few of these people can achieve. It is likely, though, that you will have experienced and recognized at least one kind of haunting in everyday life – that of a house's 'atmosphere' – but more about that shortly.

The other kind of proof is documentary evidence: and of that there is no shortage at all. The various national and international Societies for Psychical Research hold in their archives an enormous number of case-histories of hauntings of one kind or another; and while it's true that many of the events in these case-histories do have 'rational' explanations, a fair number of those supposed 'explanations' are themselves highly suspect. Too often the explanation relies on assumptions of trickery or imbecility on the part of the 'haunted', and some of the examples I've seen were no more than garbled pseudo-science, attempting to conceal that something outside of the ordinariness of science's worldview had occurred.[1] All too often there is a world of difference between what the 'haunted' saw and what some so-called 'psychic investigator' assumed they saw; so it is essential to be open-minded – literally – if hauntings are to make any sense at all.

It's true that the churches also have detailed records of all kinds of hauntings going back to the time of Christ and beyond; but the limits that Christian dogma imposes on interpretations of hauntings form the second of the two major obstacles to a more complete understanding of those hauntings and the energies they represent. It could be argued – and I have seen it argued – that the practical application of Christian dogma has been the direct or indirect cause of many types and cases of hauntings. I don't want to get bogged down in a general discussion of the merits or demerits of Christian theology, but there are two aspects of it that do concern us here. One is the inability or unwillingness of the Church to recognize anything of value in human sexuality or fertility rituals, assigning most of this side of nature and human nature to the garbage bin labelled 'human sin'; the other is the labelling of almost the entire pagan pantheon as 'devils'.

Both of these labellings may have been politically

expedient in the past, when the Church was struggling to establish itself and its identity; but from the research that I and several others have done it seems clear that both were major mistakes. There seems to be little doubt, from the results of that research, that both are major root-causes beneath the malaise of our present city-based cultures. The Church is right to warn us that certain aspects of sexuality and of paganism, if allowed to get out of control, can be unbelievably and horrifyingly destructive; but it is wrong to label them as 'evil' in themselves, for both forces undoubtedly have constructive aspects. Indeed, that labelling could itself be said to be 'evil', to use the Christian term, for it has frustrated the constructive aspects of those forces, redoubling their destructive effects. I do respect the Church and its work, and I am certain that its interpretation of hauntings is important to us; but I think we ought to be wary, for a while at least, of believing that the Christian interpretation is 'the Truth'.

Both of these obstacles – 'scientism' in the first case, religion in the other – are created by the limitations of dogma, which we could describe as a premature definition of 'reality'. Rigid beliefs produce a rigid definition of reality. But in practice and in experience reality is fluid, because of the paradox 'Things have not only to be seen to be believed, but also to be believed to be seen'. Despite the concept of the 'Laws of Nature', we do have some choice and control over the effective form of the reality we experience. And that is the point of this study, for our aim, in looking for a 'new model of nature', is to create a practical and versatile reality that can bring nature back into our lives in the cities. Realities can have value as well as 'truth'.

To construct a reality for a particular purpose, we can select or adapt useful beliefs or structures from other definitions of reality: this is what a technologist does, for example, for he uses scientific ideas and adapts them to his 'applied science', rather than following them as 'the Truth', as a scientist would. We can *use* beliefs and belief-systems, rather than having to accept or reject them in their entirety for their 'truth' or 'untruth'. The Christian interpretation of hauntings is suspect in many respects, but the categorization in the *Exorcism Report* is useful: so let us use it as a framework with which to study hauntings.

As I implied earlier, the Christian categories of 'human sin' and 'demonic interference' will need careful dissection; the others are slightly easier to discuss, although the 'poltergeist' group has a set of sub-groups within it. If we relate the six categories in the *Exorcism Report* not just to places in general but specifically to sacred sites and the apparent natural energy-matrix, research work suggests that we can ignore most of one category (ghosts proper, the 'spirits of the departed') and a sub-group of the poltergeist category (those due to 'an uncontrolled human subconscious in the house'). Although these are related to places, they are tied more to people at those places than the places themselves. There is admittedly some evidence that certain types of sites tend to 'hold' 'spirits of the departed', or to increase 'uncontrolled human subconscious' poltergeist activity, but I don't think it's particularly important to our theme; and above all I don't want to get trapped into a discussion of the existence or non-existence of the human soul or spirit. I'll leave that kind of discussion to the Churchmen: I assume they know what they're talking about in that respect.

This leaves us with part of the poltergeist category, and four others: 'magicians', 'human sin', 'place-memories' and 'demonic interference'. If we place magically induced poltergeists into the 'magician' category, and include poltergeists due to 'non-human mischievous sprites' as a sub-group of the 'demonic interference' category (for reasons that should become clear later), we are down to four categories of hauntings related to the 'earth-acupuncture' matrix.

Because we are dealing with the interaction of people and place, we can re-form these four categories into three others with a different emphasis, this time on the type of activity behind the haunting: the three new categories are 'unconscious human interaction with the place', 'conscious or deliberate human interaction with the place' and 'non-human interaction with the place'. Basically, these are the *Report*'s categories of 'place-memories', 'magical interference' and 'demonic interference' respectively, with various sub-groups of the old 'human sin' category included in the first and second, and possibly the third, new categories.

But the *Report* was only concerned with negative or destructive interaction with places, and all these three categories have constructive aspects as well. If we call them 'place-memory ghosts and ghouls', 'magicians' and 'angels and demons', these three categories form between them a framework through which we can study not only hauntings, but also the energies behind them, the energies of nature on which our 'earth-acupuncture' operates.

The first category of hauntings we'll look at is the place-memory type. According to the *Exorcism Report*, these account for some nine-tenths of all reported hauntings, but I imagine they account for an even larger proportion of the total number of hauntings people experience, for the simple reason that many of them are too minor or ordinary-seeming to be recognized for what they are. There are an enormous number of different kinds of place-memory, from stored emotion, to sounds, smells, sighs and even complete filmic sequences; but the most common type, which you're almost certain to have experienced at some time or another, is the 'feel' or 'atmosphere' of some house or place. Sometimes aptly but inaccurately described as the place's 'vibes', you can often sense a definite impression of some underlying emotion at a place: the house may seem 'happy' or 'sad', 'lonely' or 'angry' or 'sinister', or perhaps 'friendly', 'joyful'. We'll look at the theory of this in a moment, but it will feel exactly as though the house has been somehow 'painted' with that emotion.

And that is in fact a good analogy to describe it. Imagine each emotion you can think of as having a matching colour: there's a world of difference between a bright canary-yellow and a sickly lime-yellow-green, between a sky-blue and the gloomy colour that goes with the emotion we call 'blue'. Imagine, then, that each time you walk into a house, you throw a bucket of the colour of paint that matches your current feeling onto the wall in the hallway, and wherever you go in that building. Although there will be a general mixture of this colour-cum-emotion on the walls of the house, in time a predominant paint of emotion, a general tone or mood, will begin to emerge as that which you normally have in that house, or in each room of that house. It is this predominant emotional 'colour' that you and your visitors may sense as the 'atmosphere' of the house.

Because a predominant emotion tends to be painted over all that house, the emotional colour will encourage you to set up the corresponding emotion whenever you are there – and thus reinforce the predominance of that emotion in the house's 'atmosphere'. If you tend to be gloomy in a place, you 'paint' the place with that emotion, and that tends to reinforce your gloominess each time you go there. But by recognizing your tendency to be gloomy, you can deliberately 'paint' the wall with some bright and cheerful emotion, which really can help to improve things. Hence the real value of 'positive thinking'; and hence also that comment in the *Exorcism Report* – 'the blessing of a new home is a not irrelevant activity' – because in this sense its effect is like stripping off all the old paint from the walls and re-painting them with white primer.

There is a physical component in this, of course, for lighting and physical (as opposed to emotional) paint do undoubtedly affect the 'feel' of a place. So too does 'association', in that as part of mental habit you will tend to repeat emotions, thoughts and even actions at the same place because of a kind of visually- and spatially-triggered conditioned reflex. But this can't explain the whole of place-related emotions: association, for instance, is most unlikely to play a significant role where the same emotion is repeated in people who've never been to the place before. It does seem that emotions can be stored directly in the fabric of a place, or rather spread over the surfaces exactly like layer upon layer of paint.

This routine 'layering' applies to routine emotion, habitual emotion: but the occasional extreme and violent emotion can force its way right through many of these layers, sometimes breaking through as much as a few centuries'-worth of routine emotion. Given the human propensity for glumph, it seems quite rare to find a high-powered streak of joy: most of the stored extreme emotions are negative and destructive, which is why Lethbridge – whose work we'll come to shortly – labelled them 'ghouls'. To use the paint analogy, they are the emotional equivalent of a bucketful of acid or paint-stripper thrown onto the wall: almost regardless of what you lay over it, it will burn its way through. The only way you can deal with something like that is to strip off all the old paint from the walls, wash off the acid with care, and only then start again with the basic white primer: and in emotional terms, that's a close analogy to the effect of a formal exorcism and blessing of a place.

All this can make sense only if we can call emotion a force, and demonstrate or just accept that either it or its effects can be stored in the fabric of a place. For the former there is of course no physical evidence, though there is plenty of evidence for its physical effects when working through people; but for the latter, the storage of coded energy in a place, there is a physical counterpart, involving quartz or quartz-like crystals in building-stones. This was demonstrated on the popular-science television programme *The Burke Special* some time in 1973: the programme was about retrieving sounds from stone in Corfe Castle in Dorset. The theory was that sounds, as air-pressure waves, could alter the structure of quartzes and 'proto-ceramic materials' in the rocks, and thus store sounds as patterns of electro-static charge; so by exciting the stones electronically it was thought to be possible to release this stored energy as audible but near-random sound. By comparing the waveforms from the entire wall as they arrived at particular points (presumably a form of interferometry), the researchers claimed that it was possible to make out fragments of speech and other recognizable sound, possibly from five hundred or more years ago. I haven't heard any more about this process, but I don't think it was a hoax – that programme rarely goes in for hoaxes.

The point about this process was that it depended on the equipment being placed at a point where the wave-forms for a given sound coincided: and here we have another parallel with Lethbridge's work on 'ghouls' and place-memory 'ghosts'. To sense the basic 'atmosphere' of a house, you need only be in the house; but for any more complex place-memory in houses and structures, and for any kind of place-memory in open country, things get a little more complicated. The more complex the place-memory, it seems, the more important it becomes that you repeat or set up more and more complex conditions of position, time and state of mind, if you are going to be able to perceive the place-memory and recognize it as such. Tom Lethbridge studied these conditions in detail during the 1960s, and his work on place-memories now forms the central part of almost all modern research on them.[2]

Lethbridge's basic theory was that every person has around them an aura or 'field' whose strength varies with emotional strength or arousal. This 'personal field' or 'psyche-field', as Lethbridge termed it, could be said to be a product of that person's emotional being. Lethbridge described this field as being 'electromagnetic', 'electrical' and 'static' (presumably 'electrostatic'); but as he himself realized, this is not quite correct, in the strict physical sense of the words. This 'psyche-field' does resemble an electromagnetic or electrostatic field, but as with the energies involved in the complete weather-control system we met earlier, the 'psyche-field' doesn't always comply with the strict physical rules of electromagnetism and electrostatics.

But no matter: Lethbridge's concept of a personal 'field' still makes sense in practice.

Lethbridge suggested that most if not all hauntings by ghouls, ghosts or the traditional 'nature spirits' were the result of an interaction between this personal 'field' and a 'field of force' of the earth itself. The *Exorcism Report*, as we saw, agreed that this was true of most, but *not* all, hauntings. As far as I can discover, Lethbridge never recognized the very low-level type of place-memory – the 'atmosphere' of a house – as being a haunting at all: but in the terms of his theory we can see these as storage of emotional images in the ordinary 'background' level of the earth's field in ordinary places, a background 'noise' rather like the background radiation level (mostly from cosmic radiation) that can be picked up almost anywhere with a Geiger counter. As with geophysical radiation surveys, certain areas have a much higher level of activity in a ghoulish sense, and thus stand out from the 'background noise'; and it was these prominent places, concentrations of the earth's field, that interested Lethbridge. That these places of concentrations of the earth's field do in fact coincide with small areas of apparently higher background radiation levels than the 'normal' is, I think, a significant coincidence.[3] As we have seen throughout this study, there is a physical and geophysical component involved somewhere in 'paranormal' activity – but it's almost impossible to pin down its precise role in that activity.

The important part of Lethbridge's studies, from the point of view of our new model of nature, is that concentrations of the earth's field coincide with prominent natural features such as waterfalls, springs and streams, certain types of trees, and parts of woodland, deserts, moorland, mountains, sea-shores. Lethbridge noted that these 'are just the places which were peopled with nymphs and spirits by the peoples of the ancient world and by simple modern ones'. He therefore classified different types of field according to the type of nymph or sprite traditionally believed to inhabit that place:

'naiad' for waterfalls, springs and streams, 'dryad' for trees and woods in general, 'oread' in mountains and deserts, and 'nereid' in or by the sea.

Two of these groups, the oreads and nereids, we haven't met before; but we have come across equivalents of both dryads and naiads before, in Underwood's work, in Watkins' ley-hunting and in John Richards' comment on the relationship between 'ancient sites' and hauntings. Lethbridge seems to have thought that mental or emotional images stored in these places by passers-by accounted for the traditional belief in these nature spirits. While I believe that he was mistaken in this, for reasons I'll come on to later, the observations and information he left us can, like the work of Underwood, Watkins and Reich before him (whose interpretations – like mine, I suppose – were also limited by the assumptions of their times), be correlated with other fields of study, to be seen, no longer isolated, as a facet of something more coherent and complete. So we'll come back to this idea of 'nature spirits' later: for now we'll use the terms 'naiad' and 'dryad' and the like solely as labels to describe different types of earth-field.

With one exception, it seems that all the types of earth-fields are related to underground water, either in underground flows or in ground saturated with water. The exception, the oread-fields, may not in fact exist: Lethbridge included them in the list because oreads were a class of the old Greek nature-spirits, but to my knowledge he does not describe an oread-field in relation to any of the case-studies of hauntings he discusses in his books. It is not just underground water – and thus, we could infer, nodes of Underwood's patterns – that affect the 'retrievability' of place-memory ghouls and ghosts, but also water in the atmosphere, for according to Lethbridge a damp, muggy, slightly misty day seems to be best for hauntings. This coincides, of course, with the kind of weather so preferred by writers of horror-story hauntings; but it also seems to be the conditions of the atmosphere under which, according to

Reich's theories, the body's level of orgone is more easily depleted, leaving emotional strength, stamina and resistance at its lowest. This in turn does tally with Lethbridge's theories, for he suggested that the mechanism behind place-memory hauntings was one of 'leakage' between people's 'psyche-fields' and the earth-field of the place. If we suggest that at least part of that 'leakage' of energy involves Reich's orgone, the 'clustering' of phenomena like hauntings, UFO reports, fire-balls and other crazy weather – as we saw in Devereux and York's Leicestershire survey – begins to make sense.

The mechanism that Lethbridge suggested was behind place-memory hauntings went roughly as follows: In all cases a place-memory haunting involves at least two people at different times: the person who stored the place-memory

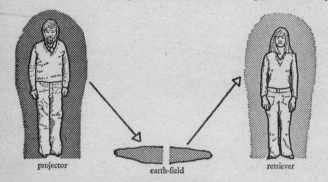

projector   earth-field   retriever

29 Lethbridge's model of ghoul-images: the coded energy that forms the ghoul leaks from a strong energy field to a weaker one.

in the place in the first instance (the 'projector') and the person or people who 'saw' it as a ghost or ghoul or whatever (the 'retriever'). The storage of the place-memory was the result of an unconscious 'leakage' of energy from the 'psyche-field' of an emotionally-aroused person – with a strong personal field, in other words – into the relatively weak field of the place. Its retrieval was the result of the same 'leakage' in reverse, from the relatively strong field of the place into the field of someone who wasn't thinking or feeling anything in particular, and thus had a weak personal field at the time. That's the basic theory: from there on it becomes more complicated, as you might expect.

The first complication is the distinction between ghouls and ghosts. Ghouls are stored emotions as we saw earlier: you could say that they are records of what someone felt – either strongly, or repeatedly, or both – at that place. Sometimes they seem to be sounds, but the sounds are always verbalizations of feelings such as the suicidal comment 'Wouldn't you like to jump over the cliff?' that Lethbridge found attached to a nereid- or naiad-field at Ladram Bay in Devon.[4] Ghosts are different in that they are records – emotionally-loaded records – of what someone *perceived* from that place: they are records of what someone felt they saw, felt they heard, touched, smelt, tasted.

So ghouls are amorphous emotions or feelings located within the area defined by the naiad-field or whatever, while ghosts are much more precisely defined, a definite image, a definite sound, often perceived as being in a particular direction from the naiad-field and not seeming to be on or part of the field at all. Even so, ghouls and ghosts aren't so much separate classes of place-memory as opposite ends of a spectrum of stored images, ranging from the storage of feelings to the storage of perceptions, thoughts and even symbolic images, all of them carrying strong emotional overtones along with them.

The symbolic imagery of some of these more complex place-memories is interesting, as it seems to account for some of the more bizarre of the classic types of ghost, particularly the headless type. There is always the possibility that one of these may be a 'ghost proper', a 'departed spirit', but in most cases it is more likely to be a place-memory. If it really is an image of someone who was beheaded, it could be a symbolic image of that person as seen by someone else – a servant, perhaps – who combined an image of the person with the idea that they were about to lose their head. Another place-memory interpretation of the headless horseman-type ghost in the forest, for example, is that the projector *thought* he saw a horseman without a head; and though perhaps a few seconds later he realized this was not so, his fright of that moment would be sufficient to project this image into a nearby and handy dryad-field. It's important to realize, by the way, that place-memory ghosts are not images of the projectors themselves, but of something or someone that the projectors saw or, as with that headless horseman, thought they saw.

What I don't understand about place-memories is why a ghoul-type emotional image should be stored at one place, an apparent sound at another, a static colourless image at another, a complete filmic sequence at yet another, and so on. There doesn't seem to be any obvious reason why a place should hold one type of image and not another, except for the 'chance' factor that the dominant part of any emotion in the projector, in a chance enounter between two people, should be visual in one case, aural in another, or just a plain feeling in a third. I don't know: that part of Lethbridge's place-memory research doesn't seem to make sense, partly because he doesn't discuss it much in any of his books.

He doesn't discuss the conditions controlling retrieval of these stored images much either, beyond this basic theory of 'leakage', but here we can build up something of a coherent theory by comparing his work with the work of others in other fields of research. Ghouls seem fairly simple, in that they seem to 'appear' to a lot of people, particularly in muggy weather, so Lethbridge's basic 'leakage' mechanism would seem to be enough. But the further the type of place-memory goes up the spectrum of complexity from ghouls to sequence-ghosts, an increasing number of conditions come into play – as is clear from the relative rarity of filmic-sequence-type ghosts compared to the simplest level of ghoul, the 'atmosphere' of a house. Again, I don't know or understand all of these additional conditions, but two of them which we can guess at – and which give us further clues as to the mechanisms involved – come from the directionality and the timing of these more complex hauntings.

The directionality of place-memory ghosts suggests that they are possibly emotional equivalents of optical holograms. An optical hologram is a three-dimensional image produced from a special photographic plate by a process that depends on beams of light coming in to each other and to the photographic plate from precise directions. It also depends on the light-beams initially being formed of light-waves precisely in step with each other – known as 'coherent' light. Since lasers are the most practical sources for coherent light, almost all optical holography is done with lasers, particularly the continuous-output gas lasers rather than the pulsed-output ruby type we looked at earlier.

A hologram is not a photograph in the normal sense, with a photographic positive and negative. The image on the holographic plate bears no resemblance to the object – it just looks like a scratchy mess of lines regardless of what the object was. No lenses are used, either: the idea is that because the light-waves coming on to the object are exactly in step, the interference-pattern formed by them as they bounce off the whole of the object (hence *holo*graphy) can be recorded and used to 'reconstruct' an image of the object later. In most holography two beams are used, both split off from one original beam by a semi-transparent mirror. One beam is aimed at the object – a knight on a chess-board, for example – while the other goes straight onto the photographic plate, to form a 'coherent background'. The waveforms reflected off the object meet up with the light from the other 'reference beam' at the photographic plate, and the resultant interference produces the scratchy lines that you can see on the plate when it is developed.

The hologram, the image on the plate itself, bears no apparent resemblance to the object; but when another laser beam of the same frequency is shone on to the plate from the

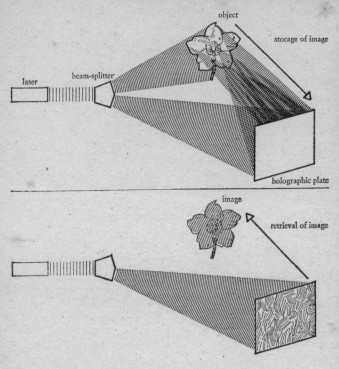

30 Laser set-up for producing and reconstructing holographic images.

same angle, the wave-fronts that were 'frozen' onto the plate carry on their travels, as it were, to form a real, photographable, three-dimensional image hanging in space in the distance and direction from the plate as was the original object. And this three-dimensionality is real, not apparent as in an ordinary photograph: if you move from side to side you can see different sides of the object – see the chessboard from different angles – as though it were a real object hanging in space. The catch is that with most holograms you can only see the image by looking through the plate, so that you can't see round the back of the original object; and because coherent light must be of only one frequency, the image will have a 'greyness' and 'flatness' that belies its true three-dimensional character.

Moving from the image to the process, there are two characteristics of holography which are particularly striking: one is that the hologram is formed by beams of light coming in to the object and the plate from precise directions; and the other is the ability of a fragment of the resulting plate to reproduce an image of the *whole* of the object – rather than, as on an ordinary plate, a small part of it – though it will be an image as 'seen' from a more limited angle. This is because, unlike a photographic plate, every part of a hologram is a record of light arriving from the whole of the object. So given these properties of the holographic image and process, we can construct a holographic analogy to describe place-memory ghosts.

The key to this will be whether or not a place can 'record' complex and normally meaningless information like an 'interference pattern'. The place, in other words, has to be the equivalent of a photographic plate. Using Lethbridge's labels for the different types of earth-field, an equivalent of a photosensitive emulsion at a place would seem to be water percolating through the surface at the place. Water, due to its odd 'bent' molecular structure – which I'll come back to later – has known information-storing properties; and we already know that water is in some way involved in Lethbridge's naiad- and nereid-fields by definition, in his dryad-fields by implication (because of the connection between certain trees and underground water, as I described in the discussion on lightning), and in sacred sites in general, as the work of Underwood and the other dowsers implies. Water can be seen in this context as an 'energy-sensitive emulsion'.

To be more precise, it would seem to be water chemically bonded to the soil that forms the 'plate', rather than flowing water, for otherwise the image stored within it would lose its coherence and fade away in a matter of seconds rather

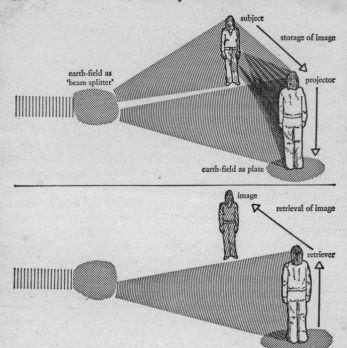

31 Holographic analogy for place-memory ghosts.

than be 'retrievable' for many years. The areas these earth-fields cover are as definite and definable as the shape of a photographic plate: one of Lethbridge's case-studies in *Ghost and Divining Rod*, of a ghost figure at the nearby Hole Mill, showed that the image was stored in and derived from a definite field formed on the inside of a curve in an underground stream by the Mill, a field whose limits were sufficiently defined to 'step over in a single stride', as Lethbridge put it.[5] It's possible that these earth-fields aren't always active in their role as 'plates': Lethbridge suggested that they were only active – for the retrieval of the image, if not the recording of it – on warm muggy days. Certainly the 'electric tingling' feeling which he describes as being on those sites in such conditions, and often coincident with a haunting, is only present from time to time, as I've discovered myself.

Other materials can also act as the 'plate', such as quartz-type crystals in building-stone, for example, and perhaps the water chemically trapped in the wooden timbers in buildings. If we use the holographic analogy for place-memory hauntings, this would explain why – as is sometimes reported – ghosts of old houses move to new houses that incorporate material from the old. The fragment of the 'plate' would still contain enough information to reconstruct the whole of the image under certain circumstances. The analogy may also explain why some sequence-ghosts (those moving around, as if seen in a short 'clip' from a film) do 'impossible' things like walking through walls and closed doors, for the walls and doors may not have been there when the original image was recorded by the place. The same analogy also explains the three-dimensionality of place-memory ghosts, their strange 'flatness' or 'greyness', and at least part of the reason why only some people see them. As with holograms, unless you're standing in the right place at the right time, standing in the same relationship to the plate as was the original projector, and with the power-source turned on, you won't be able to see the image the plate retains.

The time-factor is interesting, for it suggests that an astronomical component may be involved in the 'retrieval' of place-memory images: ghosts that repeat their appearance on the same day each year might demand, as part of their 'lighting', the same angular relationship between the place and the centre of the earth, and between the earth, the sun and some hypothetical universal 'centre'. It's also possible, particularly with place-memories at sacred sites, that the equivalent there of the laser of optical holography might be the 'leyser', which we know has astronomically-linked pulses, linked to sun, moon, planets, and perhaps even the risings and settings of particular stars, if Professor Thom's theories about star-alignment at stone circles are correct.[6]

But if we look closely at the time-factor we can see that a holographic analogy, useful as it is, is not enough, for some place-memory ghosts appear to haunt their sites *before* the event that created them took place. Lethbridge gives an interesting example of one of these from his own experience. Before he moved into his house at Hole, he was asked if he minded ghosts, because a 'Red Lady' with white hair had been seen there several times shortly before the First World War. He never saw the ghost himself; but he believed he knew how it came to be. During the late 1950s the woman from Hole Mill, just down the road, used to visit him and his wife quite often: and she was a little old lady with white hair, who invariably wore a red coat – a 'red Lady', in fact. Lethbridge also knew that she was something of a magician, in the proper sense of the word. She often came into their house without bothering to knock on the door, and Leth- bridge said she sometimes caught him by surprise, sitting in the dim hallway, unexpected and unannounced, taking off her sea-boots. He thought that it was his surprise, coupled with the woman's known projective skill, that created the 'ghost' of nearly fifty years before.[7]

None of this would matter, and place-memories would remain interesting if disturbing curiosities, if it were not for the fact that they can cause accidents of one kind or another. From the researches I've done, and from those of others I've talked to about this, there seems to be little doubt that this is so. The ghoul at Ladram Bay, the one who suggested to Lethbridge and several others that they might like to 'jump over the cliff', did in fact collect a suitably suicidal victim a few years later; and it's possible, given the crazy time-factor involved in place-memories, that the ghoul was both a cause and an effect of the same suicide. Apparently that ghoul is still there: it frightened several other people on top of that cliff before the suicide took place, and could still panic someone else into falling over that cliff accidentally.

I'm scared of heights, as it happens, so I wouldn't even go near a cliff; but I have noticed something very similar to Lethbridge's description of the Ladram Bay ghoul in a number of places on the London Underground. They are rarely 'active', fortunately; but when they are, the feeling-cum-thought of 'Why don't you jump under the train?' is unmistakable. It's probably true that most suicides of that type are at least partly premeditated; but I sometimes wonder how many times a ghoul of that kind has been the 'last straw' that pushed some unhappy person literally over the edge.

The unexpectedness of ghouls and ghosts, and particularly the emotional overtones carried with them, may well be the hidden cause behind a lot of accidents both at home and on the road. A sudden fright, a momentary irrational fear, can be all that's needed to cause a car-crash: and a ghoul based in a naiad-field under the roadway can be enough to produce that kind of fear. I've come across a ghoul of that type which could easily have caused a crash, but – fortunately for me – did not on that occasion. I was driving down from London to Somerset on the A303 with my wife and a friend in the car; and somewhere before Mere (I forget where exactly) we got stuck behind a very slow-moving car. We reached a clear stretch of open road, and I started to overtake; but just as I did so both my passengers yelled 'No!', so I had to pull in sharply – to avoid nothing.

Now this sounds like a routine complaint at my driving, but I don't think it was: the road was clear, and my car, though slow, had enough acceleration to get past with ease on that empty stretch of road. Both my passengers yelled because of a sudden fear: they had seen nothing dangerous, and realized (rationally, at least) that it was safe to overtake. Neither of them realized until later that the other had spoken and, what is more, they had called out exactly as each of them had passed over the same spot on the road, the passenger in the back calling out about a tenth of a second later than my wife, who was in the seat in front of him in the car. The weather was also warm and muggy, if I remember correctly, so the conditions do seem to have been right for ghoulish action. It's not just from defence of my driving ability that I believe a ghoul was in action there; but what worries me is that that ghoul, under slightly different driving conditions, could well cause someone to crash.

This is true not only of ghouls, of course. Lethbridge, in one of his books, gives a detailed example of a ghost car that he and his wife experienced on a country road in 1964;[8] and I remember once reading somewhere of an accident caused by a ghost double-decker bus, complete with passengers and crew. As I remember the article, two cars collided when they both swerved to dodge an imaginary bus that appeared from nowhere, crossed a junction in front of the two cars (which is why they swerved) and passed *through* two parked cars before vanishing into thin air. Both car drivers, and a witness passing by, said that they thought at first that the bus was real: it was complete with its passengers and crew, and from its number was a normal bus to be travelling along that route. It was only its strange 'greyness', and the manner in which it appeared and disappeared, that made it clear that it did not exist in a physical sense. Whether the drivers were believed by their insurance companies or the court I do not know; but assuming that their stories were true, we could infer that there was – and probably is – a strong and large naiad-field beneath that junction. The image of that bus, as caught in that field, could well have been put there by an infuriated would-be passenger whom the bus had failed to pick up, perhaps even some years before. A moment's anger in one year by one person, it seems, can cause a car-crash in another for another.

At this stage I'd better repeat that place-memory ghosts and ghouls are impersonal memories, not malevolent 'spirits'. They broadcast their stored images and emotions mindlessly whenever the conditions are right for them to do so, and for the benefit or otherwise of whoever happens to be part of those conditions at the time. In themselves they're harmless: it's their suddenness and unexpectedness, and also the heavy emotional overtones that are a necessary part of them, that can make them dangerous. To give an analogy, they wait around like tape-recordings of very loud noises, to be set off by a trip-wire or a hidden beam; and they're dangerous for the same reason and in the same way, in that they take you by surprise because you're not ready for them, not aware of them.

They're dangerous, in other words, because we try to ignore them. Many claim that no ghost of any kind, including place-memories, can exist: but that is literally ignorance, ignoring what is undoubtedly a real – and thus existent – area of human experience. But given that they do exist, and given that they can be dangerous if we allow them to take us by surprise, one of our concerns, in building a model of nature that can bring an awareness of reality back into urban life, should be to find out the natural processes and factors behind these hauntings, so that we can learn not so much how to control them as how to live with them and limit the destructive and dangerous aspects of their effects.

There are many things we can do about this. One of them, perhaps the most important, is to realize that the vast majority of hauntings are these impersonal place-memories, and that there is nothing about them to be frightened of. If we can lose our fear of them, they will lose their power to haunt us, and they will become just interesting curiosities, like pictures on the screens in the television-hire showroom that you pass in the High Street. It's not easy to lose our fear of them, but it can be done, even in the emotional 'deadness' of the cities. Another thing we can do, once again even in the cities, is to locate – by dowsing and by other means – the still-active earth-fields, and try to identify what kinds of place-memories they store and under what conditions they 'appear'. Lethbridge's theory of 'leakage of field' does explain one of the conditions – that of the 'retriever's' state of mind – in some detail, but many of the others, particularly the astronomically related ones and the weather linkage, remain poorly researched. We still need to do much more work on them.

There is one danger here: it is, I believe, foolish to try to ignore place-memories and their effects on us; but I think it is still more foolish to go 'ghost-hunting', prodding likely-looking sites in various ways to see if a place-memory appears. It's true that one may do so: but they have little choice in when or whether they appear, because they are impersonal memories, and they are anyway less likely to appear when 'prodded' because the active or 'trying' state of mind that 'ghost-hunting' implies is diametrically opposed to the 'emptiness' of mind in the 'retriever' that seems to be an essential part of the conditions for their appearance. The danger in 'ghost-hunting' is that other types of haunting may appear instead. More often than not these will be active and probably malevolent types, such as true ghosts, elementals, 'guardians', poltergeists and other oddities lying around at other levels of the mind and elsewhere; and these are more likely to appear – in your mind and imagination, if not elsewhere – if you go looking for them, for by doing so you effectively call them into existence through you. I don't want to go into all the technicalities of this here; but it is a real danger that should not be ignored.[9]

The point I'm trying to make here is this: *don't* play at 'ghost-hunting' unless you know *exactly* what you're doing – and if you're just playing at it, you won't know what you're doing. From personal experience I know how real the danger is: so *if you don't know what you're working with in this field, leave it well alone*.

The other point we have to realize is that since place-memories are simply memories of how someone has felt, or thought, or perceived at that place when it was 'active', we have to learn to be careful not only of what we do physically at those places, but also what we feel, what we think, what we perceive. In other words, we have to be careful, at such sites, of what we do at every level of our being. Place-memories can affect us, and negatively so if they happen to be negative; but it's useful to remember that we create them in the first place, for others or for ourselves to find at a later – or earlier – date. It's up to us, where we have the choice, to make sure that the 'atmosphere' of a place is left as we would wish to find it.

We can do this semi-consciously, by watching our feelings and thoughts in places, particularly if the place we happen to be at is, as the *Exorcism Report* puts it, a 'desecrated' site. But we can also do it deliberately, by constructing an emotion, a feeling, a thought, with a view to implanting it in the place. The blessing of a house is one example of such deliberate action; but so is much of magical ritual, and that's what we'll move on to look at now.

7

Magicians

We are back at the stone circle again, looking down on it from above. It's night-time: we can only just see the stones, as dull shadows in the moonlight. As our eyes adjust to the darkness, we begin to see that there are other shadows there, moving shadows that we slowly recognize are those of people dancing, weaving in and out and round the stones. Their shouts and cries and singing drift up to us through the night air; the sounds float upward, dancing themselves, as the people dance round the *Dawns Myin*, the Dancing Stones.

The dance grows wilder, the sounds sharper, shriller; but there is pattern and purpose there, even though it is hard to see quite what or where. And, imperceptibly at first, the glow, the energy-haze that we've seen before, begins to form: first as a thin mist trailing after each of the dancers, then thickening, spreading, till it forms a glowing ring rippling and moving round the dancers and the stones. The glow spreads inwards, rises, its colour changes; the brilliant ring of the dance now surrounds a pillar of electric-blue fire.

At an unseen, unheard signal the dance stops; the dancers and their glowing ring melt away into the night. All we can see is the pillar, its impossible flames licking round the circle of stones at its base. And from our vantage-point above we can see that the pillar itself is sinking, dispersing and spreading its energies underground along the water-lines and other energy-channels that centre on the circle – they all glow now with the same blue fire. The energy created by the ritual spreads the blue, the colour of healing, throughout the countryside that surrounds this ageless sacred site.

Tom Lethbridge once commented that all religious ritual is a form of magic; and it's in the study of sacred sites, the study of the major node-points of the natural energy-matrix, that we can see this most clearly. Stone circles and the like are real centres of power – in a number of senses, as we've seen – and that power can, with knowledge, be directed to an enormous range of uses. The direct physical use of the power, as power-magic, seems from traditional accounts to have been a particular speciality of the witch-cult, particularly in its later phases. One of the best-known stories concerns the destruction of the Spanish Armada in 1588 by a 'miraculous wind'.

In the version of the story that I've heard, all the Hampshire witches – a large number, according to all the accounts – met together on an unknown site to construct a 'cone of power' to send against the Spaniards. According to my magician friends, such a 'cone' would have looked not unlike the one in the image that heads this chapter. Once the cone was formed, so the story goes, the witches converted it into a violent but controllable gale that split up the Spanish fleet. What makes the story more credible is that the wind chased the fleet all the way up to the tip of Scotland, and then back down the Atlantic coast to Spain. Because of this endless storm, very little of the Armada returned intact to Spain.

It seems that as far as Queen Elizabeth was concerned, this storm did more damage to the Spanish fleet than did the harassment by her privateers, for a comment about 'this miraculous wind' has pride of place on a medallion she had struck to commemorate the occasion.[1] There's little doubt that Elizabeth's highly efficient secret police would have informed her of the activities of the witches, particularly if they were of a military or political nature, as this example of a very 'grey' piece of power-magic was. Assuming that the witches did create that 'miraculous wind', one rather wonders whether they created it from patriotism, or from hatred of the Spanish Inquisition, which would have persecuted them – to say the least – had the Spaniards won. With Catholic fanatics on one side, Puritan fanatics on the

F

other, and with Elizabeth changing her mind about them by the hour, it can't have been easy for the witches to decide whom to support.

Now this is supposedly a story, not factual record, but it may well be true. Witches were traditionally credited with the ability to control the weather, and particularly to raise storms.[2] We do know that they were the last adherents of 'the old religion', which may well have been the remnants of a pre-Druidic religion; and we've already seen that a form of weather-control seems possible through the use of the artifacts of that religion, the standing stones, barrows and the like. All this adds credibility to the story. We still don't know exactly how this storm-raising was done, but in many ways that's a good thing – for if the present-day military got

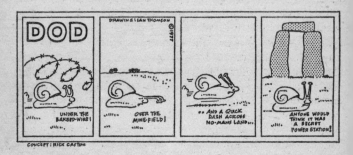

hold of the technique, we wouldn't be able to see any of the sacred sites behind the barbed wire that they'd put up round them 'for security reasons'. It's bad enough already at Stonehenge on Midsummer Day: it's no joke trying to get into a suitable frame of mind for the dawn ritual when you're surrounded by searchlights, soldiers, police-dogs and triple-coiled barbed wire. From the activities of the State, the police and the military, anyone would think that the place and the rituals were security risks.

I suppose that in a way they are, for rituals do have real effects at sacred sites. Stonehenge itself can only be described as a mess – in every sense – and its 'atmosphere' is now almost beyond repair; but at other sites it is still possible to construct 'atmospheres' consciously, and to project them into the place to act as 'filters' on energies of various kinds that pass through the place. We've seen the unconscious versions of these as the ghouls of the last chapter – and remember that there are ghouls of joy and pleasure as well as those of fear, misnomer though this may be. But here, with rituals at sacred sites, we are dealing with the deliberate construction of a sort of 'super-ghoul' which affects not just people on the site, but also much of the surrounding area, because sacred sites act as centres or 'distribution points' for 'occult forces', as John Richards put it.

According to tradition, it's not just people that rituals affect: many, if not most, of the old pagan rituals are to do with fertility of the crops and stock, the control of the weather, and the general health of the land. We have to remember that pagan cultures were not just 'close to the land', they were part of it; and we know that they believed that their health and their lives depended on the carrying out of a ceaseless round of rituals, some of which were carried out just anywhere in the fields, but others of which were carried out specifically at the sacred sites.[3] That belief is easy to laugh at, from our unnatural urban viewpoint, but the evidence we're collecting now suggests that, in some ways at least, the old pagans may not have been wrong.

Physically speaking a ritual can have no direct effect at all. But this does not mean that rituals have no effects: even at the social level, one of the few which current academia admits, rituals are recognized to tie a community together and give it hope and purpose. The energies that rituals create and manipulate are not in themselves physical, but they are made real in a physical sense by the way in which they affect people's attitudes, and thus their actions. There is considerable evidence that they can affect the general health of people, of animals and of plants by a sort of multi-level catalysis – but we'll come to that later. For now, the simplest way to understand ritual is to say that people literally 'realize' the energies that rituals create, in the sense that those energies become real through people. The energy behind a place-memory, for example, has no physical existence and no physical effect until it is realized through the mind of some person, or perhaps some other animal.

The various types of ritual seem to bear this out, in that they are as much designed to work on people's minds, and their attitudes to a situation or place, as they are to work on the place itself. One example of this was the exorcism service that was held in the Southampton flat of a school-friend of mine, when he was a student at the University there. The flat, which he shared with some fellow-students, became haunted for no apparent reason, partly by strange noises, but mainly by an excessive sense of cold in one room, which refused to warm up even in summer.

My friend, a staunch Catholic, discussed this with the local priest, who agreed to hold an exorcism service there on the condition that all the members of the household were to be present. This was done, and from that time on there was no more haunting in the flat, at least as far as the people who had been present at the service were concerned. The odd thing was that casual visitors to the house could still hear the strange noises of the haunting, and could still feel the excessive cold of that room. The energies involved could only become real, in an experiential sense if not a physical one, through people who had been 'primed' to allow them to become real – or rather, in this case, through people who had not been primed not to let them become real. Rituals change the personal definition of what reality is, or should be, and thus help to make that subjective reality real in the physical world.

The same applies to rituals like, for example, the fertility rituals connected with dancing round the Maypole. I'd agree that the present day 'version' of dancing the Maypole – small kids on the village green dithering round a gaudily-painted bit of stick – is almost meaningless, even if it is pretty; but four centuries ago it was still a matter that was taken seriously in Britain. The Puritan propagandist Philip Stubbes could, with evident disgust, still write this contemporary report in 1583:

'Against May, Whitsonday, or other time, all the yung men and maides, olde men and wives, run gadding to the woods, groves, hils and mountains, where they spend all the night in plesant pastimes; and in the morning they return, bringing with them birch and branches of trees, to deck their assembly withal ... They have twentie or fortie yoke of oxen, every oxe having a sweet nose-gay of flouers placed on the tip of his hornes, and these oxen drawe home this May-pole (this stinkyng ydol, rather), which is covered all over with floures and hearbs, bound round about with strings, from the top to the bottome, and sometime painted with variable colours, with two or three hundred men, women and children following it with great devotion. And thus beeing reared up ... they straw the ground round about ... and then fall they to daunce about it, like as the heathen people did at the dedication of the Idols, whereof this is a perfect pattern, or rather the thing itself. I have heard it credibly reported ... that of fortie, threescore, or a hundred maids going to the wood over night, there have scaresly the third part of them returned home againe undefiled.'[4]

It is in that last sentence that Stubbes reveals not only the righteous indignation of the civilized man (or is it, I wonder, just common envy?), but also the fact that he has completely missed the point of the ritual. The 'defiling' – as he calls it – of the maidens (and for that matter of the 'yung men' who were with them) was not disgusting licentiousness, as Stubbes implies, but a necessary part of the devotion, a religious act. The whole is a fertility ritual; and the energy produced by dancing round the Maypole – a still-living 'needle of wood', in the terms of our earth-acupuncture – has first to be primed to work towards fertility of the area.

The energy is primed and directed by the state of mind of the participants in the dancing: and what better way of framing a 'fertility' state of mind could there be than spending the night in the woods, engaged in 'pleasant past-imes'?

Fertility rituals aren't the only ones in pagan religion, they're just part of a complex cycle of religious events. Fertility comes into many of them, of course, but that's not surprising when we remember that people's lives depended on it. In the neo-pagan cycle of the present-day Druid Order, for example, the 'Earth Mother' character Ceridwen is symbolized by a maiden at the Spring equinox, a young woman (preferably pregnant) at Midsummer, and a mature woman bearing the fruits of the harvest at the Autumn equinox. From what I've seen of these rituals, their symbolism affects the 'colouring' of the energy stored at the place. It's possible that the different 'colourings' of the energy left behind after each festival might prime the weather-control system in different ways: I'm not sure about this, but it does seem to make sense in Reich's terms at least.

The same is probably true of the old Celtic fire-festivals. These were Imbolc (February 1), Beltane (May Eve), Lugnasadh (August 1) and Samhain (November Eve). These festivals all seem to have involved the lighting of bonfires, and one of them is still followed in Britain, now thinly disguised as the 'Guy Fawkes Night' of November 5. It's interesting to see how these key festivals became Christianized: Imbolc, the feast of the 'Earth Mother' Brighid, symbolizing purification of the earth, became Candlemas, the festival of the Purification of the Virgin Mary: while Lugnasadh, the harvest festival, became the Christian Lammas, a word which is apparently derived from 'loaf-mas', implying a feast of the harvest. The other festivals seem to have given the Christians more trouble, for their festivals *follow* the Celtic ones: All Hallows, a sort of general thanksgiving, follows Samhain on November 1, while the inconspicuous feast of St Philip and St James follows Beltane on May Day itself.

Beltane and Samhain were the pivot-points of the Celtic year, marking times of high instability. The material world seems to have been unstable at Beltane, bringing with it diseases and civil disorder: hence, perhaps, the practice of driving sheep through the bonfire at Beltane (purification by the equivalent of moxibustion, or a 'needle of fire', in our earth-acupuncture); and hence also, perhaps, the reason why May Day is now taken as a symbol of a day of bloodshed and revolution. Samhain seems to have been a time of instability in the spiritual world, when the fairy-mounds opened, when witches and warlocks were abroad, when the living and the dead could speak together, and when great good as well as great evil could be done. The sacred sites – of all kinds, it seems – were supposed to have been particularly active at these two times, and rituals held there then were believed to have a strong influence on events in the following half-year. If our hypothesis of a 'super-ghoul' effect is correct, it's likely that such beliefs were based on practical experience, not 'mere superstition'.

It seems that very few pagan festivals were not continued in a Christian guise. According to the Venerable Bede, at least, the Church in its early days in Britain had a deliberate policy not only of taking over existing sites – 'purifying them of devil-worship' first, of course – but also of disguising previous festivals as saints' or martyrs' days.[5] In some cases the entire rituals remained unchanged except for some details of names and terms.[6] Their meaning, and thus the priming effect of the rituals on the energies at the place, remained unchanged. The rituals gave meaning to a pagan way of life; and it was not the Church's suppression of paganism, but rather the increasing enforcement of a 'civilized' way of life on the whole of the countryside, that destroyed that meaning.[7] The result is the meaninglessness of life that we suffer today.

Be that as it may, rituals do still have real effects at

sacred sites and others. On a Midsummer morning at Rollright, a few years back it was discovered that some group had
held an unpleasant ceremony the previous night, for beside
the smouldering ashes of a bonfire were the dismembered
remains of a very young puppy. There was no doubt that it
had been 'sacrificed', and probably while alive. The 'atmosphere' in and around the circle could be aptly described as
hellish; and even though the owner had an exorcism service
held there within a couple of days, an unpleasant 'buzz' –
that's the only way I can describe it – could still be felt
around the centre of the circle for nearly two years. As
the *Exorcism Report* put it, 'the activity of magicians
frequently revivifies ancient celtic sites such as . . . circles
. . . and causes a general sense of "buzz" or strain which
can be disturbing, if rarely dangerous.' There's no doubt
whatsoever that that ritual had a real effect in an experiential sense at least.

In this case the ritual – and I suppose also the nausea of
the people who had to clear away the remnants of what the
'celebrants' had left behind – created a ghoul powerful
enough to burn right through the 'white paint' of an exorcism service: it really was a 'super-ghoul'. With the amount
of magical attention that Rollright has to put up with, it's
not surprising that its 'atmosphere' is best described as
'moody'.

But what of the effect of that ritual on the surrounding
area? We know that Lethbridge's earth-fields act as 'stores'
for the coded energy that is behind place-memory ghosts and
ghouls and we know of the connection between those
earth-fields and underground water, or at least water trapped
in the soil as 'water of crystallization'. We know too that
the naiad- and dryad-fields at least are likely to be on water-
lines. But we also know, from the work of Underwood and
the other dowsers, that sacred sites are centres where many
water-lines coincide with each other and with centres of
overground patterns. We could therefore suggest that
sacred sites are the centres which connect up all the earth-

fields of a given area, and at the same time connect them with the overgrounds of the ley-system.

If this is so, activation of the central site, either by ritual on that site or – as we shall see – through 'messages' coming through the overground network, could affect the attitude (so to speak) of the earth-fields of the entire area. Whether it would do so electrostatically, orgonomically, through the peculiar properties of water itself in the water-lines, by a combination of these, or by some other means entirely, I do not know: but whatever the actual mechanism involved, the idea makes sense, as far as we can make out at the present time. It does seem to be what is implied in John Richards' comment that 'the proximity of ancient sites may be the only explanation of places of disturbance which are not centred on a home', and that 'such centres act as distribution points for occult forces . . . which appear to run on power lines or "leys" between each centre'.

But here, as you can see, we run into a certain amount of confusion as to the relative roles of the underground and overground connections between sites, for both types of connection do carry a wide range of energies or codings. Assuming that the term 'ley' does mean the same to Richards as it does to us, what he is describing is not so much the local distribution of energies, covering the immediately surrounding area, as the interconnection of the centres which feed each area. The two networks have slightly different functions.

To return to our earlier 'energy as paint' analogy, the ley-lines or overgrounds are like paint-carrying pipes linking together a network of spray-heads – the sacred sites themselves. The water-lines coming away from each centre, each sacred site, are like the paths which the paint takes travelling between the spray-head and the surface it is to colour; and the earth-fields, the naiad- and dryad-fields, are like concentrations of paint, small areas where for some reason or other the central part of each stream of paint from the spray-head will land. And although the surface is unevenly painted, every part of the surface 'beneath' the spray-head should receive some paint under normal conditions. It's possible, though, that some areas, because of blockages at the spray-head or elsewhere, or because of shielding or shadowing, or some other reason, might remain unpainted, however much paint may land elsewhere.

Assuming that the paint is at first just a colourless medium, it can be coloured, by the addition of pigment, at a number of stages. It may already be coloured in the pipe, in which case the same colour will be supplied to every

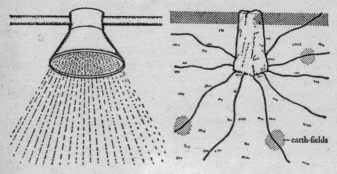

32 The spray-head analogy of energy distribution.

spray-head. It may have pigment added at individual spray-heads, in which case the colouring at each may be different; and according to the way in which the pigment is added at the spray-head, it may or may not affect the colouring of that paint-medium in the pipe that is travelling through or past that spray-head to others. There may already be some colour on the ground-surface as small local 'atmospheres', or at the concentration-points (ghouls, in other words), which may have been put there by other means – by hand, we might say in this analogy – and this would provide interesting problems of colour-mixing, much as we saw before when we looked at the earlier version of this analogy as 'emotion as paint on the wall'.

The spray-head could be regarded as an 'active' or 'passive' filter, by adding or subtracting colour respectively. There is also another way in which it could filter colour, or other properties of the paint-medium, and that is by using differing sizes of filter-mesh to separate different sizes of particles. There could be different-sized meshes at different spray-heads, or even in different parts of the same spray-head. If the pigment in the paint coming through the pipe were made up of several different colours, each of a different particle-size, they could be separated from each other by the different-sized filter-meshes; or, to twist the analogy a little assuming that the paint started as a single pigment, this filtering could be used to alter the *texture* of the final painted surface, some areas thus having a smooth finish, others a rough one, yet others a mottled finish, and so on. The spray-heads could be made to 'filter' a number of properties in this way, of which colour would only be one.

Taking this as an analogy, we can see that the overground and underground energy networks do carry the same energies, or properties, or whatever you want to call them, but the two networks carry them in different ways. The basic carrier in each case – water with the water-lines, God only knows what with the overgrounds – is basically neutral: it's just raw energy, a carrier like a colourless paint medium. This carrier carries the various properties in it, through it, by it – 'piggyback', if you like – and these properties can be added, subtracted, modified, interconverted at any point, from the basic transmission through the overgrounds down to the local level of 'atmosphere'. And this, as I said earlier, presents interesting problems of 'colour-mixing'.

The problem in geomancy, then, is to balance all the different 'colours', 'textures' and the like – many of which will be changing by themselves all the time – in a way that produces a harmony, a music, at all the levels from local to area to national to international and, we might hope,

beyond. That would be the ideal, but we haven't a hope in
hell of doing it now, or at least not until we have a better
understanding not only of geomancy but of ourselves as
well – for we are ourselves a key part of that geomancy.

But we may as well start somewhere, and one place to
start would be to clear up a few misconceptions. I hope I've
cleared away a few already; but another I'd better despatch
is the idea that at sacred sites all is sweetness and light. It's
true that at some of them there is a tendency that way, but
I think it's safer, and more accurate, to describe sacred sites
simply as 'power points'. They are distribution points for
various energies, places that collect those energies from the
overground network. Assuming a good connection between
upstairs and downstairs at any given site, we can say that,
crudely speaking, high ley-line density at a site will give high
energy levels at that site.

But note that this is probably going to be raw energy, the
colourless paint-medium in our analogy: there is no reason
at all why it must be the colour of 'sweetness and light'. As
Richards says, it is probably 'an instinctive awareness' of the
energy potential of sites that leads to 'the willingness (of
young people) to spend hours at such sites as Glastonbury
Tor', but there needs to be an awareness of the energy for
what it is, not what people would like to assume it is. Until
that 'instinctive awareness' of young people at Glastonbury
developed into something more than a bemused, naive and
often arrogant instinct, those same energies made life
pretty hellish there at times – as you'll remember if you'd
been there during the 'No Hippies Served' seasons of the
early 1970s.

Even if it is supposed to be the country's most important
magical area, Glastonbury is in most other ways a very
ordinary West Country town. So it's not at all surprising
that there should have been clashes then between some of
the townspeople and the hordes of spiritual sensation-seek-
ers who invaded the town at the time. Even if the over-
reaction of a few of the townspeople was unpleasant – it

included the dumping of tons of caustic sludge around the caravans of those 'hippy invaders' who tried to stay in the area – the arrogance and tactlessness of the newcomers and the high energy levels of the area made it only too predictable. But at the same time many of these 'invaders' met with extraordinary and often undeserved kindness and tolerance from others of the townspeople: the energies will work in whatever direction they are asked to go.

High energy levels at a place like Glastonbury can make the whole area surrounding it unstable, at an emotional level and beyond. So while it's true that those energies can indeed create a state of 'all sweetness and light', they have to be pushed and held there, cherished with care and respect. If the area's 'atmosphere' gets out of control, as it undoubtedly did in that case, those same energies are far more likely to turn themselves towards reinforcing someone's private hell.

Glastonbury is a quiet and pleasant place now: those of the 'invaders' who stayed have learnt the importance of tact, and respect for the people of the place as well as for the place itself. Most of the 'No Hippies Served' signs have gone. I often pass through the town on my travels, for business as well as personal interest, and the Tor with its weird, impossible tower seems to hold a fascination for me; but unless I'm there solely for business I can't stay there long. It is perfectly possible to live an ordinary life in the areas around the great sacred sites, you don't have to be a saint to live there – and that's something which few of those 'invaders' of Glastonbury realized. The problems only start when you turn your attention towards those energies, for then (as John Cowper Powys put it in his epic *Glastonbury Romance*) the 'invisible Watchers above the town' start to turn their attention toward you. At least part of those 'Watchers' is yourself: you have to bring to the place what you would wish to find there. The problem is the same as with the 'atmosphere' of a house, but far, far more so in this case.

This, of course, is the whole point of a pilgrimage, in that you have to purify yourself *before* you get to the holy place. The time spent in travelling to the place must be a period of contemplation and preparation, or else you just won't be able to handle what will be thrown at you by the place. In a personal sense, sacred sites can be mirrors that pick out your flaws, amplify them, and then throw them back at you in a way that forces you to do something about those flaws or go insane. It's happened to me at several sites, and it's not a comfortable experience; the ordinary people of places like Glastonbury, I imagine, stay sane only by being thoroughly civilized, ignoring the existence of those forces as hard as they can. Since I live in a city, I have to spend several days in the country before I can quieten down enough to handle the sheer power of the great sacred sites; and this is why I can't stay for long in places like Glastonbury, if I'm only passing through.

A pilgrimage, then, is as much a magical process as a religious one. You could say that it is the use of a religious mode to prime the energies at the place in order to cause a magical transformation – sometimes a physical transformation of healing, as at the holy wells, but more often a transformation of the soul, of one's attitude to the world. If that priming isn't done, the pilgrimage may be useless, or even harmful. To return to our 'paint' analogy, that kind of priming affects the colour and texture – and whatever else – of the 'paint' only in relation to you; it selects the final properties of the energies in other words, at the point where they reach you.

This assumes, though, that the 'paint' is initially a colourless medium, right up until that point of contact; and as we have seen, there are a whole range of points at which the properties of the 'paint' can be changed in its travels from wherever it comes from – which we don't know – to that final point of contact. It can be changed at the sacred site or 'power point' – the 'spray-head' in the analogy – by ritual or by some other conscious or unconscious means of changing the 'atmosphere' of the place; and it can also be changed in the 'pipe', within the overground network itself. If the place is to work as a place of healing (or literally, 'wholing') both for people at the place and for the area surrounding it, all those properties must harmonize with each other. If they don't, the resultant discord will, it seems, produce dis-ease. Some of the factors which produce discord are beyond our control – though not entirely beyond our direction – since they are, as the *Exorcism Report* puts it, 'non-human'; but all the human factors are, or can and should be, within our control. We've looked at quite a few of these human factors so far, but there are still a few others we need to look at before we go on to look at the non-human aspects. And these new human factors are particularly important, for they operate on the energies as or even before they arrive at the 'power points'.

The one major category of magical operation on the 'power points' themselves that we haven't yet looked at is that rather odd category in the *Exorcism Report*, 'human sin'. As the *Report* put it: 'a house or site used for sexual misbehaviour (often the ancient fertility-cult site), but equally the office of an organization devoted to greed or domination, can often incur trouble or act as a dispersal centre'. I think we need to regard that comment about 'sexual misbehaviour' as slightly suspect, as the Church's definition of 'proper' sexual behaviour is still a little limited; but there's no doubt that fertility rituals can be dangerous in some respects. To use the 'paint' analogy again, we could say that the 'colour' of fertility rituals is an odd one, and has to be balanced carefully by others. Fertility rituals, in other words, must be only a part of a more complete system of rituals.

If fertility rituals do actually stimulate the fertility of the land, we can see that over-stimulation – as would be the case where fertility rituals were used to excess – would cause as many problems as under-stimulation. When fertility rites are taken totally to excess, as they are in Crowley-style sex-magic, the Commission on Exorcism is probably right to suggest that 'human sin' of this kind 'opens the door for other forces to enter in'. I'm not sure exactly what those forces would be, and I'm not sure that I want to know: for in the cases that I've heard of it would be appropriate to describe them simply as 'hellish'.

This leaves us with that extraordinary comment that 'the office of an organization devoted to greed or domination may incur trouble or act as a dispersal centre'. The social and political implications of this 'throwaway' comment are, to say the least, staggering, and I'll be going into them in some detail later. For now I'll just say that it completes the range of effects of attitudes of mind of people living, working and acting upon 'power points' and lesser sites, by adding moral and ethical factors to the emotional and similar ones we've already met. Greed and the wish to dominate are attitudes of mind and being, and these, as we've seen from all our studies of hauntings so far, affect the places where those attitudes are held. A negative or destructive attitude will cause a negative or destructive effect.

This is true *anywhere*, affecting the 'atmosphere' of the place; it is more serious at Lethbridge's earth-fields, for then a true negative ghoul would be formed; and it is particularly serious at 'power points', for the 'colour' supplied to the whole area would be affected. In magical terms, as we have seen, simply being at a place is enough to implant that attitude into the place, if the other conditions make the site receptive; so in magical terms we can say that people who devote themselves to greed or domination, or particularly organizations which devote themselves to those aims – which could be said of a large number of our present-day organizations and institutions – are practising a form of black magic which is a danger to us all. I don't care whether it is done consciously or unconsciously, it is still magic; and in magical terms it is unquestionably 'black'.

The implications of that, as I say, will have to be left for later. But there is another type of 'activation of ancient celtic sites by magicians' which does seem to be important in any study of hauntings, even though it doesn't seem to affect the 'colouring' of the energies: and that is the creation and activation of what my magician friends call 'guardians'. Fortunately these are rare, for the various reports I've had of them suggests that they can be extremely dangerous. Basically, they are images which at first 'sight' seem to be ordinary place-memories stored in a place, or in some cases in an object. They do resemble place-memories in that respect: but there the similarity ends. As far as I can decipher from the reports, they are not impersonal memories, like the place-memory ghosts, but rather the storage of a protective function or idea – but an idea that is active, in that it has a limited amount of choice and intelligence both in the choice of form in which it appears and the movements and effects it can have.

Unlike place-memories, which are planted into the place unconsciously, these 'guardians' are implanted into the place or object by some deliberate process. They are then, like place-memories, left to be activated by anyone who happens to fulfil certain conditions, such as, in the case of a barrow-guardian, breaking open, and thus 'short-circuiting', the barrow. It may be that a fair number of the legends of 'divine retribution' against barrow-robbers and the like are due to these elemental 'guardians': no matter how crazy it may sound, these 'active images' do have a real force, and are not to be taken lightly.

One well-known recent example of an active 'guardian' was that of the Hexham Heads, a pair of Celtic carved stone heads that had a werewolf-like figure associated with them; there is little doubt from the full report that this image was too active, too free and too physical in its movements and effects to be a place-memory ghost.[8] What is interesting is that although the two heads were removed from the house as soon as the connection between them and the figure was recognized, the hauntings continued. Dr Anne Ross, the archaeologist in whose home the majority of the hauntings took place, called in the Hampshire exorcist, and he advised her to dispose of her entire collection of more than twenty of these carved heads, because the two original heads had somehow activated them enough to be able to sustain the haunting by the guardian from the original heads. It was only after all the heads were removed that the hauntings ceased. This incident is doubly interesting to researchers on our 'lunatic fringe of archaeology', in that it's one of the rare instances of a professional archaeologist publicly describing a subjective experience of this kind.

Another incident, closer to our current theme of sacred sites, concerns the 'guardian' of a barrow. I came across this case because a friend of mine, then a psychiatric social worker, had to deal with its aftermath. It happened a few years back. The incident began when a group of students found or bought an old book of gramarie: a book of spells, if you like. For a joke – as they thought – they decided to hold a conjuration on top of a barrow at night, 'just to see what happened'. Something did. My friend wasn't able to get a precise description from the students of what suddenly appeared on top of the barrow, since its appearance was slightly different for each of them. (This is a characteristic of 'guardians' and many other kinds of 'thought-forms', as we shall see later.) As one of them put it, it was like a horror-movie monster, but it seemed to them to be very real, and right in front of them. Not surprisingly, they panicked and scattered; but for several days afterward they were haunted by the fear that it was stalking them, and might appear at any moment, even when they were back in the city. My friend had to talk them out of their fear, and thus protect them from further haunting. In some ways this incident is reminiscent of M. R. James' ghost story *Oh Whistle and I'll Come To You, My Lad*; but I think it does show that magical rituals, even if only performed in jest, will still work if the right conditions are fulfilled.

Dangerous as they might be, the 'guardians' don't have much effect on the 'colouring' of the energies passing through sites like barrows. They have much the same relationship to that 'colouring' as an alsatian guard-dog has to the product of the factory it guards, and – so I'm told – about the same level of persistence and intelligence. So with these we leave the sites themselves, and turn to the transmission of energies to the sites through the ley-system, the overground network.

But first we'd better look at the transmission of energies in general. The concept of 'colouring' or 'texturing' of the energy assumes, first, that there is an energy to be 'coloured', and second, that the energy is capable of carrying 'colouring' or some other coded information of a high degree of complexity. On the first point, I have no doubt whatsoever of the existence of some kind of energy associated with sacred sites, as my being knocked flat by the release of the 'spin' at Rollright made only too clear. Even if the energies themselves are 'subjective', they have been experienced by enough people for them to be called 'objective' in one sense at least. The distribution and 'channeling' of those energies in pathways both above ground and below seems to have been established, at least from the results of a fair number of dowsers; but the ability of these 'channels' to carry coded information of any degree of complexity had not been so well established. Following some clues given me by various dowser friends, I set up a series of experiments on this; and the results do show that these 'channels' are capable of carrying coded information up to the complexity of Morse Code at least.

My experiments started when two dowser friends from Wales pointed out that if one dowser stands on a water-line, holding a pendulum in neutral oscillation, that pendulum will react when another working dowser crosses the same water-line. Following their suggestion, I found a suitable testing-ground where a water-line passed under a wall close to a door, allowing us to place a dowser on either side of the wall, with an observer able to watch both dowsers by standing in the doorway. The two dowsers took turns to be 'transmitter' and 'receiver', to see if there was any difference between transmission upstream and downstream. I suppose

Needles of Stone

33 The water-line-as-cable experiment.

we took the theory to be that the transmitter interfered with some kind of tuned circuit inherent in the water-line, and it was this interference which the receiver recognized as the 'signal'; I'm not sure now, we changed the theory so much as we went along. The point was that it worked.

The results were interesting. First, we found that the pendulum was definitely the best type of dowsing instrument for the job, as all the others we tried required the receiver to be moving about, in order to break their starting friction. In the technique we used, the pendulum's 'neutral' position is one of constant oscillation, and so it doesn't have that problem. Second, we found that it *was* a little easier to get reliable results if the receiver was downstream of the transmitter, but we could still transmit both ways without too much difficulty. And third, a lot depended on the skill and continuous concentration of both dowsers, which I admit didn't surprise us much. The most serious problem in this was certainly that of concentration, for if either dowser allowed it to lapse for more than a moment the receiver's reactions went 'out of phase', with the pendulum reacting when the transmitter walked *off* the water-line instead of when he walked onto it. But the results seemed to show that, with practice and with skilled dowsers, this technique could be used with water-lines to work a crude but effective medium-range Morse-Code-type communications system.

Later, when we were experimenting with multi-way communications of this type, attempting to transmit between several dowsers on the same water-line, we came across a simpler technique. Instead of having the transmitter building up the Morse-Code pattern by walking on and off the line, all the dowsers involved in the communication stood still directly above the same water-line. The receiver or receivers held their pendulums in neutral oscillation, as before; but this time the transmitter swung his pendulum in gyration, simulating a reaction. This gyration repeated itself in the receivers' pendulums. This system demanded even more concentration than the earlier one, particularly to keep the reactions and 'neutrals' in phase; but it also allowed us to use a more sophisticated and reliable set of reactions for the Morse-Code pattern, using a clockwise gyration for 'dot', an anti-clockwise gyration 'for dash', and the neutral oscillation for the spaces.

Up to this point we'd only done these experiments with water-lines; but in experiments at Rollright we found that we could use the same technique with the overgrounds. We first tested this with a very short section – only a couple of yards – of the 'spin' overground at the eastern 'gate'. When these tests were successful we tried it with two of the major stones (stones 3 and 37 on the official site-plan), about a hundred feet apart on opposite sites of the circle, which I knew from my earlier work were connected by an internal overground, probably a fourth-band one. Two of my students found that for them it was actually easier to get reliable results from the overgrounds than from the water-lines. Neither of them had done more than a few hours' practical dowsing before that time, but on a cold November day they kept transmission and reception accurately in phase through a short 'test-run' of about a dozen changes of gyration. Towards the end of that run, it seemed that the receiver reacted more to the transmitter's *intention* to gyrate her pendulum rather than the actual movement, as she picked up the correct reaction about half a second before the transmitter's pendulum gyrated in the relevant direction. This suggests that the coding of the energy in the overground in this case was more mental than physical; and in turn this implies that the overgrounds at least are indeed capable of carrying coded information of the complexity of the 'colour' and 'texture' that seem to be involved in the various 'earth mysteries'.

So far we've only tried these experiments with short- to medium-distance communications – no more than a few hundred yards – as we haven't been able to borrow the transceivers of field-telephones we'd need to do running checks on the results; but I have little doubt that longer-distance communications based on these techniques would be possible. Assuming that the dowsers involved were skilled and well-practised, the main problem would seem to be that natural pulsings of the energies in the lines, both above and below ground, would produce a background 'noise' that could obscure the transmitted 'signal' at times. But this is a problem that dogs more physical communication-systems like short-wave radio – and as with short-wave radio we could no doubt devise 'noise-reducing' systems to get over it.

If we take the original cable-type telegraphy as an analogy for the kind of communications described above, we can see that the same cables were used later to carry teleprinter messages, telephone messages and 'wired' pictures by using more complex codings and modulations of the same energy in the cable. So by analogy we can at least suggest that although my experiments dealt only with a crude Morse-type code, there is no reason why the same 'cables' should not carry more complex codings. As the results from the Rollright experiments suggest, these may be codings not just of physical energies, but of other levels of energies as well. No matter how little sense that makes in physical terms, it does make sense in terms of the research we've seen so far.

The emotional 'colour and texture' coding that seems to be

responsible for the hauntings we've looked at are probably not the only kind of non-physical coding that the over-grounds and water-lines can carry. A number of my correspondents have told me that the transmission of complete mental images – telepathy, in other words – is much easier between sacred sites than elsewhere, and this seems to be borne out in some of my own experiments. Magician friends have told me that in their experience both forms of what they call 'astral travelling' – projection of the imagination and projection of the entire personality – are made easier by 'hitching a ride' on the energy that passes along ley-lines or overgrounds; and Carlos Castaneda described in one of his books an incident in which his personality 'travelled' along water-courses, apparently for hundreds of miles, which suggests that water-lines could be used to assist 'astral travelling' as well as the overgrounds.[9] The Feng-shui concept of 'spirit paths', clearly-marked pathways on which the spirits of the dead travel, suggests that 'astral travelling', as the projection of the personality, may not be limited solely to the personalities of the living.

Mention of Feng-shui brings me back to the problem of interference with the transmission of the coding of the energies passing through the energy-matrix. The nineteenth-century European writers on Feng-shui all commented on the way that the Westerners' 'rational' exploitation of China was constantly hindered by Feng-shui 'superstition'. As Eitel put it, 'when it was proposed to erect a few telegraph poles, when the construction of a railway was urged upon the Chinese government, when a tramway was suggested to utilize the coal-mines of the interior, Chinese officials would invariably make a polite bow and declare the whole thing impossible on account of Feng-shui.' At first this just sounds like conservatism, a use of Feng-shui superstition to prevent or limit change, and indeed most of those writers on Feng-shui regarded it as such – but there is more to it than that.

A comment by Dukes helps us in this, for it is more explicit and more revealing: 'The first railway in China, from

Shanghai to the port of Wu-Sung nine miles away, was purchased and destroyed by the Chinese on the plea that the speed of the train destroyed the Feng-shui of tens of thousands of people on both sides of the line'.[10] This doesn't appear to be simple conservatism, for the same Chinese authorities had allowed the line to be built in the first place; and it is stated specifically that it is the *speed* of the train that is causing problems. In other cases it is the straightness of the lines of telegraph poles, for example, that are said to damage the Feng-shui of an area. So the complaints are almost always about specific aspects of a development rather than the developments as such, and Feuchtwang cites cases where development had been permitted to take place on the proviso that care should be taken not to damage the Feng-shui of that area.[11]

We have seen earlier that a close parallel can be drawn between the apparent British system of geomancy and a combination of Chinese geomancy and acupuncture. To strengthen that parallel, evidence is now arising from a number of sources to suggest that many modern developments in Britain are having exactly the effect on the flow of natural energies in the energy-matrix that a combination of Feng-shui theory and acupuncture theory would predict – namely, a highly destructive one. Most of this evidence is coming out of dowsing work on a form of environmental medicine, which we'll be looking at in some detail later. Unfortunately, much of the information remains unpublished;[12] but from discussions I've had with a number of the dowsers involved a number of key points have come over. One of the most important of these is that most of the problems they have to deal with stem, as in acupuncture, from blockages and other disturbances in the energy-matrix; and most of these disturbances arise from man-made causes, not natural ones. Among the most common causes of these problems in recent times are motorways, pylon lines and mining and quarrying.

The effect of motorways is odd. The structure of the

motorway itself probably doesn't do much damage, being the earth-acupuncture equivalent of a relatively minor scar. It seems to be the vehicles travelling along the motorway that cause the worst problems, for the energy in any over-grounds crossing the motorway and close to its surface 'catches' on the vehicles as they go past. In the terms of our 'energy as paint' analogy, we could see the energy of the overground as a horizontal pipe or rod of luminous liquid crossing the road: and as each vehicle passes by, it breaks the stream of liquid, splashing the liquid over the road, the vehicle itself, everywhere, reducing the amount of liquid that can carry on, and introducing surges in the flow as it tries to even itself out on the other side of the road.

This is only one half of the problem, for as well as re-ducing the total amount of 'coloured' energy that arrives at its proper destination, this constant interruption by one vehicle after another would also break down any time-based coding in the energy-flow (a coding like a telegraph message, as opposed to something more constant like 'colour'). The overall result, as you can imagine, would be a mess, but most of these problems with motorways can be alleviated if not solved. The usual solution is to divert the over-ground either under the motorway, or higher, or in a slightly different direction, by processes which we'll look at later. In most cases motorways aren't too bad – from an earth-acupuncture point of view – apart from their permanent scarring of the landscape. They do cause a lot of hidden problems, but those problems can usually be resolved without too much difficulty, and without affecting the effectiveness of the motorway as a mode of transport com-munications.

Unfortunately, we can't say the same about pylon lines. The two problems with these are their straightness (with occasional bends) and their height. As with motorways, the lower overgrounds 'catch' on them because of their height; but unlike motorways the interruption they cause is not intermittent but continuous, lasting as long as there is an energy-flow in the overground. Basically, pylon lines split the energy-flow, allowing part of it to continue on its way, but sending the remainder down the pylon line itself. The proportions 'stolen' by the pylons vary enormously, for no known reason. At each bend in the line of the cables some of the energy that originally ran down the overground 'spins off', effectively forming a new low-powered over-ground. The result is that in some areas – like the area around Yarnley, just to the north of Glastonbury – the web of pylon lines, large and small, produces large numbers of 'unofficial' overgrounds, allowing energy of the wrong kind to arrive at the wrong place at the wrong time and probably from the wrong direction.

The result, in other words, is not just a mess, it's absolute chaos. In some cases and areas it may be possible to divert the major overgrounds upwards so that they are above the power lines; but in others the dowsers I talked to felt that the only satisfactory solution would be to put all electrical power cables underground. Even given the enormous cost of doing so, they reckoned that it would still be worthwhile in every sense to do so, because of the pylons' hidden effects on the health and fertility of the land.

Probably the most serious problems in this respect come from quarrying and mining, because of the near-permanence of their effects. For a start, an open-cast quarry could be said to be the equivalent of a massive scar or open wound, in acupuncture terms; and that means that such a quarry would prevent any energy in its immediate vicinity from passing through, either below or above ground. The same goes for spoil tips and slag-heaps: they are literally scars on the landscape. It's true that some of the blockages, particularly of overgrounds, can be reduced by 'massage', in the form of filling-in and grassing when the quarry or tip is no longer used as such; but the underground damage is permanent. Mining of any kind breaks up the sub-surface flow of water, and thus of energies: the deeper the mine, the deeper down goes the damage.

This affects not just our near-magical energy-system, but people's water-supply: one recent case the British Society of Dowsers had to deal with was where blasting – believed to have been done by the National Coal Board – had shaken up and re-fissured the sub-strata in a small area, with the result that all the wells in three villages went dry overnight. But it's not just the damage to the water-supply that concerns us: there is the energy aspect too. One stone circle I went to, at Dinnever Hill in north Cornwall, is now completely dead, both below ground and above, because all the water in the immediate area has been drained away into the vast china-clay works that starts a mere fifty yards away.

Damage of that kind to a previous 'power point' means that no energies can come into the point, or be distributed from it; energy that is already there cannot escape, and the whole area stagnates. In Feng-shui terms, the *ch'i*, the living energy, is converted to *sha*, stagnation, 'noxious breath', 'stinking exhalations'. Such an area cannot breathe, say the Feng-shui manuals, and ill-health and ill-fortune will result. From what I saw of the area around Dinnever Hill, the Feng-shui manuals are right.

But it's no use complaining about this: the quarries, the pylons and the motorways are there, and that is that. And it's no use calling for a ban on all future development: in the present economic circumstances of the country, and with the present politico-economic system we have to put up with, that would be more than a little unrealistic. What we can do, and do need to do, is to learn to repair the damage that we cause, to learn how to reduce the impact of our grubbings and burrowings. To do that we need to know much more than we do about the energies and their interactions with nature, with places and with ourselves.

So far we've looked at the various ways in which we interact directly with the energies and with places. But there is another factor which we cannot ignore, no matter how ludicrous it may seem in a materialistic and humanistic age, and that is the non-human factor: forces outside of our control, impossible forces or entities which the *Exorcism Report* describes as 'the activities of non-human sprites' and 'demonic interference'. It seems that the forces which produce balance or imbalance of the energies in the natural energy-matrix, producing Feng-shui's *ch'i* and *sha*, are the same as those which are reflected in the Christian vision of the battles between the angels and demons – and they are thus important to our aim of a more complete understanding of nature.

8

Angels and Demons

The stone circle seems as we left it, with the pillar of blue fire sinking and spreading outward through the water-lines. But there is something else there too, something we didn't notice before: for though the 'fire' spreads easily along some of the lines, there is definite tension in one of them, where the 'fire' moves onward only with evident difficulty. From our vantage-point high above the circle, we look more closely; there is something odd about that line, beyond the limit of the 'fire'. It seems to be radiating 'blackness' in the same way that the 'fire'-laden lines radiate light. The blue 'fire' is *ch'i*; the black line, the black stream, carries *sha*; and some kind of conflict is taking place at the point where they meet. We see this at first in terms of colours, in terms of whorls and vortices and edges of coloured light, that spin out from that point of contact. But with one of those changes of vision to which we've become accustomed, the scene changes: and we see the conflict now as a battle between angels and demons, each fighting for control of the line.

In Chinese terms *ch'i* and *sha* are products or processes of the interplay of the two primal forces of Yin and Yang. *Ch'i* occurs where Yin and Yang fuse together in harmony, and *sha* occurs where they are out of balance, where the primal energies are separated or stagnant. I'm almost certain that it's this imbalance that produces the 'sense of "buzz" or strain' that the *Exorcism Report* describes as the effect of 'demonic interference'; and this 'interference' seems to be a *force*, capable of disturbing the natural tendency to balance of Yin and Yang.

At the same time, there is another force or agency, which

I suppose we could call 'angelic interference', which tends to bring out-of-balance Yin and Yang into equilibrium. It is this quality which, when associated with a well, for example, makes it into a holy well, for the water from such a well will tend to re-balance the energies in people, making them 'whole'. As we've said, linguistically, 'holy' is allied with 'whole' is allied with 'healthy'. It's 'angelic interference' that makes an otherwise ordinary site both holy and healthy. This was literally the case at Lourdes in France in 1858, for 'angels' and other sacred personalities of an equally ephemeral nature showed the fourteen-year-old Bernadette Soubirous where to find the springs whose water has been behind all the subsequent miraculous cures in the town.[1] The curative effects of 'angelic' water – presumably water laden with *ch'i* – are well-known and well-attested; but what about the effects of *sha* water, 'demonic' water?

Dowsers have known about what they call 'black streams' and their effects for more than fifty years. A black stream is an ordinary water-line whose quality, as assessed by a dowsing tool called a 'Mager disc', is represented by the colour black, meaning that the water is dangerous, worse than merely polluted. In effect, the water in a black stream is water that carries *sha*. This may be so only at the physical level, as literal 'stinking water' carrying sewage or industrial pollution; but it may also be so at other levels, of emotion, of mind and beyond. These other levels are the more dangerous, simply because in a physical – and thus 'scientific' – sense they do not 'exist', so we therefore try to ignore them. (This is the same problem of 'existence' as with place-memories, which we looked at earlier.) Physical poisons carried by the water can only be dangerous through physical contact such as, for example, when the water is drunk. But the other levels of 'blackness' – of emotions, of ideas, of images, of the spirit and the like – act directly on those levels of emotion, of mind, of spirit, without needing physical contact. They have to be dealt with accordingly, in ways more closely allied to magic than to the Westerners' conventional physical medicine. We'll look at treatment later; for the moment we ought to look at the symptoms and the effects.

There seems to be little doubt that there are several ways in which water can carry energies or 'codings'. The most obvious of these is the way in which it can carry other physical substances in solution or suspension. But there are others, and the key to one of those others is the strange 'bent' structure of the water molecules. Water, as you'll probably know, is formed of a pair of hydrogen atoms straddling an oxygen atom; the strangeness of the structure comes from the fact that the three atoms do not form a straight line, as we would expect, but form a shallow angle, which is normally around 140°. Water ionizes easily because of the tension created by this angle, and that's one of the reasons why it's such a good solvent for so many substances.

But note that the angle can change. The angle varies a little from one molecule to another, which I'm told is the reason why snowflakes come in such a bewildering variety of forms. But it can also be made to change a lot, not so much by conventional physical means, but by what would seem to be magical ones. One example is Pavlita's anti-pollutant 'psychotronic generator', which made the angle about 20° shallower in clearing pollutants from a water sample; and water blessed during a blessing ceremony has been shown to change its molecular angle by about the same amount.[2] Water, then, can carry such a non-physical 'substance' as 'blessing', within its physical structure.

This use of water as a carrier for an 'idea' or 'image' is one of the basic principles of homoeopathic medicine. As in conventional medicine, homoeopathic prescriptions are supplied in liquid or tablet form; but unlike conventional medicine, the homoeopath reckons that the *less* there is of the 'active ingredient' carried in the water-droplet that went into the liquid or tablet, the greater will be its effect – or rather, the higher the level at which it will act. Homoeopathy works on the principle of '*like cures like*', in that to deal

with a given problem the homoeopath will prescribe a substance which, in its normal state, will reproduce in a healthy
subject the same symptoms as the patient shows.

This is why so many homoeopathic remedies are derived
from poisons: quinine for malarial symptoms, for example,
and foxglove (digitalis) for some heart complaints. Having
chosen the substance, it is diluted, and diluted, and diluted,
shaken hard each time, until – in some homoeopathic
remedies – there is almost no chance that a single molecule
of the original substance is present in the solution that is
taken by the patient. And yet it still works. It doesn't seem
to be a variant of the 'placebo effect' of conventional drug-
testing: from my own experience I know that homoeopathic
remedies have more definite and predictable effects than that.[3]

In homoeopathic circles the theory seems to be that as the
physical substance is reduced in each dilution, and as it is
shaken with each dilution, the 'idea' or 'essence' of the
substance is strengthened. The stronger the 'essence', the
higher the level of being at which the remedy acts. So for a
complaint which is mainly physical, the homoeopath will
prescribe a fairly mild dilution or 'potency' of a given substance, such as a potency of '3 $\times$', a dilution to 10^{-3}; for a
problem more on an emotional level, $10 \times (10^{-10})$; for one
on a more mental or intellectual level, $30 \times (10^{-30})$; and for
one on what we might call a spiritual level, $200 \times (10^{-200})$.
Since the average density of molecules in a liquid is around
10^{23} per cubic centimetre – plus or minus a couple of orders
of magnitude – you'll see what I mean about there being
little or no chance of any of the original substance being
present in some of the higher-potency remedies. But, say the
homoeopaths, the 'idea' or 'essence' of the substance is still
there, and more so with each increase in dilution.[4]

There is an interesting piece of confirmation for this.
George de la Warr, one of the pioneers of 'radionic' medicine – a variant of medical dowsing that uses a radio-like
'black box' as a 'tuning device' – developed what he called
a 'radionic camera', based on the 'radionic box'. This, he
claimed, was able to take photographs of diseased parts of

the body by what seemed to be a kind of controlled thought-photography. There is still some controversy over his claims, and the camera itself was unreliable, being subject to such usual vagaries of magical or near-magical equipment as refusing to work at all when a sceptic came near it. But in addition to producing X-ray like photographs of what appear to be the insides of people and animals, de la Warr also took some photographs of the 'essences' of homoeo-pathic remedies. In one set that have been published, 2 x-potency aconite pilules showed up on the photograph as large, diffuse, but recognizable aconite flowers; while 200 x-potency aconite showed up as smaller but much clearer images of the flower.[5] So the 'idea' or 'essence' of the substance in a homoeopathic remedy does seem to become more refined with increasing dilution of its physical counterpart.

Perhaps more interesting, de la Warr took some photographs of the 'radiations' of ordinary tap-water before and after a blessing ceremony.[6] Before the ceremony, the pattern shown on the plate looks something like a photograph of a cosmic-ray strike in a nuclear-physicist's 'cloud-chamber'; after the ceremony, the same pattern is still visible, but almost obliterated by a massive glowing three-axis cross. The trouble with de la Warr's photographs, though, is that they are useless as 'proof' for anything, for it becomes a case of ascribing one unknown to another.

But radionic practice does provide us with another clue about the ability of water to carry other energies or codings of energies. In conventional homoeopathic practice, the remedy – and thus the energies carried by the water within it – comes into the body by being swallowed; but many radionic practitioners 'broadcast' homoeopathic remedies to a patient by placing together the remedy and a 'sample' of the patient – usually a blood-spot, a urine sample or a lock of hair. Again, crazy as it sounds, this modernized witchcraft does work: the idea of the idea of the substance travels to the patient by means of an image or 'idea' of that patient.[7]

It's on this level of 'ideas' and 'broadcast ideas' that *sha* is

G

most dangerous. Even the 'idea' of underground water
causes problems: quite a few dowsers get rheumatic pains in
their joints if they track water-lines for too long, and they
reckon this is due to the water below. Traditionally, rheumatism is brought on by damp weather; a water-line is an
image or 'idea' of a stream, and implies dampness; and it
seems to be the idea of dampness, rather than any physical
dampness, which brings on the rheumatism in these cases at
least. Studies by a number of medical dowsers over the past
fifty years extend this, and seem to show conclusively that
rheumatism and arthritis in people and animals can often
be linked with water-lines of any kind passing below. These
studies were detailed enough to show that in one case of
arthritis in a knee-joint, for example, a fine water-line passed
under the patient's bed at the level of where her knee rested
in her normal sleeping position; when the patient moved
her bed a few feet, clear of the path of the water-line, the
arthritis cleared up within a matter of days.[8] It's probable
that these allergy-type reactions to water-lines are not the
only causes of rheumatism or arthritis, by the way: there are
other more conventional explanations in many cases. The
water-lines certainly seem to be one of the causes of these
illnesses, but they are equally certainly not the only cause of
them.

It seems that a water-line of any 'colour' can trigger off
rheumatism or arthritis; but it's when we look at black
streams that the links between water-lines and disease start
to get disturbing. The same studies of water-lines and disease found cases of a wide range of illnesses, particularly
degenerative diseases like polio, multiple sclerosis and some
cancers, associated with the 'noxious radiations of black
streams' running beneath the beds, couches, desks, even
kitchen sinks, of the patients studied. In other words, the
sha of a black stream could affect those people if the water-
line ran below any place at which they spent a large part of
their day or night. I'd often wondered about this myself
before I read these reports, for in my parents' medical prac-

tice (a conventional one) there was one house in which three unrelated people – the successive owners of the house, in fact – had died of different cancers within two years there: and cancers, according to conventional medical theory, aren't supposed to be infectious.

There was an interesting experiment carried out on this in Germany in the early 1930s. The local hospital drew up a map of 'cancer houses' of this kind, and compared it with a map of black streams that the local dowsers had plotted out independently: the two maps coincided exactly. As the writer of the article I found this in said, 'a better or more final confirmation of the "noxious earth rays" theory is scarcely necessary'; but he forgot to mention which town this test was supposed to have been held in, which was awkward of him.[9] In spite of this, more modern evidence does back him up:[10] the equivalent of *sha* in underground water-bearing fissures does seem to be a causative factor in an as yet undetermined proportion of cases of a range of degenerative diseases. More research is needed: and it *is* needed, and now.

In the same research on 'noxious earth rays', the dowsers involved found some interesting coincidences which bring us back to our current theme of 'demonic interference'. As one of them put it, 'while looking for "noxious earth rays", I also tested haunted houses: every time I found that such a house stood over crossing streams. In such formations the low Elementals enjoy to live!'[11] Another commented that a 'geological fault in the ground will produce bad reactions, and also ghostly phenomena'.[12] So if *sha* is producing hauntings as well as illnesses, what is it? And more to the point, what creates it, and what can we do about it?

I said earlier that *sha* was the product of an imbalance of Yin and Yang; but I think it's time we turned to the Christian terms 'angelic' and 'demonic' in order to study this in more detail. This unfortunately brings us some problems of definition, because of the inherent ambiguity of Christian values, so I'd better deal with those first.

In some Christian writing I've gone through, it's implied that the demonic half of the angelic/demonic duality was and is feminine, the equivalent of Yin. Particularly since the Pauline and Augustinian distortions of the original teachings of Christ, women seem to have been regarded as the main representatives of the Devil in tempting men away from the True Path; and the Yin mode, as the 'dissolver', constantly threatened the stasis which the Church, until recently at least, seems always to have been aiming for. This lopsidedness of the doctrine of the Church – which cannot in honesty be called Christian – seems to have been inherited from the early days of the Jewish patriarchy. The Jews invented this idea of the willingness of women to side with the Devil as a means of bolstering up the new patriarchy at a time when many Jewish women still preferred the old matriarchal Earth-Mother religion: the idea was derived more from political expedience than religious truth, as far as I can work it out. This over-rating of Yang and near-hatred of the Yin mode must have been and must be productive of an enormous amount of *sha*, so much so that it's best to describe that aspect of Church doctrine itself as 'demonic' – so we will have to look elsewhere for a better understanding of angels and demons.

Angels and demons, whatever they are or represent, are not themselves *ch'i* and *sha*: rather, they are the forces which produce the respective balance of *ch'i* and the imbalance of *sha*. We can even define different kinds of *sha* if we use two of the names for the Devil, namely Ahriman and Lucifer. To modify Rudolf Steiner's more mystical terminology, we could say that ahrimanic *sha*, *sha* produced by ahrimanic action, would be an imbalance caused by excess Yin or a severe shortage of Yang; a luciferian *sha* would be an excess of Yang. Ahrimanic *sha* carried in a black stream should create an excess of Yin in anyone above, and thus, from Chinese theory, will tend to give rise to degenerative diseases: an excess of Yin will give a mixture of 'change for change's sake' and constant dissolution. Luciferian *sha* would lead towards rigidity, and thus, we could theorize, 'rigidity' diseases like hardening of the arteries (arteriosclerosis) and all the problems associated with excess fat. The connection between Yin-biased disease and black streams seems to be well-established, but no-one, to my knowledge, has done any work on the streams and Yang-biased disease. It would be worth doing.

The effects of these two senior demons on emotions are also interesting: luciferian *sha* should produce stubbornness and complacency, while ahrimanic *sha* should produce impatience, power-lust, tyranny. That brings us back to that category of 'human sin' in the *Exorcism Report*: 'the office of an organization devoted to greed or domination may incur trouble or act as a dispersal point', followed by the comment that 'human sin opens the door for other forces to enter in'. We could say that the force that enters in in such cases is symbolized by a demon called Ahriman: so while those in the organization may be killing themselves with coronaries in trying to dominate others, the demon they've called up by doing so will be busy killing the people in the area around that office by giving them cancers. As an example, we can see that, given the kind of total social control that both military and civil nuclear power projects will have to demand if they are to be at all safe, it may well be that the anti-nuclear protesters, and the priest who recently performed a public exorcism service in front of a Polaris base, are reducing the world's cancer risk in more ways than one.

We have here given names to the two different types of *sha*: but in the past they would have been personified not just with a name but with a visual appearance as well. In an illiterate or semi-literate culture, pictures symbolize things and ideas better than words can. People 'saw' these forces not as abstract energies, but as entities; and once we look into the folklore behind this we can see that most of the aspects of the primal energies, those which we've so far labelled Yin and Yang, *ch'i* and *sha* and the forces which produce or arise from them, also have names and personifications. All of them clothe themselves, as far as we are concerned, in images that they borrow from our minds: images which the occultists call 'thought-forms', since that is exactly what they are.

The various thought-forms include not only the Church's angels and demons, but also fairies, goblins, elves, dragons, devas, dwarves, nature spirits and the rest of the mystical menagerie. Under normal circumstances we can't see these images, as they are personifications of otherwise abstract, obscure and ephemeral forces: they do not 'live' or 'exist' in the generally-accepted sense of the words. On the occasions when we can 'see' them, or perceive them, rather, we do so in the same way as with place-memory ghosts, and under much the same sort of conditions: so some people may see them at a time when others around them may not.[13] They exist in personal or subjective realities, but at the same time exist in a world outside of those realities, a world which the Jews called *sheol* or 'invisible world', which is the proper meaning of the derivative word 'hell'. But though to us they can only be seen as part of our subjective realities, it's important to realize that those subjective realities can become physically real in many ways and senses, yet still remain subjective: poltergeists, apportations and all manner of unpleasant things can follow the unwary investigator if he calls too much into existence.[14]

Perhaps it might be useful to look at these assorted 'spirits' in terms of their functions. If we take the words back to their linguistic roots, we find that angels, for example, are 'spirit messengers', and demons are 'spirits, possibly evil'. In the original Persian sense a 'deva' is a nature-spirit, an aspect of nature; while the word 'devil', which is derived from 'deva' via the Jews, was taken by the Jews to mean 'fallen angel', so we could say that devils are also 'spirit messengers' of a kind, even if somewhat unreliable ones. We could say we have two classes of spirits: those who ferry messages around (though from and for whom remains another question), and control the balance of the primal forces regardless of place; and the nature spirits, which also control energy-balances, but which seem to be more closely tied to places, to things or to species.

If we see this vast range of spirits not as entities with fixed appearances, shapes and sizes, but as personified 'representatives' or messengers of otherwise abstract forces whose appearance varies according to the form in which we want or expect to see them, some intriguing coincidences begin to emerge. The 'spirit messengers' have, it seems, been with us from the time mankind emerged on this planet. In the past they appeared as gods or 'sons of god', as angels, as demons, as nature-spirits, as anything which would make sense to us, as anything which would give them 'authority' to make us listen to them. Since we were the ones who supplied the images they used, angel-images and demon-images were the ones they used then; but our expectations have changed, so the images in which they appear to us now – and they do still appear to us – have also changed.

The forces remain the same, and the characters of their representatives remain the same; but their appearances change to match the times, to match our expectations of those times. A clue to their real identities comes in the names with which these entities call themselves, for they seem to change little with the time or the gambit. There was of old a goddess called Astarte, the destructive aspect of the feminine mode; and an old senior demon called Ashtaroth, a trickster who specialized in supplying misleading prophecies: now a 'spirit guide' called Astar supplies misleading prophecies to present-day spiritualist seances, while 'spacemen' under the 'Ashtar Galactic Command' give identical messages to UFO contactees.[15] The angels use the same 'flying saucer' gambit: messages like 'put a stop to all atomic tests for warlike purposes – the balance of the universe is threatened' and 'the inhabitants of your planet will upset the balance if they persist in using force instead of harmony' are handed to people all over the world by 'visitors from outer

space'.[16] As I said earlier, 'visitors from inner space' seems
more likely.

But it's only when we look closer at the 'flying saucer'
data that we can get a clear idea of the power of these
'imaginary' entities, these modernized angels and demons.
The angels appear skilfully to have contrived religious re-
vivals throughout history, by displays of 'miraculous' lights
in the sky and 'miraculous' cures on the ground: there are
plenty of well-documented incidents of that type, as at
Lourdes in 1858, Knock in Ireland in 1879 and the 'Lady of
the Rosary' incident at Fatima in Portugal in 1917.[17]

The demons play other games, more suitable to their
apparent aim as 'forces tending to unbalance': they issue
sequences of unerringly accurate prophecies about private
and public events, and then, as John Keel put it, 'when (the
contactees) are totally sold, they introduce a joker into the
deck'. The 'joker' is usually some kind of 'end-of-the-
world' prophecy that has the contactee shouting from the
rooftops or organizing attempts at revolution.[18] According
to Keel and other researchers, there is a whole range of
phenomena associated with sightings of UFOs: sometimes
when someone reports a sighting, their phone seems to be
tapped, which in the past led to claims about 'government
censorship' of UFO sightings. But this is only part of the
apparently demonic activity, which includes classic but
'modernized' poltergeist activity in the homes of contactees,
and visitations by 'three men in black' who, in the United
States at least, always travel round in a black Cadillac that
vanishes with them inside soon after they threaten some
contactee. Sometimes the 'men in black' turn up *before* the
contactee has had time to report a sighting, and demand all
records of the incident immediately; and their knowledge
of the personal details of the contactee, as Keel describes,
makes it clear that the whole set-up goes well beyond the
limits of what any 'government censor' could do. The demons
seem to contrive every incident as carefully and apparently
meaninglessly as did the angels the incident at Fatima.[19]

People have been healed by UFOs, people have been killed by them. The 'spacemen' have left behind elegantly engraved visiting cards in one case, religious relics and symbols in another. They have handed over very ordinary pancakes in one case, dropped lumps of tin and slag in others. A 'man in black', it seems, handed Thomas Jefferson the design for the reverse of the Great Seal of the United States, and then vanished; while a 'man in white' led Joseph Smith to the place where the strange gold plates – whose inscriptions were later deciphered and translated by Smith as *The Book of Mormon* – were hidden underground in a stone box.[20] Angels and demons in their various disguises have meddled with our history and our health in meaningless and meaningful ways. It just doesn't make sense.

It probably isn't meant to. The angels and demons are messengers, as their names imply; and whatever they are messengers for undoubtedly has intelligence of a kind. But we have to realize that it is an intelligence that works under different rules to ours, a totally alien intelligence. By 'alien' I don't mean von Daniken's clumsy and materialistic concept of 'aliens from outer space', but rather the pagan concept of an invisible parallel world coexistent with ours, the Jews' *sheol*. Angels and demons, as I see it, are aspects of the primal forces of nature, so the intelligence for which they act as messengers is nature itself, in its constructive and destructive aspects. That is the 'pagan solution' which I mentioned earlier. That which haunts us, and that from which we hide in the artificial environment of our cities, is nature itself. Materialists may dream of 'man's increasing control over the blind forces of nature': but nature, anything but blind, plays the same mysterious games with us that it has always played. We think we use it, while all the time it is using us.

The games have remained much the same throughout time: it's only the tactics and gambits, the outward forms, which change to suit our changing world-views. Despite initial appearances, the energies involved remain the same as always: for we can see the games of the currently most popular gambit, the UFO tactic, fit the same geographical networks behind the natural energy-matrix whose form and effects we've been studying so far. This is true of the 'hard' phenomena, the 'flying saucers', and of all the 'soft' phenomena – coloured lights, glowing shapes, fireballs and the like – that go with them.

This comes out most clearly in correlation of UFO sightings – and particularly 'landing-sites' – with ley-lines, the overground part of the energy-matrix. This seems from recent research to be so in Britain, as I'll describe in a moment; but it was first noticed in France in the 1950s, by the UFO researcher Aimé Michel. In an analysis of the Bayonne-Vichy 'flap' of 1954, he found that the sightings all fell into straight lines. Several sightings implied that the UFOs in question had used the intersections of these lines as 'junctions', changing direction at those points, changing height by the often-noted 'falling-leaf' manoeuvre at the same time.[21] Michel published the details on these 'orthotenies', as he called them, in 1958; but after initial interest in UFO research circles the idea of alignment was dismissed on the same dubious statistical 'refutation' as was later applied to ley-lines.

The problem with sightings of airborne UFOs, as was the case with Michel's work, is that it's impossible to plot out their precise positions relative to the ground. It was this vagueness that allowed the statisticians to 'prove' that orthotenies were meaningless. But 'landing-sites' and other ground-based UFO phenomena are a different matter, for not only can their apparent positions be plotted with a high degree of accuracy, from the relationship of the 'craft' to nearby hedges and trees, but visible impressions and even – in some cases – deep holes have sometimes been left at the points of contact. There seems little doubt that in the few cases of this type that have been fully researched in Britain, the landing-sites can be correlated not just with leys, but with other Fortean phenomena as well. Paul Devereux of the *Ley Hunter* magazine kindly supplied me with details of two recent examples: one was of leys related to three closely-linked UFO incidents near Winchester in Hampshire, and the other of a UFO landing-site from the 1920s correlated with a classic ley through the city of Leicester, and with a wide range of other Fortean phenomena.[22]

The Winchester incidents are interesting in that they all centre around one woman, a Mrs Bowles, who had suffered so many poltergeist and similar incidents occurring around her, over the years, that she and her family treated them as part of the normal way of things. In the first of these UFO incidents, in November 1976, the car she and a Mr Pratt were travelling in was 'jerked' across the road and on to the opposite verge, where a 'spacecraft' and then a man-like figure appeared. This humanoid walked round the car – the car's engine and headlights flaring into life at one point while he did so – and then vanished, as did the 'space-craft' itself. The second incident, which occurred in December 1976, was a 'rather less tangible contact' in the car park at the Devil's Punchbowl, a few miles from the first site on the Chilcomb road.

By the time Paul Devereux was asked to study the case, a Mr Frank Wood had already noticed that the first site, that of the 'landing', lay on an alignment of six prehistoric sites (mostly tumuli), on which that section of the Chilcomb road and its very wide verge also aligned. Paul found to his surprise, that according to the map, both the Chilcomb road site and the Devil's Punchbowl car park fell on another precise alignment of prehistoric sites (once again mostly tumuli, but most of them with specific names this time) which crossed the first line at an angle of about 4° precisely at the Chilcomb road site. A section of the A272 road aligned on this second ley, and both leys passed through modern 'trigonometry points' (small concrete pillars used in map-survey work), which were built by the Ordnance Survey Service at the highest points in each area – another correlation with Watkins' formulae for leys.

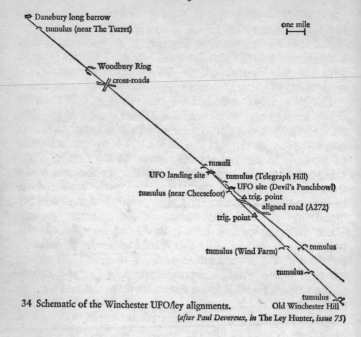

one mile

34 Schematic of the Winchester UFO/ley alignments.

(after Paul Devereux, in The Ley Hunter, *issue 75)*

The third UFO incident, early in 1977, was even more
bizarre than the first, for Mrs Bowles and Mr Pratt claimed
they were 'beamed aboard' a UFO while they were travelling
along another minor road, the B3404. This site is not on the
first two leys; but as Paul explained, that section of the
B3404 is dead straight for nearly two miles as it approaches
Winchester from the east, and is visibly aligned with two
churches in Winchester itself, and a tumulus just to the west
of the city. These three incidents, which can all be pin-
pointed precisely in relation to the ground, do seem to have
occurred on leys, and thus on the overground part of the
energy-matrix.

The Leicester ley that Paul Devereux researched is in
many ways a classic type. It starts at Oadby Church, just to

the south-east of the city of Leicester, and runs for ten and a half miles to the trigonometry point at the top of Green Hill, to the north-west of the city. On its way it passes through two more churches, a standing stone, an obvious ridge-notch and the middle of a copse that looks like a 'tree-clump' grown round a mark-stone. Careful walking of the ley showed up other classic details, such as a mark-stone near Frog Island, now the industrial area of the city; the line ran through the site of one of the ancient city gates, next to a modern cross-road on the main A50 road, and up the side of one of the roads that led to that cross-road; it ran up an ancient stretch of bridleway before coming to the ridge-notch at the Old John Folly; and it then ran through paired footpath gates where it crossed the next road. In many ways a classic ley.

But the line showed some not-so-classic aspects of leys as well. Part of Oadby, just by the church, had been subjected

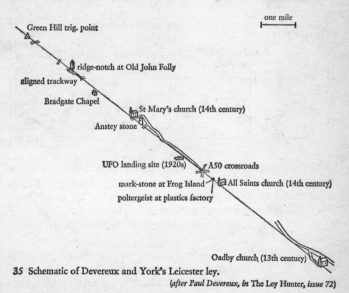

one mile

Green Hill trig. point

ridge-notch at Old John Folly

aligned trackway

Bradgate Chapel

St Mary's church (14th century)

Anstey stone

UFO landing site (1920s)

A50 crossroads

mark-stone at Frog Island

All Saints church (14th century)

poltergeist at plastics factory

Oadby church (13th century)

35 Schematic of Devereux and York's Leicester ley.

(after Paul Devereux, in The Ley Hunter, *issue 72)*

to a clear-blue-sky deluge in June 1976; the UFO landing-site I mentioned earlier was apparently beside a section of road near Anstey which aligned on the ley; and from the Anstey standing stone and three other points towards the Old John Folly, as series of apparent lines ran off to the south-west, converging at Barwell village, about seven miles away. Several incidents have centred on the point at which the lines converge, between Barwell's two churches: a large meteorite strike in 1966 damaged a factory there, and a fireball demolished a house in 1975 – and both incidents preceded UFO 'flaps'. The oddest aspect of the line was by the mark-stone at Frog Island, for there there is a factory which straddles the line, whose work-force have the unusual distinction of having gone on strike until the place was exorcised. A poltergeist and hauntings by a 'hideous monster' had damaged machinery and caused several accidents, so the work-force regarded them as a safety hazard. (The

exorcism was successful, apparently.) This seems to be a general pattern linking leys and the underground part of the energy-matrix with Fortean phenomena like hauntings, 'impossible' weather and not-so-natural 'natural' events like meteorite strikes, and the modernized hauntings by UFOs and mysterious lights in the sky.

If we equate Reich's 'orgone radiation' and 'deadly orgone radiation' with *ch'i* and *sha* respectively, we can see, from our earlier look at that possible weather-control system, that airborne OR and DOR could account for much of the 'impossible' weather phenomena. We could suggest that those phenomena are aspects of the workings of the energy-matrix, side-effects of its now rather erratic working. Much the same could be said of the 'soft' UFO phenomena, the strange lights in the sky: we could suggest that they are side-effects of the passage, or possibly disruption of the passage, of energies in the overground part of the energy-matrix. The 'hard' phenomena, like the poltergeist and haunting in the factory at Frog Island or the meteorite hole in the factory at Barwell, could be regarded as 'messages' of a very crude sort, or as distortions of the natural energies, or both. Either way, when we see this kind of activity in relation to the energies in the energy-matrix, it does seem that the 'non-human mischievous sprites' that the *Exorcism Report* refers to may not just be mischievous: they may, in their crude ways, be acting as 'messengers' of a kind. So we could see them too as angels and demons, representatives of that 'intelligence' which seems to be behind the energy-matrix.

That, of course, was the pagan solution: that the earth, that nature itself, was alive and intelligent. The earth was the 'earth mother', from whom all things came, and to whom all things went; nature was Pan, literally 'everywhere'. If we are to understand nature, we have to understand the pagan approach to nature – an approach based more on keen observation than on 'mere superstition'. Paganism was and is a way of living with, and perhaps rationalizing, man's real and inescapable relationship with nature; while civilization, the city way of life with its dream of 'man's increasing control over nature', was and is nothing more than an attempt to ignore that relationship. If we are to get out of the mess to which civilized ignorance has brought us, we must prepare ourselves, in some ways at least, for the return of paganism.

9

The Return of Paganism

'It had incredible shimmering colours, and as it changed its shape it could easily be imagined to be fluttering multi-coloured wings. It was a living control mechanism, controlling energy in and out of a growing plant, varying its shape with this control. If I'd seen this thing without my scientific background, I might have thought I'd seen a classical fairy.

'Talking with other people who've had this kind of experience, I believe that there are vortices of energy (of some kind), which are reported as elementals, fairies or whatever, depending on what space the observers are in themselves. Because of the great 'thought-form' of fairies set up in the West over thousands of years, when people get this type of experience, they say 'I have seen a fairy'. It may 'only' be an energy field, seen partly with the imagination, but it's still a straight-forward account of a physical observation'. (An electronics engineer, now a member of the Findhorn Community.)[1]

It's a characteristic of pagan cultures that they 'people' the world around them with angels, demons, spirits, fairies and the like; and it's a characteristic of civilized cultures that they sneer at this pagan 'ignorance'. But the research we've been looking at suggests that the pagans weren't far wrong in their beliefs in animism, in spirits and in the life and intelligence of nature: it's the citizens who are 'ignorant', not the pagans. Civilized anthropologists seem to have assumed that pagans see spirits because they're trained to see them; but in reality it's more likely that we in civilized cultures don't see them because we're trained *not* to see them, to rationalize away any vision of them that might be so uncivilized as to appear. We need to look at things from a pagan point of view before we can dismiss paganism as 'mere superstition'.

As that engineer said, those fairies and the like may 'only' be energy-fields interacting with us, but they are still aspects of the reality that nature imposes on us, and they are still realities that operate upon us, which we cannot ignore. Almost the whole of our civilization is based on an ignorance of that reality, a deliberate ignorance of that reality; and that is the reason why life in this civilization, which at the present time is undoubtedly at its zenith as far as civilizations go, is particularly devoid of both meaning and hope. If we are to recover anything from that civilized carnage, we have to unlearn that ignorance, and learn once again to recognize nature both within and without ourselves. Hence the *need* for a return to paganism, or at least to some of the pagan values and respect for nature, in our culture.

The re-introduction of paganism would at first have to be somewhat limited, and adapted to suit modern terms and limitations, to give us time to unlearn our ignorance. It's not going to be easy, not just because of the sheer power behind the forces of nature (particularly at the emotional level, which is probably why that ignorance developed in the first place – life was more comfortable if you ignored nature and reality), but also because one of the side-effects of the so-called 'Age of Reason' has been to destroy most of the experimental meanings – in English and probably in most other civilized languages as well – of all the key words we need to describe the phenomena we're dealing with. Without them, we cannot meaningfully describe what we see.

Angels, demons, fairies, goblins, dwarves: these have all been relegated to nursery tales, for according to civilized 'reason' neither they, nor anything that might be behind them, can exist – except as a 'figment of the imagination', perhaps. In other words: we've already seen how the present meanings of words like 'coincidence' and 'existence' limit our understanding of the concepts behind those words –

concepts which are vital if we're to understand anything of the pagan view of nature. We also run up against the ubiquity of 'scientism', the near-worship of an irrational 'rationalism', when we try to describe fairies and the like in terms of 'frequencies', 'vibrations' or 'radiations': for although such terms make sense in describing what we perceive, they don't make sense in terms of any material energy, and thus in the current social view of science. We have to watch the meanings of words all the time in studying these fields, for all the time we run into traps of modern meaninglessness; it's often best, whenever a word seems meaningless, to look up its meanings in the old languages from which the modern word is derived; for then the pagan reality was still real.

The other problem we have to face is the effects of the highly successful propaganda campaign that the Roman Church in particular waged against pagan religions from the time of Constantine, in the fourth century, right through to the present day. The short-lived Celtic Church can be excused from this, I think, for there is little doubt that St Patrick, St Cuthbert and the other great Celtic saints made a sincere effort to graft the original Christian ideas on to existing pagan beliefs; but to my knowledge it was the only Church that bothered to do so. The other Churches tried to obliterate all previous beliefs, dismissing as 'ignorant heathenism' the whole of the reality of the peoples whose territories they invaded.

And invaded is the right word. The Council of Nicaea of 325 AD was convened by Constantine to construct an ideology that would unify the peoples of the ailing Roman Empire – his concern was political, not religious, and it has been a characteristic of the organized Church ever since.[2] Within two centuries of Constantine's time, when the Empire had already collapsed, the Roman Church was engaged in an attempt to reconstruct the old Empire by ideological rather than military conquest. The parish system, the central facet of the Church's administration system, is identical to that of the old Empire; and the Church went to great pains to suppress the old oral traditions, replacing them, through its jealously-guarded monopoly of literacy, with its own manufactured 'history' of 'the Truth'. The fact that 'history' now changed with each succeeding Pope was conveniently ignored.

By the time that the Roman missionary Augustine came over to Britain, in the early part of the seventh century, the Roman Church had re-written church dogma several times, Constantine-style, and had conveniently forgotten almost all of the original teachings of Christ. It preferred narrow authoritarianism to the gentle humanity of the Christianity of the Gospels. By the seventh century the Church was, from all the evidence I've seen, little more than a voracious, fast-expanding political bureaucracy operating under a thin disguise of religious concern. Its concern with 'conversion' of the 'heathens' seems to have had more to do with increasing the Church's tithe-revenue than it ever had to do with the saving of souls. That's a cynical view, I admit; but from what I've seen it's probably not far off the truth.

So it's interesting to see what happened when Augustine came over to Britain. The first time he came over, to Kent, in the south-east corner of Britain, he was 'seen off the premises' by the local heathen king. He came back a few years later, slightly less over-confident, and slightly less arrogant; but his instructions from Pope Gregory the Great, if somewhat conciliatory, were as arrogant as ever:

'I have come to the conclusion that the temples of the idols in England should not on any account be destroyed. Augustine must smash the idols, but the temples themselves should be sprinkled with holy water and altars set up in them in which relics are to be enclosed. For we ought to take advantage of well-built temples by purifying them of devil-worship and dedicating them to the service of the true God. In this way, I hope the people (seeing their temples are not destroyed) will leave their idolatry and yet continue to frequent the places as formerly, so coming to know and revere the true God.'[3]

The Roman Christianity of that period was a mixture of

political intrigue and expediency, mixed with a large amount of arrogance and hypocrisy. The 'conversions' that took place in England then were more for political security than religious faith, and in one case the king was converted in order to escape the endless preachings of his Christian wife. So much for the glory of the true God!

But the Celtic Church was still very much alive and active at this time. It's noticeable that until his eastern 'power-base' was well established, Augustine never dared to travel west or north to meet with the Celtic Church, which had been there for the best part of six centuries – assuming that the stories about Joseph of Arimathea at Glastonbury and in Cornwall are true.[4] There's an apocryphal tale that says that the Celtic Church were wary of Augustine, and representatives who were due to visit him in the south of England wanted to know how they could recognize if Augustine really was the 'man of God' that he claimed to be. They consulted their scriptures, and decided that a true man of God would, like Jesus, welcome them after their travels and wash the road-dust off their feet when they arrived at his residence. Going on their own practice, they expected that residence to be a hermit's cell.

The 'hermit's cell' turned out to be a gaudy palace; and Augustine, far from greeting them, stayed seated in his raised up 'cathedra' or bishop's throne, demanding that they bow down to him as the true representative of the 'one true God'. They didn't: they walked straight out, and walked back to Wales again, wiser and warier men. It's an apocryphal tale, but, again, it's probably not far off the truth. Certainly the Celtic Church avoided any dealings with the Roman invaders until the latter forced the convening of the Synod of Whitby in AD 664. The enforced death of the Celtic Church that stemmed from that meeting spelt, to my mind, the death of any true organized Christianity in Britain, and the reinforcement of the cant and hypocrisy that much of organized religion in Britain has spread around itself from that time until now.

Looking back, there is just no way in which the Roman dogma could have made sense to anyone living, as a pagan would, as part of nature. The whole Roman system of belief centred round a nebulous and not particularly benificent Father-God, a sexless Son, a Virgin Mother, and Joseph, an impotent physical foster-father. No birth, no recognition of death as physical death, and no rebirth either, since the doctrine of reincarnation, an original part of Christian belief, had been expunged from Roman doctrine by Augustine's time. Life was a one-way trip to heaven or hell, and what happened to the land that you tilled meant nothing to you after your death. That attitude is the direct ancestor of modern agribusiness monoculture: it destroys the land, but no-one involved gives a damn, because they know the land will last out just beyond their own lifetimes before turning into a desert. The pagan attitude, which is still quite strong among family farmers, was and is one of 'live as if you'll die tomorrow, but farm as if you'll live for ever' – ecologically a far sounder approach.

At least the Celtic Church had a realistic attitude to sex, for although its monks and nuns were celibate, as in all Christian organizations, it was common for people to join the Celtic religious orders after they had brought up their families. They joined those orders when they were mature, when their thoughts turned naturally to wonder about meaning in life – not, as in other Christian orders, when they were too young to have any knowledge of who they were. Apart from the Celtic Church, most of the Christian organizations maintained a ludicrous attitude to the fact of human sexuality. In the excesses of the Middle Ages, when even the Popes kept prostitutes on call, such an attitude became merely farcical; while in the excesses of the Puritans and the Victorian neo-Puritans it was totally destructive of all the joy of living, productive of much suffering, and often beyond the borders of the barbaric.[5] It is still ridiculous to expect a celibate priest to give reliable advice on sexual problems, as Catholics are daily asked to do; and the costume of the present-day Anglican priest, with the head separated from the black-covered and shapeless body by a circle of light, nicely symbolizes the inability of many priests to handle any matters outside the artificial limits of their head-based religion. What is missing in religion is a sense of joy, as the litany drones on; what is missing in civilization is a sense of meaning, as the rush-hour drones on; and these are things which the pagan reality can provide.

The Church labelled most of the pagan pantheon as 'devils'; and if we can forget for a moment the Church's hatred, and therefore their labelling as 'evil', of anything which they didn't understand or which didn't fit their current system, that description was, for a change, accurate. The term 'devil' was a Jewish corruption of the Persian word 'deva', which literally means 'shining one' – without connotations either of good or of evil. And the concept of 'shining one' describes exactly the energy-forms that people have always seen, and still see, as 'gods', 'demons', 'angels', 'fairies', 'spacemen' or whatever. The term 'deva' tends to be used in a more specific sense nowadays, as we'll see shortly; but I think it's fair to say that the early English gods were indeed 'devils', in this sense of 'shining ones'. We have another Christian confusion to sort out before we can move on, though, and that comes from the fact that the Old English word 'godi' meant both the god, the 'shining one', and its wooden representation in a temple, through which the god or its attributes could be invoked. Hence Christian harangues like this:

'The profound guilt of those who wilfully adhere to insidious superstition and the worship of idols is openly shown in the damnable images they adore. The Psalmist says of such; "All the heathen gods are devils; it is the Lord who made the heavens." And again, "They have ears and hear not; they have noses and are not able to smell; they have hands and cannot feel; they have feet and do not walk. Therefore, those who make them are like them, as are all who put trust and confidence in them." How can such stocks and stones have power to assist you when they are made to order from perishable materials by the labour of your own subjects and journeymen? Even their lifeless resemblance to human form is due solely to man's workmanship.'[6]

That the same could be said of an altar or crucifix, or a statue of the Virgin or some Christian saint is, I think, a point that should not be missed. But forget that, for what matters here is that the Church once again shows its remarkable ability to miss the point. The idols, the 'godi', are tools for the invocation of a god or its attributes: they are not the gods themselves. The concept of invocation, or literally 'calling into one's-self' the attributes of something, is a standard part of magical practice throughout the world, and a standard part of many religious practices and meditations. It's a key part of the Christian ritual of the Eucharist, in which the wine and wafer of the Communion are seen as the blood and flesh of Christ: so if we are to take that writer, Pope Boniface, seriously, we must also call the wine and wafer of the Communion 'damnable images'. But the Eucharist is of real value and has real effects on many people, bringing, as they see it, the spirit of Christ within them – cannibalistic practice though it may be, as one astute heathen pointed out. We can say the same about the pagan 'godi': that as tools for invocation they brought the spirit, the attributes, of the respective god within the people who took part in the ritual around that 'damnable image'.

The concept of invocation is difficult to understand if you haven't done it yourself. It's a kind of possession, in the traditional sense; but if it's done properly the whole operation and the type and level of the 'possession' remains under the operator's control, or at least under his direction. One everyday example of this is in dramatic acting: a good actor does not so much interpret the part as let himself be interpreted by the part, by the character he is 'playing' – and, more important, he must be able to drop that part when he walks off the stage. In a sense, a good actor must be a good magician or medium.

So the aim of religious invocation, for which those 'damnable images' were tools, is to take on the characteristics of a god-form in the same way that an actor takes on a part in a play. The names given to the various god-forms, in religious and magical invocation at least, are simply labels for groups of characteristics. The names are traditional, but any label can be used for any set of characteristics, as long as they are recognizable as such to the operator: an eccentric magician friend of mine once used the names of two commercial glues, Uhu and Araldite, as labels for 'a pair of very sticky goddesses' that he invoked for a group to whom he was teaching the rudiments of magic. But it's more normal, in both religious and magical practice, to use a recognizable name, if only to make sure that the set of characteristics you are about to call up are the ones you want.

And that is an important point: *you* call up those characteristics in an invocation. In essence, an invocation is a way of emphasizing certain characteristics within you, a way of changing both the inner and outer effects of your subjective reality. An invocation, if it really works, will alter the whole structure of your personality. Most of the god-forms dealt with in current magical practice, and in fact most of the named gods, as in the old Norse, Greek and Roman cultures, are sets of entirely human characteristics – groupings which Jung termed 'archetypes'. I've read that on one occasion Jung also evoked an archetype, a far more difficult magical operation, for during a detailed study of one particular archetype he found himself 'walking and talking in the garden' with what was to him a visible personification of that archetype. The conversations he had with that 'entity' enabled him to gain a great deal of information about that archetype. If the archetypes are groupings of human characteristics, we could say that in a very real sense the gods, as archetypes, created man in their own image.

But this accounts for only one class of god-forms, a class which is not particularly important in a study of the energy-matrix of nature and those aspects of it which impinge directly upon us. A god-form is a collection of factors and characteristics which, when operating together as a kind of 'personality', perform some function: Jung's archetypes are good examples of these. But there are other classes of characteristics linked to functions, such as the angels and demons. In their roles as messengers they are sets of characteristics of a kind with functions of a kind, and forms with which they 'clothe' themselves according to the circumstances. Beyond these, there are other sets of characteristics more of the forces of nature than of man, but which also have recognizable functions and forms, and can thus be said, in the magicians' sense of the word, to be 'god-forms'. Angels and demons, in their roles as messengers, are archetypes that arise from an interaction between man and nature; while this other class of archetypes or 'god-forms', which are usually called 'devas' in the more recent use of the word, are archetypes within and of nature itself, sometimes archetypes of a place (the *genius loci*), of a plant or animal species – even, it seems, of classes of machines.

Much of the recent data on this comes from the early days of the Findhorn experiment. Like Jung, the Findhorn community learned to converse with archetypes in various ways and on various levels; but these were archetypes of the natural rather than the solely human world. Like Jung, the community were able, by conversing with these 'entities', to obtain a great deal of practical information and advice: specifically, in their case, on how best to grow each species of plant in the initially hostile climate of a caravan park in a cold Scottish bay. From their work we can construct what would seem to be a hierarchy of levels within the natural world – a hierarchy that exists almost entirely independently of man, but without which mankind could not survive.

There appear to be three levels or, as Findhorn would put it, three 'kingdoms' in this hierarchy: the nature spirits or 'elementals'; the devas and landscape angels; and nature itself, of which we are necessarily and inescapably a part. The nature spirits are best described as energy-forms, manipulating the movement of energies in and around plants, animals, minerals, everything; the energies they manipulate are the same as those we've seen in studying the energy-matrix of the landscape. The devas and landscape angels are the archetypes and essences behind each thing or place, laying the patterns on which the nature spirits build. And nature . . . nature just *is*, I suppose, in the same way that we just *are*.

It's important to realize that each of these levels or king-doms has intelligence of a kind, taking 'intelligence' to mean 'adaptability' rather than the distorted civilized sense of 'logical intellection'. Within each level are many sets of characteristics, and thus many different 'personalities'; so each level contains many different entities, each with person-alities and each with more or less intelligence and scope of action. And all of this is independent of almost anything that we may do. The complexities are enormous, but I think it's simplest to say that if we are to understand nature and our relationship with it, we will have to develop a kind of psychology of nature in the same way as we have developed a psychology of man – for each of these levels has parallels within man. The work at Findhorn is important to us because it lays the groundwork for a modern version of a psychology, and perhaps a sociology, of nature. I can't go into the details of Findhorn's work here because of the scope of this book, but I think I can summarize it as follows.[7]

In the sense that Findhorn describes them, the nature spirits are elementals, similar to the 'barrow-guardians' we looked at earlier: but they are natural rather than artificial. Another way of looking at them is to say they are, like the guardians, constructs, but constructed by nature rather than by man. All are concerned with what we might call routine maintenance work; they rarely have any physical existence, operating on levels outside of such existence, and are traditionally classified according to the symbolic images and forms as which they are sometimes 'seen'. Fairies are associated with plant life in general; goblins and dwarves with the slow changes of minerals (hence the pick and shovel in the classic image of the dwarf), and the provision of the mineral needs of plant life; naiads and dryads are associated with water-supply and with trees; and so on.

Like the barrow-guardians, these nature-spirits seem to be limited in their movements and the scope of their activity, and to have little individual intelligence; but the group-intelligence is enormous, and is traditionally represented by the nature-god Pan. Pan is unlimited in movement or scope of action – in the original Greek he is literally 'everywhere' – and his form, half animal, half human, represents the marrying of the forces of nature with a kind of intellect. The apparent form, again, is symbolic, rather than representational of any physical entity. The elemental archetype is more often sensed than seen; and it's likely, as one of the community explained, that it is only seen when it 'wants' to be seen.

The same is true of the devas, the archetypes of species. It's best to understand them as personalities that operate on things and on places, in the same way as it is easiest and best to understand human archetypes as discarnate personalities that operate on people. Man's civilized ignorance of nature, and thus of these higher 'personalities', means that the latter – to put it in human terms – are sulking, and co-operating only where necessary for the maintenance of nature rather than the needs of man. On a physical level, we could suggest that one result of this non-co-operation is the current spread of desert areas throughout the world. We could also see it in the odd fact that human life expectancy, after infancy, remains substantially unchanged from time immemorial even in civilized countries, despite the technical advances of civilized medicine. On another level, we can see that what Reich termed the 'emotional plague' is pandemic in cities on an enormous scale, and usually coupled with a degree of stress

that we could say is literally Panic, a meaningless and irrational fear that is now more a characteristic of civilized
cultures than the pagan ones from which the term first came.

The Church must, I believe, take a large part of the blame
for this non-co-operation of nature, for it was its use of the
Pan symbol as its main symbol for the 'forces of evil' that
formed the justification for the deliberate ignorance of
nature that now typifies civilized cultures. To the civilized
man, that symbol 'proves' that nature is nasty. But Roman
Christianity, as we have seen, was an urban ideology *par
excellence*: its weird emasculated view of reality could not be
squared with the pagan view, and the Church made sure, in
its various ways, that it was the pagan reality rather than its
own monstrosity that was buried under the junkpile labelled
'evil – do not touch'. Pan is the symbol of our relationship
with nature: if we pour hatred and negativity into that
symbol, as the Church has always told us to do, we should
not be surprised or complain if we get negativity thrown back
at us from that relationship. What is surprising is the tolerance that Pan and nature continue to show us: but I doubt
if they can remain tolerant for much longer.

The Findhorn experiments make it clear that we have
everything to gain by co-operating with nature, and little to
lose except our arrogance. The early years of the Findhorn
experiments, when the legendary forty-pound cabbages and
eight-foot foxgloves were grown, were exceptional. Some
people have interpreted them as a kind of 'publicity stunt'
on the part of nature, to show that true co-operation could
bring spectacular results. They're probably right, and I don't
think we ought to expect results of that kind again – it was a
publicity exercise, not a 'normal' mode of operation.

But even in a 'normal mode', the Findhorn results suggest
a number of other possibilities that could arise through a
closer co-operation with nature at all levels. We could take
the traditional intuitive 'green fingers' approach to garden-
ing up to a conscious level, for example, and 'ask' each
archetype or deva for practical advice on the best planting

and culture for the plant species it represents under the immediate conditions. Findhorn also suggest that we could 'ask' the archetypes to modify the form of the plant at an archetypal level where necessary, to produce a new version of the plant with special characteristics for special conditions – such as desert – that would be sturdier and more reliable than one modified artificially by man. Plants could be made more resistant to diseases or pest attack by the same approach; and Findhorn claim that they have done this on several occasions through their co-operation with the respective devas.[8]

In *The Findhorn Garden*, Dorothy, Findhorn's main 'contact' with the devic kingdom in the early days of the experiment, gave several interesting examples of 'pest control' through action at the archetypal level. One was when they had a serious problem with moles, who were uprooting their plants in search of the enormous worms that were growing there. Deciding that it would be wrong to try to trap or kill any of the moles, she tried another means of dissuading them from wrecking the garden. She tried to visualize the archetype or essence of 'mole-ness', and received, as she put it, 'the impression of a rather scary King Mole with a crown on his head, sitting in a cavern underground'. She 'explained' to this archetype – which we could say was 'merely' an image in her mind – that the moles it represented were damaging her garden at Findhorn. Promising that none of the moles would be threatened or harmed, she asked the King Mole if he would be so kind as to ask his 'subjects' to move to a nearby piece of scrub-land, where they would not disturb or be disturbed by anyone.

This archetypal mole 'sort of grunted', said Dorothy; but for several weeks there were no moles at all in the garden. Each time they re-appeared, Dorothy repeated her request to the King Mole image; and in time no moles wandered back. They weren't bothered with moles again. Not, that is, until the garden was expanded to take in that nearby piece of scrub-land, some years later, for the moles were, of course, all there. Dorothy was no longer working in the garden then, but I do think it was unfair of the gardeners of that time to use Dorothy's way of asking the moles to move on again. They had been told that they would be left alone there – an important part of this 'pest control' technique – and the fact that it worked, that the moles did move on, says a lot for the tolerance and co-operation of nature in those circumstances.

The key to all of this is love and respect for nature and all life in nature; and in this the Findhorn experiments are hardly new, as Tompkins and Bird showed in their excellent book *The Secret Life of Plants*. It's true that we have to kill in order to live, in order to eat; it's true that we can't possibly avoid killing myriads of minute creatures every time we move; and we'd go insane – as some people have done – if we tried, impossibly, to avoid killing *anything*. But there is a world of difference between killing as a necessary fact, and killing as wanton destruction; and there is a world of difference, too, between killing a stock-animal yourself, and paying someone else to do your killing for you as you pick up your meat from the butcher or from the supermarket fridge.

I'm not suggesting that meat-eating is somehow 'wrong' – in fact from the evidence I've seen it would seem that vegetarian diets are ecologically unsound except in small mobile cultures, which hardly applies to ours – but rather that meat-eating should be done with respect, with awareness of the fact that the corned beef in your sandwich didn't just come out of a tin, it came out of a once-living animal. Recent research seems to show that plants have feelings too, so vegetarians have no reason to maintain a smug 'holier-than-thou' attitude about 'murderous meat-eaters': vegetarian food is still murdered at some stage, just like any other food-source.[9] The fact remains that whatever you eat, whether it came from the garden or from a tin, you – or someone you hired – killed it first. So treat your food with respect, and with thanks for what it gave you. From its death comes its rebirth as part of you: that's how nature works.

Try looking at nature with a sense of wonder, for that's

what much of the pagan attitude to nature is about. Learn not to take everything for granted; learn once more, as you knew as a child, to recognize the miraculous in nature. I've talked at times with people who say there are no such things as 'miracles'; but I honestly believe that they need their heads – and hearts – examined, for I have no trouble in seeing the wondrous and the miraculous in nature everywhere. I don't only mean the obvious natural miracles, like the growth of trees and plants, the delicate balances and cycles of nature in the countryside; these are important, but they are by no means the only ones, and they aren't so obvious or so visible in the depths of a city. The miraculous is still there in the city, and you can see it clearly once you have unlearned your ignorance of it. Watch a child go past you, for example, riding a rattly and battered pushbike: see that for the miracle it is. Birth itself is a denial of entropy, the constant running-down of things; and yet here before you is a child, capable even before it goes to school of complex physical motion and balance, of play, of communication, of subtle rational thought. If that's not a miracle, what is?

And see miracles in the workings of man-made things: see the miracles behind them. Even an ordinary light-bulb is miraculous: for no amount of theory, no amount of 'explaining' how it could work, can explain *why* it should work at all. I find the naturally-coded pulsing of the overgrounds in the natural energy-matrix miraculous; but the pulsing that can be put down a telephone wire to carry a message across a vast distance is no less miraculous. Man's ingenuity, however great, does not create those properties of wires in light-bulbs and in telephone systems: it simply makes use of them. Even such an obviously man-made thing as a car is miraculous, for it is still a miracle that such an enormous mass of metal can be made to move by the explosion of a tiny amount of a simple hydrocarbon compound.

Despite those miracles, there is, it seems, a touch of the demonic in everything that man touches. The orange glare of the city lights obliterates the beauty of the night sky; the telephone carries messages of hate as well as of love; the car poisons, pollutes, maims and kills; and the Concorde aircraft, rightly called a miracle of engineering, is beautiful to watch but makes a noise that can only be called hellish. We admit the miracle of the growing and maturing of a child; but yet, to make sure that the child grows up suitably 'civilized', we force that child through our 'education' system, a compulsory non-education whose main function seems not to be to 'out-lead' the qualities of the child but to stifle them, limit them, until the child can be turned out into the civilized world classified as one or other type of civilized factory-fodder. There is little or none of this in nature: there is savagery and death in all manner of guises, it's true, but this deliberate cruelty, deliberate evil, seems to be a characteristic of man alone.

I suspect that the 'force of evil' which the Church describes and from which it purports to protect us is not only man-made, but also to a large extent Church-made. Remember the 'barrow-guardian' I described earlier: it was a constructed 'idea' with a function. Once something like that is constructed, it will continue to operate until it is dismantled – which is, to say the least, a tricky job. Demons – personified agents of imbalance of the natural energies – are constructs like the 'barrow-guardians'; and it's probably true that minor demons can be dismantled in much the same way as the 'guardians', either through exorcism or through what the occultists call 'absorption by love'. But the major demons are a different matter, for they are more than mere 'ideas': they are complete archetypes which have been built up over millenia. They exist (and that is the right word) in something akin to a 'collective unconscious', and they operate on the forces of nature as part of our interaction with nature. We cannot complain about the evil of demons, for we created them, and we maintain them. They are the personifications of our own imbalances – our greed, our ignorance, our self-aggrandisement and such like – and they are more part of our nature than part of nature.

These imbalances within us are essentially anarchic, and they would normally fight each other for our attention. But it is here that the Church has done its greatest evil to us, for in constructing an image of a demonic hierarchy, comparable to the hierarchy of the natural Kingdoms, it has effectively unified those inchoate forces behind one massive super-archetype, *the* Devil. Look again at what the Church's Devil really is: the symbol used is that of Pan, but it is better described as a sort of 'dustbin' for all the aspects of human nature that the Church preferred to hide.

The doctrine of the infallibility of the Pope – as the Pontiff, the bridge between man and God – meant that the inevitable mistakes and prejudices of each Pope were concealed as being the effect of the interference of the Devil and its 'forces of evil'. Protestants took the whole idea a stage further, declared the Papacy itself to be the work of the Devil, and effectively declared a doctrine of the infallibility of *man* rather than God. A reversal occurred, implicit, but never stated: for man was no longer seen as 'being made in the image of God'; rather, God was seen as an extension of man, an image of man. God was and is assumed to 'rule' the universe in whatever way is currently believed to suit man best; and it is the Devil – and thus nature, through the equating of the symbol of Pan with that of the Devil – who is blamed for those little inconsistencies that led to the witch-hunts, the persecution of heretics, and the whole mess that civilized arrogance has led us in to.

We can see exactly the same attitude maintained throughout the development of science, and particularly its religious aspect, humanistic 'scientism'. God rules the universe in whatever way science sees fit; science assumes that the universe *must* have a logical order behind it, so inconsistencies are not allowed to exist. God and nature are forbidden by man to be illogical; and the logic is man's, not God's or nature's. The whole aim of science is the same as that of the old theologians – to define how the universe '*really* works' – in other words the aim of both science and religion has been to define what man will permit God and nature to do.

Every so often, the theologians and scientists have claimed that they have finally defined the workings of the universe; but every time they have done this there have been one or two inconvenient inconsistencies that have broken their so-consistent logic. In physics, the atom was at first the 'indivisible building block of the universe'; but the atom has been divided and sub-divided until it is obvious that nuclear physicists are seeing what they want to see – an apparent order – rather than admit that they do not know.[10] In all its history, science has brought us no closer to finding out how the universe '*really* works'; and its key principle of 'reductionism', of dissecting the universe into ever smaller and smaller parts, is probably taking us further away from understanding the universe all the time.

The fact remains that if the universe is logical, it follows its own logic, not man's. A system of logic is destroyed if even one inconsistency is allowed to exist within it; and as Charles Fort and his followers have shown, there is a mass of 'damned' phenomena that have been observed throughout history – like freak weather, and horrors such as spontaneous human combustion – which, once admitted as facts instead of being conveniently ignored, destroy not only science's tidy logic, but science itself.[11] Once we admit the 'damned' phenomena to exist, we can see that science, as *the* way to define reality, has been an expensive fraud from the moment of its inception as a system of belief.

The problem with both science and religion, in their Western forms, is that both claim to define 'the Truth' – and the concept of Truth, when taken to its limit as both science and religion do, cannot admit the concept of Value, of the 'truth' of something under some circumstances but not others. The same holds good for political systems, which are, if you like, social religions: the variants of Marxism, to take one example, are seen as 'true' or 'not-true' in an absolute sense by their adherents and opponents, with no realization of their varying value or lack of value in varying circumstances. When technology is seen as 'applied science', and thus as 'true' and 'value-free', no-one bothers to think about the total value, the wider or long-term effects of the application of that technology. Our present technology therefore tends, at best, to be value-less, but far more often destructive of value, taking the value away from life and living. To say that life in civilized societies has lost its magic is correct, for magic is essentially concerned with values, with the value and use of things and ideas in a personal sense; and the whole aim of science, and thus the 'applied science' of our technological cultures, has been to ignore and destroy the concept of subjective or personal value in its search for its illusory 'objective Truth'.

The Church's construction of the Devil, as a means of concealing its own fallibility, created the very 'force of evil' it fights in its unbalanced way; and scientism, in its effort to conceal its own limitations, has done its utmost to deny the existence of any miracle, any magic, any value or meaning in life, other than its own mechanical, mindless, valueless simulation of 'Truth'. God, both say, is Truth; Truth is God; but if we look more closely we can see that their monotheism, their professed service of the 'one True God' and the 'one god Truth', turns out in practice and in reality to be little more than a garbled and imbalanced worship of the arrogance and ignorance of man – for both Church and Science demand that God and nature should obey man-made logic and man-made 'laws of nature'.

Demons are agents of imbalance in nature; and we could say that as we try to separate ourselves from nature, as we claim we are 'above' it, but yet necessarily remain part of it, we are ourselves the only agents of imbalance in nature. The demons are our creations. Our civilized arrogance, our civilized ignorance, and our civilized denial of nature and our nature, have created the demonic archetypes that harass us; and they will and must continue to do so as long as we try to maintain our illusion of separation from nature. We have ourselves created the hell that we live in, in our so-civilized culture: no 'force of evil' is at work but ourselves. And we could say that until we learn to recognize – to 'know again' – the unity of nature, recognize the constructive archetypes or gods within nature, and live in accordance with what our inescapable relationship with that unity, those gods, demands, we will always be troubled by the very real effects of demons. We could say that until we abandon our arrogant and ignorant monotheism, our worship of ourselves, and re-adopt the pagan knowledge of nature, the pagan pantheism, life in civilized societies will continue, literally, to be pandemonium.

There is another pagan concept that we need to recognize if we are to regain a balanced relationship with nature: we need to recognize that nature itself has a high degree of intelligence, far higher than ours, and entirely independent of ours. That is not just a concept, that is a *fact*, no matter how much we may try to conceal it behind our wall of arrogance and ignorance. We try to think that we control nature; but there's no shortage of evidence that nature controls us or uses us for its own inexplicable purposes. The various devas and the like that were involved in the Findhorn experiments made it clear that they were using the Findhorn community for experiments of their own; the community were well aware that they were being used, but their previous lengthy spiritual training made them only too happy to oblige – and reap an extraordinary harvest as their 'reward'.

There is certainly an element of 'reward' and 'punishment' in our relationship with nature. The 'reward' element is not all that obvious, except in the more spectacular examples like Findhorn; but as the Feng-shui practitioners put it, where nature is balanced, where people are living in harmony with nature, 'health and good fortune result'. The 'punishment' element is rather more obvious, not only in the Feng-shui case-histories but in a large number of folk-tales, in Britain at least, that describe the 'retribution' that follows the destruction or desecration of a site. John Michell cites some of these tales in his *View Over Atlantis*, and Janet and

Colin Bord made a special study of them in their *The Secret Country*, so I don't think I need to go into the details of the various tales here. In some cases the effects described would appear to be the result of damaging the barrow-and-stone weather-control system, as I described earlier; in others – the 'Pharaoh's curse' type – the effects would seem to be the result of the activation of a 'guardian'; but there is a hard core of tales whose effects are apparently outside that range, and which would seem to be the result of tampering – accidentally or deliberately – with the forces of nature, at an archetypal level or beyond.

It is here that we come back to our earlier study of the energy matrix, for the majority of the 'retribution' legends that Michell and the Bords cite are connected with key sites of the matrix or else, as in Ireland, with the obstruction of 'fairy paths', which we could take to be the ground-lines of overgrounds. It may be that these stories are in the majority only in Michell's and the Bords' books, reflecting their interest in these fields; but either way, and whether 'factual' or 'invented', the stories do imply that tampering with ancient sites is a mistake. And as in English law, ignorance of the power of the sites is no valid excuse: retribution still followed, and follows, whether the tampering was done accidentally or deliberately. It seems to be assumed by nature that you should know when you're liable to run into trouble of this kind.

The innumerable church-siting legends suggest that in some cases nature was willing to give man a certain amount of help in deciding where the 'best' site for a new church should be, to be best in harmony with the area and with its energy-control needs. There are few obvious common factors in the stories, but most simply say that 'the stones of the half-built church were moved during the night' to some other site, up hill, down dale, on a marsh or island (as with a fair number of the great cathedrals, such as Durham, Ely, Salisbury, York Minster and Westminster Abbey), but always at a distance from the original site, and usually to one that is apparently more 'inconvenient' in some way or other. The legends have been interpreted in many ways: some historians have suggested that the resiting was due to differences of opinion among the villagers; the Bords and Michell suggested that the differences were between representatives of the Christian clergy and the non-Christian geomancers they employed, or else, as Underwood would have suggested, that geomancers were called in by the villagers during the building of the first site because that site somehow didn't *feel* right.

These theories all assume that the people *knew* what they were doing, but I'm not sure that we can assume this. Particularly with the stories of divination by animals' movements, the coincidences involved are such that if the sites are to be 'perfect' in a geomantic sense (which many of them are) and to tie in with both the underground and overground parts of the energy-matrix (which most of these moved-sites and divined-sites do), then something would have to have been manipulating coincidences for the divination to work properly. Animals don't think in the same way as we do, after all. That 'something' that is manipulating coincidence would seem to be nature itself, for by getting people to build in the right places, it ensures that those places and structures help to maintain the harmony of nature by maintaining the flow of energies within it.

The siting-legends tail off sharply after the Reformation; and Michell, for example, has said that he thinks this to be so because the continuity of the geomantic tradition was broken by the religious upheavals of the time. But as he himself pointed out, the Reformation coincided with the rise of humanism and the development of the concept of the city as something apart from or above nature. We could suggest, then, that the geomantic continuity was broken from nature's side, not the clergy's: nature withdrew its co-operation with man because of man's ignorance of it. The few known cases of geomantic layout after the Reformation – such as Wren's churches and Inigo Jones's 'Queen's

House' at Greenwich (which is sited on a right-angled intersection of two major overgrounds, according to several independent dowsing surveys that I've seen) – can be seen as
coming from people who combined the new humanism with
a deep love and respect for nature and its forms. Certainly it
is true that most post-Reformation religious architecture is
'dead': as Michell put it, 'while our older churches are still
capable of use as precise instruments for spiritual invocation, many of those built in modern times are nothing
more than empty halls.'[12]

That, as I see it, is nature's side in the complex business of
geomantic layout of sacred sites, such as we first saw in
Underwood's work. Unlike Underwood or Michell, I see no
need to postulate the existence of some kind of elite secret
brotherhood of geomancers in Britain, travelling up and
down the country to ensure that sacred – and secular –
structures were correctly sited. It's possible that there may
indeed have been such a brotherhood: the Masons and the
Templars are both likely candidates for the job in the
Christian period, and the archaeologist Euan MacKie has
shown evidence for the operation of a similar group in the
prehistoric period.[13] But I think in many cases the geomancy
was more a matter of feeling on the part of the local inhabitants – with a little assistance from nature – rather than
cold logic and systems supplied by an outside elite.

Consider, too, the complexity of the complete system of
geomancy – which includes, as recent studies show, not only
the placing of each site so that it matches with the underground and overground parts of the energy-matrix, and
harmonizes with the surrounding landscape; but also astronomical alignment, geometrical and numerological structure, musical resonance and much, much more. It seems to
be far too complex, and to contain too many factors, to be
handled by the kind of systematic analysis that Underwood
and some others assumed to have been used by this elite
corps of geomancers. The marrying of just two of the many
factors in the geomancy – geometry and astronomy – with

the surrounding landscape stretches even the present-day capacity for analysis to its limits, as Professor Thom showed in his study of Castlerigg, near Keswick in Cumbria. As he says:

> 'How was a position found which would permit (the geometry of) a Type A circle to be orientated to give so accurately the four declinations (of sun and moon)? Ask any engineer with experience of field-work to locate a site with similar properties and he will want a large group of surveyors working for an indefinite time fully equipped with modern instruments and calculating facilities. Add that the ring must occupy a level piece of ground and he will ask for equipment to level the ground when he has located the exact spot. It will be realized that it is only the mountainous nature of the country which makes it possible to find a site with the necessary properties, and yet Castle Rigg, as tens of thousands of visitors know, is beautifully situated on a flat level part of the field.'[14]

Analysis just isn't up to handling the complexity of the complete geomancy – so how indeed was it done? There is, as Colonel Bell pointed out to Underwood, no evidence that anything like the present-day practice of dowsing was used in the layout of churches or previous sacred sites. There is no evidence that the Masons, the Templars or MacKie's 'astronomer-priests' included systematic divination or a conscious knowledge of the energy-matrix in their practical work. Michell, in his *View Over Atlantis*, seems to imply that this knowledge was carried on by the ultra-secret remnants of some post-Atlantean 'supercivilization'; while others have suggested that the work was all done by von Daniken's 'ancient astronauts'. But there is little or no evidence for the former from archaeology or even from folklore; and the latter 'theory' can be seen clearly to be the materialistic fantasy that it is, once the paraphysical nature of UFO phenomena is fully understood. And that seems to leave us without a theory.

However we try to juggle the evidence to fit those various more 'convenient' theories, we are always brought back to that pagan solution: that nature is intelligent, and is using people, through the forms that people in those siting-legends described as 'fairies', 'angels', 'the Devil' or just 'something', to help it maintain its energy-matrix, its nervous system, its veins and arteries. The sacred sites, as we have seen, are on node-points of the energy-matrix; and the structures at those sites were built where and how they are, and with the extraordinary properties they show, not through analysis and logical systems, but because the builders understood and obeyed that 'something' beyond them, through dreams, through divination, through 'coincidence', through feelings.

Our ignorance of our feelings, our ignorance of 'coincidence', of dreams and divination and of our relationship with nature, has left us wide open to attack by the demons we have created and maintained since time immemorial. Sacred sites we can see as being at key nodes in the energy-matrix: when the structures at those sites are used for true worship, for reinforcement of and respect for our relationship with nature, they direct the energies passing through those sites towards creating and maintaining the harmony and health of the area. Literally, such actions at those sites are 'holy'. But what if the node-site is occupied by a 'profane' structure, such as, to quote the *Exorcism Report*, 'the office of an organization devoted to greed or domination'? We would expect, from the comments in the *Exorcism Report*, that such a structure could 'incur trouble or act as a dispersal centre', would tend to direct the energies passing through that site towards destroying the health and harmony of the area. Going on our previous definition of the term, we could call such a structure 'demonic'.

And that would be an accurate description of the use of the site in more than one sense, for it seems likely that the structure will be where it is – on a site that should be occupied by a sacred structure, not a profane one – because our man-made demons have 'suggested' that use of the site

in exactly the same way that nature 'suggested' the sacredness
of node-sites in the first place. Our demons' aim is to destroy
the harmony of the energies in the energy-matrix: they
would therefore, we could suggest, encourage 'offices of
organizations devoted to greed or domination' to take up
residence at node-sites, so as to promote and increase that
destruction.

It's not easy to find evidence for this suggestion, mainly
because no-one has yet – to my knowledge – studied the
geomantic aspects of the siting of 'offices devoted to greed
or domination': but there are several clues which point in
that direction. During his Leicestershire fieldwork Paul
Devereux found that almost every mark-stone, however inconspicuous, was marked – and presumably 'short-circuited'
– by a steel post of one kind or another rammed into the
ground beside it, for a sign, a fence or whatever. In ley-
hunting work I've been struck by the number of times that
railway stations, of all things, fall onto precise alignments
of prehistoric sites – there may be demonic Feng-shui-type
reasons for that – and by the way that military research
establishments and other military oddities both on and off
the map fall onto the same lines. There is a small military
post within fifty yards of Rollright stone circle, for example,
and a whole network of military establishments surrounds
Stonehenge on Salisbury Plain. But the clearest example of
this possibly demonic siting is the layout of the towers of the
military microwave chains in Britain.

Officially, the towers form a major part of the Post
Office's public telecommunications network – but this is only
a secondary function for use in peace-time, a function which
can still be switched off at the touch of a button. Their
primary function was and still is to provide the Government
and the military with a 'secure' system of communications,
to enable them to maintain their control over the civilian
population in case of war or civil insurrection. As Peter
Laurie explained in his book on the towers, *Beneath the City
Streets*, the fact that the designers were told to make the

deceptively strong concrete towers of the main 'Backbone' chain proof against attack by civilians makes this quite clear. So the towers' primary function was, and probably still is, one of domination – they are thus 'offices of an organization devoted to domination'. So, we are entitled to wonder, what are the geomantic aspects of these rather demonic towers?

We saw earlier, when first looking at Watkins' work on the ley-system, that the main principle of the towers – straight-line communications between high points, with minor points 'tapping in' to the straight line – is the same as that of the ley-system, particularly if we can equate leys with overgrounds. At first I took this just to be an analogy; but as time went on evidence began to collect that suggested that the analogy was too close for 'mere coincidence'. It seems, on looking more closely, that at least some of the towers are built on or very near to node-points in the natural energy-matrix. Many times when driving around the country I've seen one of these 'Watchers on the skyline' form part of a

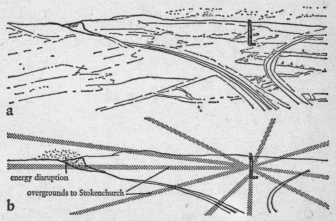

36 Earth-energy activity on the Chiltern ridge: (a) Stokenchurch tower and the M40 cutting, seen from the east, and (b) showing energy activity at the same place.

visible ley-type alignment. My clearest example so far is to the steel mast at Kelvedon Hatch near Brentwood in Essex, for at night-time the red warning light on its tip can be seen to be exactly in line with the centre-section of a classic ley-type road-zigzag round the church at High Ongar, about five miles away to the north; while the results of some experiments at dowsing from the air that I did recently suggest that at least five overgrounds converge on the concrete microwave tower at Stokenchurch.

But it's particularly on feelings that the towers' analogy with the ley-system seems more than an analogy. For me, a ley, or rather the overground it represents, has a definite feeling as I drive through it, 'pulling' my eyes round to look at the point it comes from. There's a particular point on the A38 main road a few miles above Lichfield where a line from Lichfield Cathedral crosses it, on a low hump in the road; for me, and for several others I know, the ley 'pulls' me round to show me that the central axis of the cathedral, from whence the line comes, is aligned precisely on that point. (This may be one reason, by the way, why that point on the road is classified as an 'accident black spot'.) Time and again, I've had this effect happen not just with churches and barrows, but with the towers as well. Still more interesting is the way that sections of new road or motorway 'coincidentally' align with the towers – as does a section of the M40 to the Stokenchurch tower – in the same way that sections of old road align on churches and cathedrals. Given the destructive effects of motorways and other high-speed roads on the energy-matrix, as reported by many dowsers, it would seem that these too had a certain amount of demonic 'assistance' in the choosing of their routes.

The aim behind a return to pagan values is to reconstruct our relationship with nature – and it is this, of course, that our great demons of ignorance and arrogance, of pride and profanity, fight so hard against. Profane structures, the 'offices of organizations devoted to greed or domination', now occupy many of the node-points in the existing energy-matrix; so if we are to limit their destructive effects we have to take not just remedial action against the results of their discord, but also, if possible, protective and preventive action. We need to isolate them from the energies, by-passing those energies around such 'desecrated' sites. It is here that our earth-acupuncture becomes both useful and important; in using it we can heal not just the land and its energies, but also our relationship with nature, and with ourselves as well.

10

Healing the Land

Three people sit on the ground of a Cotswold farmyard, discussing intently the work they are about to do. One of them, evidently the leader of this group, seems to be foreign, but speaks with a rich Oxford-academic accent; the other two are more obviously English. Discussion over, but still sitting on the ground, one of the three picks up what seems to be a bow, loops a stick through its string and, rocking the bow back and forth, rotates it to grind the tip of the stick against a block of wood on the ground. A wisp of smoke rises from the block, then flames as the tinder round the tip of the stick catches light. Lighting a spill from this tiny flame, the leader reaches over and lights a paraffin storm-lamp. A lamp lit by an ancient and awkward method, on a bright and sunny day.

A short while after, the three can be seen on the hillslope above the farm. One is kneeling on the ground, another is holding the lantern, and the third, the leader, has his hands raised to the sky. He *is* foreign, despite his excellent English; he is chanting in Persian, a Zoroastrian fire-ritual. But it's more than the ancient ritual, for at a signal the kneeling man hammers the stake he is holding into the ground. The short ritual comes to a close, and they move on to another of the sixty-odd points they have marked out in this valley. A complex process of earth-acupuncture, to heal and make holy the 'atmosphere' of this small Cotswold valley.

The operation above occurred a few years ago, when I was visiting a small religious community in the southern part of the Cotswolds. It was actually the last part of a very complex piece of earth-acupuncture, in three stages, that had taken two years to complete. The process started soon after the community had bought the farm, for they found that the place's 'atmosphere' was in such a bad state that not only was the valley devoid of wild-life, but every person staying for more than a couple of hours picked up some kind of 'stomach-bug' – whether they had drunk the water there or not. The leader of the community and another member – the Persian with the Oxford accent – were both dowsers, and I was told that they had traced the source of the trouble to a new quarry about fifty miles away. The energy imbalance this created had somehow focused on the valley; and though the problem could not, for practical reasons, be dealt with at source, it could be dealt with by 'isolating' the valley from energies arriving from outside the immediate area, and then 'restructuring' the energies as they arrived at that point.

The first stage – the 'first aid', we could say – involved placing about twenty wooden stakes, with copper wire wound round the top of each, into the ground at various points selected by dowsing: the 'stomach bug' disappeared within days. The second stage, the repair operation, involved staking the ground in more detail, patching up gaps and loopholes: the wild-life began to return. The final 'cosmetic' stage, which was the one I saw, used copper-sheathed iron stakes to 'restructure' the energy-flow, removing the imbalance rather than simply isolating the valley from its effects. The balanced energy-flow that came into the valley brought with it deep peace and quiet – the deep silence of a cathedral. Earth-acupuncture, and a large amount of commitment on the part of the community, had changed the 'atmosphere' of the place from hellish to holy in just two years.[1]

It was an impressive piece of work, but I'm not sure how much of the 'trimmings' of the operation were essential to its working. The community insisted that the ritual and the chanting were an essential part of the process; but since I've seen dowsers doing similar work – though admittedly on a smaller scale – with just the basic 'staking', I think that while the ritual was useful and valuable 'priming' in a magical sense, it probably wasn't as essential as they believed it was. Dowsers have been using stakes to neutralize 'noxious earth radiations' from black streams for more than fifty years, in a variety of ways and forms; and their work can be seen as part of a more complex system of earth-acupuncture that is now being developed as a means of healing the land.

The idea of earth-acupuncture has strong roots in European tradition; and these traditions begin to make sense once we realize the interaction between people and the natural energies, and realize that most of these energies are non-physical 'codings' carried by and within physical energies, as we saw earlier. The best-known of these traditions, and the ones that tend to make 'rationalists' dismiss the concept of earth-acupuncture without even looking at it, are those about the staking of vampires or about witches sticking pins into models of people or of land. The horror-movie images that these traditions conjure up are, to say the least, a little erroneous compared to the reality behind them: but we do need to recognize that there is a reality behind them.

The blood-sucking variant of the vampire legend we can, I think, ignore for our present purposes. But the idea of something draining away a kind of 'lifeblood' is very real, for in various forms and modes it can be seen in action around us all the time. We talk of people or places or situations that 'drain' us: a 'tiresome' person, for example, is literally a vampire in the sense of draining away physical or emotional energy. We don't deal with such people by staking them through the heart, of course (though from practical experience I know that the traditional magical 'banishing' rituals are usually more efficient at keeping them at bay than physical restraint); but extreme forms of social 'vampires' – particularly suicides or, to a lesser extent, executed murderers – were buried at crossroads, often with a stake through the heart. Church law forbade the burial of suicides on consecrated ground; this can be seen in Shakespeare's *Hamlet*, in the discussion about the burial of Ophelia. The crossroads, as an 'un-sacred' node-point in the energy matrix, was and is a more sensible place to bury such a focus of negative and destructive energy, for it should allow the dispersal of the *sha* attached to that person well away from inhabited sites. Much of the traditional lore about crossroads only makes sense when seen in this kind of energy context.[2]

This crude manipulation of energies was almost certainly organized at an intuitive level; it's only in the last fifty years or so that Western dowsers have built up a systematic form of energy manipulation, both isolating and restructuring 'bad' energy, *sha*. The isolators and insulators used are usually physical insulation materials of some kind, such as asbestos or plastic sheeting. These are placed directly over the black stream at key points such as beneath a bed or desk, to protect the area above it. The various dowsing studies I've seen state that these do work, but only for a matter of months at most, as the insulator itself becomes 'charged' with *sha* and has to be replaced and disposed of.[3] Isolation is at best a temporary palliative measure, and should only be used while a more permanent means of protection is being worked out.

The only permanent means of protection – or at least as permanent as can be expected when every new development alters the structure and interactions of the energy-matrix – is to re-structure the local energy network. Most dowsers use stakes or coils or similar gadgets for this, and the process resembles acupuncture, as the term 'earth-acupuncture' implies. Like acupuncture, the principles are very simple; but the practice is anything but simple, for the right kind of stake has to be sited at exactly the right place, and even – in some techniques – at exactly the right time. Diagnosis of the problem in any given case is as complex as diagnosis in acupuncture, if not more so; at the present time there are only a handful of dowsers in Britain with the skill and experience needed to do a safe and reliable job. It's probably illegal to do it at all in the United States on the usual pseudo-scientific grounds that block the development of most unconventional medicine there. I know quite a lot of this work goes on in France and Germany, and some probably goes on in most of the countries of Europe.[4]

From my own knowledge of this earth-acupuncture, and going on the published case-histories of the more recent work in Britain, it seems that this staking with stakes or coils can indeed restore the energy-balance and the health of quite large areas of land. One dowser claimed that he had stablized more than twenty square miles in one operation, but that, if true, would be exceptional: a couple of acres or so at any one time is more usual.[5] Ideally, the 'needle' should neutralize the wayward components of the *sha* all the way downstream (or downline in the case of the over-grounds) of its point of insertion; but in practice, partly because of the difficulty of siting the needle precisely on the line, most of the case-histories I've seen describe the pro-tected area as a comma-shape spreading downline from the needle's point of insertion. The size of this comma-shape is dependent more on the accuracy of the siting of the needle than on any other factor, so the skill and experience of the dowser is critical to the success of any operation.

In principle, the needle staking a black stream is like an upside-down version of Reich's cloudbuster, in that it selectively removes and 'earths' aspects of the energies from downstairs; or else, in some cases, it 'unscrambles' the tangled coding of the energies that comes out as *sha*, to convert it to a stable *ch'i*. How it does so is still obscure, but then so is the effect and operation of acupuncture needles applied to the human body.

If we look at earth-acupuncture in Reich's terms of orgone – which is both a coding of physical energy and a non-physical energy in itself – we can see 'cloud-forming' work with the cloudbuster to be a shifting of orgone from the cloud into an 'ordinary' stream. DOR-cloud-busting trans-fers the DOR/*sha* into the water-lines below ground, and may in fact convert it to a black stream in some cases: I don't think Reich had any way of knowing where or how the energy he 'drew' from DOR-clouds went. To make sure that sky-borne *sha* is not just transferred underground, so causing further problems elsewhere, it would probably be best to neutralize it by taking it into the ground at a point with a high level of *ch'i*, a holy place – which is where we come back to sacred sites and sacred structures.

Before we leave Reich's theories, I'd better mention one misapplied aspect of Reich's orgonomy that has caused quite a few problems in the recent past. A number of would-be acupuncturists, recognizing the connection between DOR and *sha*, connected earthstakes to small orgone accumulators. For a while a black stream so treated will indeed be neutralized – but only while the accumulator is being charged by the *sha* drawn up through the earth-stake. Once the accumulator is fully charged, the problems caused by the 'blackness' of the stream will re-start – and the earth-acupuncturist will be left with an orgone accumulator that is fully charged with *sha*.

Since this represents a disposal problem as serious as – and possibly identical with – that of the disposal of radio-active wastes, it's not a good idea to use orgone accumulators for earth-acupuncture work without the back-up of a suitable and safe means of disposing and dispersing the collected *sha*.[6] It's possible that the observable effects of the barrow-and-stone weather-control system described earlier are in fact side-effects of just such a dispersal system. The Fortean phenomena associated with the sites may be the result of erratic and inefficient dispersal of *sha*, caused by the ruinous state of the system. Again, assuming this to be so, I don't think it's likely that the network of barrows and stones was deliberately set up with this in mind. It's more likely that the builders put them where and how they did because it 'felt right' to do so. At a time when people recognized their dependence on nature, those feelings could well have been seen and recognized as the direct instructions of nature and its gods.

Much the same could be said of historic (rather than prehistoric or modern) structures at sacred sites. Buildings were constructed far more to some preconceived system, such as the old Quadrivium of Number, Music, Geometry and Astronomy, but there was still the same deep concern with feeling – a concern that is largely absent in modern buildings as a result of the inhumanity of civilized cultures. We can see, by looking at the work of Underwood and his contemporaries in a slightly different way, that the great sacred structures of the historic period do operate as gigantic earth-acupuncture needles; and their effects seem to be far more selective and sophisticated than in the simple, ancient 'needles of stone', because of the far greater concern with shape, and thus the shape-power effects of the structure.

The same interest in the shape-power effect can be seen in the bewildering variety of different gadgets and constructions that modern dowsers have used for this earth-acupuncture work. Comparing this with conventional acupuncture, we can also see that the concern with materials in the barrows and standing stones, the churches and cathedrals and the modern earth-acupuncture needles, has a lot to do with the elemental attributions of the various materials. Each different element (wood, earth, metal or whatever) has a different effect in controlling the balance of the energies behind *ch'i* and *sha*.

An interesting theoretical and practical problem is whether the various needles should be left in place or, as in conventional acupuncture, be inserted and then removed after a short period. Much of this has to do with the tidal ebbing and flowing of the energies and the levels of those energies. It is here that the known astronomical aspects of sacred sites and their structures – historic and prehistoric – may come into earth-acupuncture. Where the needle cannot be removed from the site – as is obviously the case with a permanent structure like a cathedral – it may be that the astronomical aspects of the structure were designed (again, probably unconsciously) so as to handle the constantly changing energy-patterns through astronomical alignments, and possibly through the elemental attributions of the astronomical and astrological aspects and functions of the structure. This is, I admit, rather outside my field; but the attributions and interactions of the various aspects and functions of Number, Music, Geometry and Astronomy are known to have formed the major part of Medieval university studies, and are still used a great deal in present-day magical practice.

Until recently, most earth-acupuncturist dowsers simply stuck their gadgets in the ground in what they hoped was the right place, and left them to work in peace, coming back from time to time to check if they were still having the desired effect. But a number of dowsers involved in this work have recently insisted that earth-acupuncture stakes should be removed soon after insertion, in the manner of conventional acupuncture needles, and that the old practice of leaving the stakes in place is wrong. They point out that a needle left in a patient in conventional acupuncture could have the opposite effect to the one intended at the opposite end of the daily cycle of energy-flow. In reply, other dowsers have pointed out that in much conventional acupuncture the needle is left in the patient 'until the flesh no longer clings to it'. It then drops out of its own accord, having done its job. One dowser even said that the ground pushed out the stake when it was no longer needed. From my own practical work, it seems that both sides, as usual, are right. In one case at a stone circle, for example, I was 'told' by my pendulum to remove some of the stakes after insertion, but to leave some of the others in place, pushed just below the surface. To my knowledge, they are still there now.

But the use of needles, you'll remember, is only one part of acupuncture: conventional acupuncture includes moxibustion, massage and diet as well. Moxibustion, as we have seen, is paralleled in this earth-acupuncture by the controlled use of fires as wend- or need-fires and as the beacon-fires on the old Beacon Hills. Our civilization has completely concealed the magical use of fire; it's something which comes out in children's sometimes lethal fascination with matches and bonfires. In our civilized culture, the Beacon Hills seem to be regarded as nothing more than pretty view-points from which people can look out over a countryside that is now so civilized and so ignored. But the Beacons were and are something more than that.

Something of the power of the Beacons was seen recently in the lighting of the bonfire chains for the Queen's Silver Jubilee. It was nothing like as powerful as it could have been, since few of the bonfires were on the ancient Beacon sites (the National Trust, among others, would not allow it), and the glare of orange streetlights obscured the official and unofficial bonfires in many areas; but some of the power was still there. I was with the *Ley Hunter* team at the Dunstable bonfire at the time, and we all felt the extraordinary sense of unity and non-verbal communication – so rare in a civilization – that was brought home as each bonfire in succession was lit and linked with others.

Even so, civilization had to meddle in the process to make sure that everything 'still worked', for the firing of the first few bonfires in the chains radiating out from Windsor was controlled not by visual sighting but by portable microwave links. The Windsor bonfire wasn't even visible from Dunstable, supposedly the first bonfire in the northward chain – a pity, but never mind. I feel sure that if we were to reactivate the old Beacon Hills, and use them for their proper magical and communications purposes instead of leaving them dead as 'pretty viewpoints', then they would have a highly beneficial effect both on the natural energy network and also – as was clear at the Jubilee bonfires – on the national morale.

Massage of the landscape is easier to see and to understand. In conventional acupuncture massage is used to reduce the damage and blockage caused by bruising and scarring: so by analogy we can see that the filling-in and returfing of quarries, and the grassing-over of slag-heaps and spoil-tips, does a great deal for the energy aspects of the landscape as well as for its visual appearance. The same is true of careful 'landscaping' of new motorways and building developments. Feng-shui's concern with the shape and harmony of the landscape can be seen in earth-acupuncture terms as the landscape equivalent of massage.

If we are to restore some kind of balance between civilized people and the landscape, we also need to do a kind of 'massage' on their minds. We need to instil a greater respect for the natural harmony of the landscape, and a realization, particularly among architects and 'planners', that man-made systems and man-made 'convenience' will only work in the long run if they take the natural forms of the area into account. The planners need to be made to realize just how fragile and artificial cities and city 'conveniences' are; they need to have a true education to show them the limitations and destructiveness of their civilized 'solutions' to civilized problems, and to show them how pagan experience, far from being 'primitive and mindless', is far better suited to handling the total reality imposed on us by nature than is their civilized arrogance and ignorance.

One example is whether we really need motorways. A study of earth-energies redoubles the doubts about their necessity: concrete and tarmac have disastrous effects on the 'colouring' of energy-flows both above and beneath, for one point, since both materials are essentially sterile and sterilizing. The process of constructing a motorway often crushes and blocks underground streams; and the speed and continuous flow of the vehicles on the completed motorway, as we saw earlier, breaks up any time-based coding on overgrounds that pass close to a motorway's surface. When we couple these worries with those of the neo-pagan ecologists – worries about the twenty or more acres per mile of farmland that disappear beneath the motorway, and the efficiency (or lack of it, in any terms other than the artificial and constantly changing terms of economics) of moving so many passengers and so many tons of freight in so many vehicles –

the doubts about the viability of motorways in real terms
become even stronger. But as I would reply myself, as a car-
driver and motorway user, motorways cut down the time
we have to spend in that unimportant inter-urban space;
they allow us to travel at a civilized (in other words excessive)
speed; and besides, now that the railway system in Britain is
all but demolished, how else can I or the freight of trade get
about the country? No matter what we feel, no matter what
we do, a civilized culture forces us to be hypocrites.

It certainly wasn't very intelligent, except in the terms of
the economics of the now-gone days of cheap fuel, to
demolish two highly efficient networks that we already had –
the canals and the railways – which had already consumed a
vast amount of land between them, in favour of yet another,
but highly *in*efficient, transport network, the motorways.
And it's even less intelligent to continue destroying thousands of acres each year of our best farmland – on whose
produce once more we are soon going to have to rely for our
survival – in favour of what is proving to be a very short-
lived convenience.

This is only one area in which pagan practicality clashes
with civilized suicide; and it's only one of several areas in
which our 'unimportant' study of the earth-energies and the
earth mysteries is forced into the political arena. There's no
point in studying the past as a means of escaping from the
harsh realities of the present: the only valid reason for studying the past is to learn from it, to apply those lessons to the
problems of the present day. That we will have to return to
before we leave this study; but for now we'd better return to
the practice of earth-acupuncture.

One of the controls for the energy-matrix, as we have seen,
is ritual; and this would suggest that 'diet' in a landscape-
scale acupuncture would be the ceaseless round of rituals
kept up by pagan communities. Those rituals have a real
effect on the matrix. Our civilized culture has made sure
that not much meaning is left in the old rituals that still
survive; those that do retain some meaning, such as the

Padstow Hobby Horse and the Abbot's Bromley Horn Dance, are in danger of being defused into civilized tourist attractions. About the only ritual attention that the earth receives is the weekly libation of dirty soapy water in the urban ritual of 'wash-day' or the suburban ritual of 'washing the car'. Once we see rituals for what they are – not as superstitious games, but as tools or constructs with real effects – we can see their importance and their value as part of a re-introduction of pagan awareness into our ailing civilized culture.

So far we've only looked at ways of manipulating the energies in their existing 'channels'. But in some cases this is not enough, for to repair completely a piece of damage we

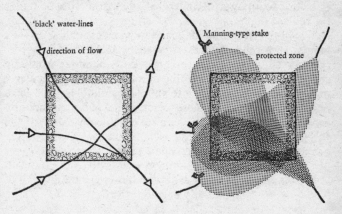

37 Staking black streams round a house.

may need to isolate a small area, or to divert the energies around it. These diversions use much the same tools as in routine manipulation of the 'colour' or 'texture' of the energies, but need slightly different techniques. In the routine staking of black streams, only one stake is used on each stream, and they are regarded as being independent. A typical, badly-affected house may have five or more black streams crossing beneath it, and so the same number of stakes would be used, one placed upstream from the house on each of the streams. Diversion is rather trickier, depending on where the problem lies. In some cases two stakes may be used on each stream, on a 'spark-gap' principle, to move an energy-flow from below ground to above for a short distance, or vice versa. In others the effective course of the energy-flow may be altered by hammering, by the orientation of quartz-based crystals, or by connecting a series of stakes in a chain or ring.

The 'spark-gap' diversion is particularly useful with roads. There have been a few cases where 'accident black spots' on apparently clear stretches of road have been shown to be due to a powerful underground stream crossing under the road at that point. A car's steering wheel, like a dowsing rod, is designed to amplify small movements of the driver's hands; so a reflex twitch triggered by the stream in someone who slips unconsciously into a dowsing mode would be enough to send a car travelling at a fair speed – particularly on a wet or greasy road – into an uncontrollable spin. I have heard of one or two of these 'black spots' being successfully exorcized, which we could see as a 'psychic diversion' of the energy of the stream; but the usual dowsers' solution to the problem would be to insert a pair of stakes into the ground directly above the stream, one on each side of the road, to divert the energy of the stream itself above ground instead of below, where it apparently has less effect.

The same technique has been used in reverse with overgrounds crossing motorways near ground level. The 'coding' which the cars were breaking up is sent underground, below the motorway, and then lifted back overground again by the stake on the other side. The different types of energy, the 'idea' of the stream and the 'coding' in the overground, are different in their effects upon us, and need different techniques to neutralize their unwanted side-effects without neutralizing the energies themselves. We have seen much the same with the standing stones, which both mark and are the points through which energies and 'codings' are interchanged between the overgrounds and water-lines.

Several dowsers I've talked to have suggested that there were at one time several independent standing-stone networks, each constructed at a different period for a different purpose. They suggested that the ruinous state of the networks, and the 'melted' appearance of many of the stones, might be due to a late tampering with these networks, at a time when the intuitive knowledge of how to handle them was lost, and which didn't work in quite the way the meddlers expected. We should never forget that the energies the stones operate on are real, can do real – and sometimes immediately physical – damage if we are not careful in what we do with them; so we need to approach any redirection or reconstruction of these energy-networks with care and with caution.

It seems to have been the late Evelyn Penrose, the one-time Official Dowser for one of the Canadian provinces, who discovered about twenty years ago that hammering on a stake above an underground stream appeared to change the stream's course. It's been a matter of some controversy among dowsers ever since, whether it does or does not work, and what it can or can't do.[7] The idea is that by banging a large number of times on a boulder or stake directly above a water-line, a dowser can block the water-flow down the line and divert it along whatever alternative route may be available down there. The problem, which has been much aired in the dowsing journals, is whether the physical water-flow itself can be diverted in this way – and if so, how, since as with all this kind of work the stake only goes a few inches into the ground – or whether it only diverts the water-*line*, the image of the water that the dowser sees. Either way, it is the water-line that carries much of the 'coding' which concerns us in a system of earth-acupunture, and so we could say that this hammering technique could be used as a diversionary tool in this respect. I have heard of one or two earth-acupuncturist dowsers who use it as part of their regular 'armoury', but I haven't yet been able to find one who has been willing to discuss the details of how it is done and under what circumstances it can or should be used.

I have had more of a chance to discuss the use of quartz-based crystals as 'needles' with an earth-acupuncturist dowser. According to him, the different quartzes have different properties. Amethyst, for example, is a slow-acting but long-term stabilizer for the 'colour' of energies travelling both below and above ground. I had an opportunity to try this use of amethyst in an experiment I did with the Druid Order at a stone circle. They said that although the crystals, which I had placed on all the water-lines and overgrounds around the perimeter of the circle, seemed to make little appreciable difference to the 'atmosphere' of the circle during the ritual they held that day, they did notice that the crowd of spectators was the quietest and most respectful they had had for more than five years – so the amethysts did seem to have affected the 'atmosphere' in some ways.

Some of the other quartzes change the 'colour' of energy-pathways they are placed above or below in other ways: one of the other quartzes (I won't say which) changes an ordinary water-line to 'black', for example. The dowser I discussed this with suggested that the intersections of two water-lines, one white, one black, crossing beneath church altars at right-angles – something he'd found in several cases – was due to the 're-colouring' and diversion of existing energy-pathways by this means. It's possible: but again, as with the hammering technique, we need to do a lot more work and experiments on this before we will know how to use them accurately and safely in a system of earth-acupuncture.

The last diversionary technique, using a 'chain' or 'ring' of stakes or needles, comes more closely to conventional acupuncture practice. The standard procedure in acupuncture for dealing with a spontaneously painful point, or a swelling of any kind, is to surround it by placing needles on the nearest approachable acupuncture points on the appropriate meridians – never on any part of the painful area itself. As the pain subsides, the needles are moved into acupuncture points closer to the centre of the original area, but outside any area that is still painful. The idea seems to be that the ring of needles around the swelling allows the energies to by-pass the area without being affected by the problems of the area itself, and also allows the swollen area to get on with the job of healing itself without being bothered by other energies that would only be passing through.

Taking this as an analogy, it should be possible to isolate 'scarred' areas in the landscape, such as quarries and slagheaps, by placing stakes or needles into the ground on minor node-points of the lines of the water-lines and overgrounds that pass through the area of the 'scar'. The idea would be that the 'scar' not only causes less interference to the 'colour' of the energies passing through, but is also allowed to get on with repairing the damage of itself without hindrance from outside. It was a more complex variant of this technique that the religious community I mentioned at the beginning of this chapter used to stabilize their valley. They defined an area with the stakes they used, and then worked on repairing the energy structure of that area – through ritual and through the other religious and magical means at their disposal – before re-connecting it with the rest of the natural energy-structure, the energy-matrix, outside the ring of stakes. It seems likely, from the dowsing results we saw in the early chapters of this study, that the ring of stones in a stone circle acts as a 'shield-ring' in this way, isolating the inside of the circle from the outside world, and insulating the outside world from whatever may go on inside the circle.

The principle of the shield-ring is thus analogous to that of shielding electronic apparatus from stray magnetic fields (with soft-iron casings) and electromagnetic radiation (with a Faraday cage). As far as the outside world, as seen by those forces, is concerned, that which is inside the shield does not exist, for the forces bend round the surface of the shield; and conversely, as far as the equipment is concerned,

the outside world of those forces does not exist either –
which is, of course, the whole point of the shield in the first
place.

This use of stakes to provide a by-pass shield for the
energies to use in by-passing a defined area could resolve the
dilemma posed by 'offices of organizations devoted to greed
or domination'. In an ideal world such places should not
exist: but we don't live in an ideal world, and while the
present crazy international systems of politics and economics – which are based on 'greed and domination' – continue to exist, they will unfortunately continue to be
necessary. But at the same time, as the *Exorcism Report* put
it, such 'offices . . . incur trouble or act as dispersal centres;
they also open the door for other (demonic) forces to enter
in'. As we saw earlier, there are strong suggestions that they
adversely affect the health of the areas surrounding them, so
we do need to do something to reduce their impact. The
shield-ring technique may provide us with a way of doing so.

Ideally, as I say, our aim should be to eliminate the need
for such offices: but this is definitely a long-term aim, for it
would demand a total overhaul not just of our political and
economic systems, but of our own attitudes to ourselves, to
each other and to nature. In the meantime we could reduce
the impact of such places on the energy-matrix – and thus
on the health of the surrounding areas – by constructing
shield-rings of earth-acupuncture stakes around them. A
stake would need to be placed on most, and preferably all,
of the energy-lines that pass through the sites of such
'offices'. It's possible that a side-effect would be that the
'bad vibes' created by such an 'office' would be trapped
inside such a shield-ring, in the same way that the religious
community carefully built a 'holy atmosphere' within their
shield-ring before re-connecting it with the outside world.
If so, we would expect that the 'atmosphere' within the
shield-ring would rapidly become intolerable, more or less
so depending on how much the organization was 'devoted'
to greed or domination. This could perhaps be seen as a

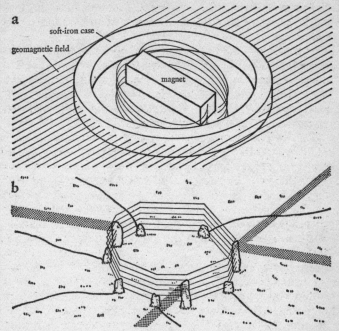

38 A soft-iron analogy for the shield-ring principle: (a) a soft-iron magnetic shield, showing magnetic fields inside and outside the shield, and (b) water-lines and overgrounds meeting a simple shield-ring.

form of 'aversion therapy' – it's certainly an interesting prospect.

With military sites, particularly those parked by demonic assistance or otherwise on node-points of the energy-matrix, the picture is slightly more complicated. Isolation of offensive sites by shield-rings should produce the same results as above – good for the community, but not too comfortable for the military. But defensive sites, if truly defensive and so ethically speaking neutral, should not have the same buildup of 'bad vibes' inside a shield-ring: an interesting deterrent against offensive military intent! The dilemma for the military is that apart from the safeguard it provides for the health of the surrounding community, there are good military reasons why both offensive and defensive sites need to be shielded. If such places are sited on node-points of the energy-matrix (which, as I suggested earlier, many of them would appear to be) they are far more liable to damage by magical or demonic attack at crucial times than are ordinary sites. A shield-ring gives a certain amount of protection against such bizarre forms of attack.

To the materialist, such a suggestion will seem ludicrous; but from what I've heard I would be surprised to find that it is not being taken very seriously in senior military circles. The military risks presented by human or non-human magical action, particularly on electronic apparatus, are recognized and real, and cannot safely be disregarded. UFOs are known to have a keen 'interest' in military activity, dating back at least to the 'foo-fighters' of the Second World War, and typified by the repeated 'flaps' at Warminster, in the military area on Salisbury Plain in the south of England. Their well-documented ability to stall or start car engines and confuse electronic apparatus such as radar and radio sets could cause disaster in a crucial military situation. As for the reality of magical action, my recording engineer friend Richard witnessed, about five years ago, a magical operation which was useful to him and his friends at the time, but which has disturbing implications in military terms:

'It was quite late one night, and a couple of acquaintances in the music business and myself had returned from the pub to the recording studio complex not far from Ladbroke Grove. A member of our small party of travellers had left his bags in the studio reception area, and needed to pick them up before moving off homeward. Unfortunately, on arriving at the studio, we found the door locked. A heavy door, solid, about ten feet high by four feet wide I would guess, with a circular window in it.

We peered through the window at the empty reception area where the security guard usually sat after hours, watching TV or listening to the radio. We rang the bell, and waited. Probably the guard was in one of the studio control rooms, chatting to tape ops as they cleared up after the last sessions of the night. Perhaps he was otherwise engaged. Whatever the reason, he did not answer the bell. We rang several times, but nothing happened.

Finally, one of our little group walked forward, inscribed some brief designs on the door (with his finger), and mumbled a few words under his breath. With a loud bang, the door swung almost wide open. The amount it opened was surprising in itself, as the door was on a very strong return spring. I reckon it would have taken the simultaneous impact of three people on the door to have the effect of opening it so far. In such a case, however, it would not have opened so rapidly as this one, which was just closed one moment and open the next. We went in before the door closed on its spring, and went over to the bags.

The door didn't close completely, however: it couldn't, as the tongue of the lock was still in the locked position. It could not pass the plate set in the door-frame, and hence could not close. Neither lock, door or frame were damaged, or marked in any way. It was as if the door had been unlocked, pushed open, and relocked in the open position. But this had not occurred . . . Neither had I been hypnotized, and so persuaded that the door had been opened by an invisible agency: that would not have got me past the door, and it would not have explained the bewilderment of the security guard when he finally arrived. What *had* occurred was a magical operation with an objective result.'[8]

Combine this magical lock-picking with directed poltergeist from children and the known ability of some psychics

I

like Matthew Manning to tamper with or eradicate information from computer tapes from an indefinite distance, and you'll appreciate why the American and Soviet governments have suddenly started spending vast sums of money on 'useless' ESP research.[9]

An earth-acupuncture shield-ring is a defence against most kinds of demonic attack because the area inside the ring 'disappears' as far as the energy-matrix is concerned; and human magical action against sites on node-points in the matrix is made more difficult, because it has to be done without 'hitching a ride' on the energies of the matrix. Just making things more difficult for magical action would seem to be an adequate defence in many respects, for it seems to be a fact that as magicians develop the awareness needed to handle increasingly complex problems, they also become increasingly aware of the relative pettiness and pointlessness of political and military squabbles, and try to avoid becoming entangled in them. The real if magical action and re-action of the 'law of *karma*', the natural law of inescapable responsibility for the results of your own actions and in-actions, soon brings home the necessity of that to every magician, master or novice – and in some senses we are all magicians, whether we like it or not.

Traditionally, a magician's training has just one aim, 'to know thyself'. The aim of the post-Druidic witchcraft in Britain, 'the craft of the wise', was the same; and the same is true of all forms of mysticism, including the Christian ones. Knowledge, 'Truth', is a personal matter as much as a common one: it's only when the organized religions like scientism and the Church try to define and enforce their version of 'the Truth' that that knowledge, and the chance of knowing one's-self, dies. No true mystic or magician is fool enough to believe that he can define nature or 'Truth', or to believe that he can control it or be above it: and that isn't a matter of belief, as it is with the man-made religions, it is a matter of personal experience, personal knowledge.

The final aim of both the mystic and the magician is to

know his nature, and thus become 'at one with nature'. To try to control nature, to fight against it, is simply to fight against one's own nature. But by knowing nature, aiming to 'become at one with it', we can work with nature instead of against it, and come to know our nature in the process. We have, throughout time, created and maintained those demons which harass us; and the more we continue to fight against nature and our nature, the more power we give to those demons, and the more hellish life becomes in civilized society and elsewhere. In healing the land, in healing our relationship with nature, we need to 'become at one with it': and to do that we need to recognize and develop, in and for ourselves, a magician's awareness and a mystic's knowledge of nature and our nature.

We need to remember this in using the techniques of earth-acupuncture. We are not, and cannot be, 'above' nature: the most we can do, with earth-acupuncture, is help nature to heal itself. No system of medicine ever cures a patient; it can only provide conditions under which the patient (whatever it is) can heal itself. Meddling or tampering, without the total knowledge of the nature of the patient that only 'being at one with nature' can provide, can only make things worse. If we remember our limitations, earth-acupuncture is a useful tool for limiting the effects of the damage we have already done to the earth, and which we are still doing today.

But this is not enough: we cannot continue to ravage the earth in the way that we have been doing, and still hope to survive for long. Earth-acupuncture is a palliative, not a cure. We should be looking to the future as well, looking to other ways of reducing our impact on nature, on the earth and its energy-matrix. Most of all, we need to change our civilized arrogance and ignorance of nature. We need, like the pagans, to recognize and realize that our relationship with nature can only be one of lord and servant – and that we are not the lords of that relationship.

11

A Reality for the Future

'And God said, Let us make man in our own image, after our likeness: and let them have dominion over the fish of the sea, and over the fowl of the air, and over the cattle, and over all the earth, and over every creeping thing that creepeth upon the earth.

So God created man in his own image, in the image of God created he him; male and female created he them.

And God blessed them, and God said unto them, Be fruitful, and multiply, and replenish the earth, and subdue it: and have dominion over the fish of the sea, over the fowl of the air, and over every living thing that moveth over the earth.'

(Genesis 1, v. 26–8)

This short passage from the King James version of the Bible has been used time and again as the 'justification' for our rapacious plundering of the earth. Since this passage states that we have been given dominion over the earth – so the argument goes – and told to subdue it by God himself, surely that means that we can do whatever we like with it, to bend it to our will?

The answer is No. There are other ways of interpreting this passage, interpretations which civilization has until recently been very careful to avoid. This section of Genesis comes before the 'Garden of Eden' story, with its inherent 'proof' that women are the cause of all problems in the Judaic male-dominated view of nature and the world. In this earlier story, male and female are equal: 'male and female created he them'. The pagan view of God is that he or it is nature, the union of Mother Earth and Father Sky, and all the aspects and archetypes they symbolize: for 'let us make man in our own image' must include woman as well, or God would be unable to encompass the totality of nature.

This section of the Bible was written by a pagan culture, not a civilized one. So we need to look a little more closely at the whole of that passage, and not just at that so-useful word 'subdue': 'Be fruitful and multiply, and replenish the earth, and subdue it: and have dominion ... over every living thing,' 'Be fruitful, and multiply': so if we are to be realistic about our relationship with nature, we cannot deny our own sexuality, as the civilized wisdom of the Church has taught us to do. And our 'dominion ... over every living thing' must not, it is clear, solely be one of subjugation, for we are ordered in that passage to 'replenish the earth' as much as to subdue it.

It's all too obvious that we haven't done this. Our 'dominion' has been that of the domineering tyrant: we have, as the definition of 'domineering' puts it, 'ruled arbitrarily and despotically, feasted riotously and luxuriously' while others, and the earth itself, have starved. We have taken none of the master's responsibilities to replenish the earth; we have merely played at being the master. But however much we may strut and crow, however much we may pontificate about the 'progress of science' and the 'march of civilization', the fact remains that that dream of mastery, as we are well aware, is nothing more than an arrogant illusion, fostered and maintained by our careful ignorance of reality.

We seem to be proud of our ability to maintain that illusion; and from that pride, that arrogance, that ignorance, have arisen the demons that harass us in their subtle and not-so-subtle ways. Our civilization is pandemonium, born of pride. But as Thomas More put it, 'the Devil, that proude spirit, cannot bear to be mocked': so nature 'moves in its mysterious ways', sending us imaginary spacemen in flying saucers, showers of frogs and fishes, poltergeists and all manner of meaningless and meaningful things to mock our pride and to show us that 'there are more things in heaven and earth than are dreamed of in our philosophy'.

We call such things 'supernatural', and say they cannot occur or exist, since they are outside the boundaries of the limited view of nature that science and religion demand. But as we have seen, such things are aspects of the reality of nature: they are not 'unnatural'. What *is* unnatural is our science, our religion, our politics and economics: for all are carried on in complete and deliberate ignorance of nature, in the belief or hope that nature will conveniently change itself to suit our whims. It gives us a pleasant illusion of control – but it's unnatural, and it's insane, in every sense of the word.

Idealists are just as ignorant. The communards' beautiful slogan 'From each according to his ability, to each according to his need', applied without awareness of the reality of human nature, becomes in practice 'From each according to facility, to each according to his greed'. Revolutionaries are the same: they fail to realize that, in society as in mechanics, a revolution is a circular motion, and that going round in circles doesn't get anyone anywhere or do anything other than waste energy, or lives, or both. Within our civilization greed and domineering are allowed free rein; so we need ideals and utopian dreams if we are to limit the effects of those unrestrained aspects of human nature. But those ideals and dreams, in practice, have to be tempered with an awareness of reality; without it they can be – and usually are – worse than useless.

If the view of reality we use is to be sane, not just to us but in its effects on the outer world as well, it needs to be constructed so as to take into account the reality which nature imposes upon us – whether we like that reality or not. The reality includes the energy-matrix we can see behind and beneath the old standing stones; it includes ghosts and ghouls, angels and demons, fairies and flying saucers, and all manner of other things which, as we have seen, are outside the common definition of reality but yet are still real. In a sense we could sum up this other reality in one word, and say that it is magical.

It is magic, in every sense, that our civilization has lost, buried by the inadequacies of ignorant science and arrogant religion. And it is magic, in every sense, that our civilization needs, if it is to regain its sanity, its joy, its reason for being. An awareness of the magic of the earth has much to offer us in this respect; as we have seen, that magical world-view is of more value than those of science or religion when dealing with the whole of the reality of nature. Paganism can teach us a great deal about that magic, but we need to use it with care; civilization has its flaws, but I've no wish to see a return to a culture run by half-crazed witch-doctors instead of half-crazed politicians. We need to go beyond civilization, beyond paganism, to something that combines the intellect of civilization with the joy and magic of paganism. We need, in effect, to regain our collective wisdom as well as our collective sanity.

So if our culture is to regain its *magi*, its 'wise men', we need to redevelop our awareness of nature, our magicians' awareness. Like magicians, and as magicians, we need to learn to know ourselves; we need to learn to feel for the needs of the earth, so that we can learn not just to subdue it, but to replenish it as we do so. This will and must demand radical changes in our world-view; necessarily and literally radical changes, since we will need to regain an awareness of our roots, in our past and in nature, in order to bring them about.

But it is here that the standing stones can help us, by symbolizing our different attitudes to nature. As part of the past, they symbolize both the time of man's closest 'at-oneness' with nature, and his breaking away from nature, the birth of his belief that he could control nature and thus be 'above' it. From that came the birth of civilization, and the death of magic. But as research goes on into the 'earth mysteries', we are regaining our respect for paganism and for the old magic, and so those same stones are gaining a new meaning, both symbolic and practical. For as 'needles of stone' they symbolize both a way and a means of returning to a realistic relationship with nature.

And that, I believe, is our one great hope for the future.

Notes

Publishers and publication dates for books referred to are given in the bibliography. Journal titles are abbreviated as follows: *JBSD*, *Journal of the British Society of Dowsers*; *TLH*, *The Ley Hunter magazine*; *JSPR*, *Journal of the (British) Society for Psychical Research*.

1 Introduction

1 Such as that of the American Indians: see T. C. McLuhan, *Touch The Earth*.
2 For examples, see the books of George Ewart Evans, such as *The Pattern Under The Plough*.
3 See T. C. McLuhan, *Touch The Earth* – particularly the first section.
4 Quoted in John Michell's essay in his study *The Old Stones of Land's End*, in which he discusses the qualities that make up the 'sacredness' of a site.

2 Dowsing and Archaeology

1 See Leslie Alcock, *By South Cadbury is that Camelot* (the 'popular' report on the Cadbury-Camelot 'dig'), particularly pp. 72 and 78.
2 See Francis Hitching, *Pendulum*.
3 See Francis Hitching, *Pendulum*, particularly pp. 159–88.
4 James Plummer, *Dowsing for Roman Roads*, in *JBSD* XXV, No. 174, Dec 76, pp. 205–14.
5 Captain F. L. M. Boothby, *The Salted Track*, in *JBSD* IV, No. 26, Dec 39, pp. 46–9.
6 Helmuth Hesserl, *The Earth Rays and their Importance*, in *JBSD* IV, No. 26, Dec 39, pp. 52–60.
7 Louis Merle, *Radiesthesie et Prehistoire*, 1933; Charles Diot, *Les Sourciers et les Monuments Megalithiques*, 1935; publishers not known.

8 Captain F. L. M. Boothby, *The Religion of the Stone Age*, in *JBSD* II, No. 10, Dec 35, pp. 115–16.

9 Reginald A. Smith, *Archaeological Dowsing*, in *JBSD* III, No. 24, Jun 39, pp. 348–56.

10 Underwood's articles on these patterns are: *Archaeology and Dowsing* (*Part I*), in *JBSD* VII, No. 56, Jun 47, pp. 192–205; *Archaeology and Dowsing* (*Part II*), in *JBSD* VII, No. 58, Dec 47, pp. 296–306; *Archaeology and Dowsing* (*Part III*), in *JBSD* VII, No. 59, Mar 48, pp. 354–60; *Track Lines*, in *JBSD* VIII, No. 60, Jun 48, pp. 22–8; *Spirals*, in *JBSD* VIII, No. 62, Dec 48, pp. 162–77; *Aquastats*, in *JBSD* IX, No. 71, Mar 51, pp. 279–86; and *Further Notes on Dowsing Aquastats and Prehistoric Sites*, in *JBSD* X, No. 73, Sept 51, pp. 40–6.

11 It's important to realize that Underwood's work was nearly twenty years out of date when it was finally published: he had it published posthumously because of worries about bitter sarcasm from professional archaeologists.

12 W. H. Lamb, *Old Churches Over Streams*, in *JBSD* XIX, No. 129, Sept 65, p. 85.

13 Muriel Langdon, *More About Old Churches Over Streams*, in *JBSD* XIX, No. 130, Dec 65, p. 150.

14 See *JBSD* IX, No. 71, Mar 51, p. 286 and *JBSD* X, No. 73, Sept 51, p. 46. Colonel Bell *was* the Society at that time: as well as being editor of the Journal, he was the Society's president, secretary, treasurer and librarian!

15 First mentioned in his article *Track Lines*, in *JBSD* VIII, No. 60, June 48, pp. 22–8.

16 This is well illustrated in Underwood's diagrams in *The Pattern Of The Past*.

17 See *Pattern Of The Past*, pp. 46–7 and 58–9.

18 See *Pattern Of The Past*, pp. 34–59.

19 The clearest example he gives is on his Fig. 45 on p. 131 of *Pattern Of The Past*, showing patterns on and round the Slaughter Stone at Stonehenge.

20 This is his main theme in Chs. 8–17 of *Pattern Of The Past*.

21 For a practising scientist's view of what science and scientific research is and does, see W. I. Beveridge's excellent *The Art of Scientific Investigation*.

22 The Journals of the British Society of Dowsers are the most reliable British source on this: 'official' research in the past has had too much of a vested interest in the classical view of

'science' to allow them to design experiments based on dowsing practice rather than pseudo-scientific theory.

23 See my book *Dowsing: Techniques and Applications* for practical details.

24 See Maby and Franklin, *The Physics of the Divining Rod*, or Tromp, Psychical *Physics*.

25 Underwood did recognise Creyke's system of depthing: he mentions and describes it briefly on p. 51 of *Pattern Of The Past*, and refers to an article of Creyke's in *JBSD* II, No. 9, Sept 35, p. 86. See also Trinder, *Dowsing*, p. 27.

26 Particularly, for example, the detailed patterns at Stonehenge which Underwood shows in Figs. 32–5, 39, 40, 43 and 44 in *Pattern Of The Past*, which cannot match the archaeological facts if they are interpreted in terms of his theory of the 'pattern of the past'.

27 See, in particular, T. C. Lethbridge, *Ghost and Ghoul*, and *Ghost and Divining Rod*.

3 As Below, So Above

1 See Francis Hitching, *Earth Magic*, pp. 105–6.

2 See Maby and Franklin, *Physics of the Divining Rod*; Maby, *Physical Principles of Radiesthesia*; and Tromp, *Psychical Physics*; then compare these with Arthur Bailey's article *Fact and Fiction in Dowsing*, in *JBSD* XXIV, No. 168, Jun 75, pp. 252–60.

3 See Colin Brookes-Smith's report on research into psycho-kinesis in *JSPR* XLVII, No. 756, Jun 73, pp. 68–89.

4 See Evan Hadingham, *Circles and Standing Stones*, pp. 174–5.

5 See *Pattern Of The Past*, pp. 58–9, and a comment on work by Andrew Davidson in Paul Screeton, *Quicksilver Heritage*, p. 185.

6 T. C. Lethbridge, *Legend of the Sons of God*, pp. 21–2.

7 See Peter Laurie, *Beneath the City Streets*.

8 Alfred Watkins shows many photographs of markstones in his books, particularly in *The Old Straight Track*.

9 See, for example, Sir Norman Lockyer's study of Boscawen-un circle in *Stonehenge and other British Stone Monuments Astronomically Considered*, and Michell's extension of Lockyer's thesis in *The Old Stones of Land's End*; see also the

survey of Stonehenge by Professor Thom and family in *Earth Mysteries: a study in patterns*.

10 The Old Straight Track Club's vast but disorganized files can be studied in the city library in Hereford.

11 Watkins gives an excellent example of one of these, through a pond at Holmer in Herefordshire, in Fig. 59 in *The Old Straight Track*.

12 For a typical example, see W. G. Hoskins, *Fieldwork in Local History*, pp. 136–7.

13 The first part of Francis Hitching's *Earth Magic* is a good but pre-MacKie summary of the clash between the old archaeology and the new. For detailed studies, see Thom's *Megalithic Sites in Britain* and *Megalithic Lunar Observatories*, Renfrew's *Before Civilization* and MacKie's *Science and Society in Prehistoric Britain*.

14 This information comes from work currently being organized by Dr G. V. Robins at London's Institute of Archaeology.

15 See *TLH* 14, Dec 70, pp. 81–8. The heading harks back to the title of Michell's earlier book, *The View Over Atlantis*.

16 See *Undercurrents* magazine, issue 17, pp. 14–17.

17 See, for one set of examples, Bob Forrest's 'studies' of leys, published in various issues of *TLH*, *Undercurrents* and elsewhere.

4 Sinuous and Straight

1 For a more complete study of Feng-shui, see Eitel, *Feng Shui*, or Feuchtwang, *Chinese Geomancy*: the latter is more detailed and more up to date. Both have their limitations: Eitel's book suffers from Christian arrogance, particularly in its summary; and Feuchtwang's study is blinkered by current notions of anthropology. But if you can 'read between the lines', both books are useful in a study of the energy aspects of Feng-shui.

2 See *Chinese Geomancy*, pp. 151–71.

3 See, in particular, two articles by Steve Moore in *The Ley Hunter: Leys and Feng Shui*, in *TLH* 72, pp. 11–13; and *Mirroring*, in *TLH* 73, pp. 6–9.

4 Mary Austin's *Acupuncture Therapy* is one acupuncture manual that usefully explains the practical aspects of acupuncture terms and theories.

5 See Ostrander and Schroeder, *Pyschic Discoveries Behind The Iron Curtain*, pp. 233–7.
6 This is the impression given by almost all the articles on acupuncture that I've read in British medical journals, such as the *Lancet*, the *British Medical Journal* and *World Medicine*.
7 See Edward de Bono, *Practical Thinking*, pp. 94–6 and 118–24; see also the anonymous *SSOTMBE*, p. 17.

5 Needles of Stone

1 Most ley-hunters have ignored modern sites, because it seemed ludicrous to suggest that they fell in with the same pattern as the prehistoric sites. No published information is available on this as yet, for that reason. But it's something I've noticed time and again in my own work; and in discussions with several ley-hunters I've found that they too had noticed the connection, but had dismissed it as 'mere coincidence'. The problem is not whether it is 'coincidence' – which it is – but whether the coincidence is meaningful: and much more research is needed if we are going to be able to answer that question.
2 See Brian Branston, *The Lost Gods Of England*, p. 54.
3 See the article by Martin Puhvel, *The Mystery of the Crossroads*, in *Folklore* 1976 ii, pp. 167–77.
4 See J. G. Frazer, *The Golden Bough* (Papermac edition), pp. 835–9.
5 See Janet and Colin Bord, *Mysterious Britain*, pp. 71–2.
6 See, for example, J. T. Lesser, *Sacred Geometry*.
7 See, for example, Critchlow's articles on sacred geometry in the Research Into Lost Knowledge Organization's studies *Glastonbury: a study in patterns*, *Britain: a study in patterns* and *Earth Mysteries: a study in patterns*.
8 Michell and Critchlow discussed this in their articles in the RILKO studies. Michell covers number-symbolism in more depth in his *City of Revelation*, while Critchlow has shown the interaction in architecture of number, music, geometry and astronomy in many lectures and books, and in his Arts Council exhibition *Working Order* (1974).
9 See Figs. 24–5 in *The Old Straight Track*; also 'Alignment for Issue 73' in *TLH* 73, p. 12.
10 See *The Old Straight Track*, p. 96–9 and Figs. 95–100.

11 See Ostrander and Schroeder, *Psychic Discoveries Behind The Iron Curtain*, pp. 368–89.

12 See *Psychic Discoveries Behind The Iron Curtain*, pp. 358–67; also Lyall Watson, *Supernature*, pp. 97–101.

13 See Frazer, *The Golden Bough*, pp. 99 and 296 for examples.

14 The original article, in German, was by Peter Reiser in *Radiasthesie, Geopathie, Strahlenbiologie*, Issue 114, May–June 1973.

15 Some examples in *JBSD* are Colonel F. H. Iles, *The Question of Protection Against Lightning as Affected by Earth Rays*, in *JBSD* II, No. 11, Mar 36, pp. 164–70; M. H. Chipperfield, *Observations Regarding Lightning*, in JBSD III, No. 22, Dec 38, pp. 275–7; and Helmuth Hesserl, *The Earth Rays and Their Importance*, in *JBSD* IV, No. 26, Dec 39, pp. 52–60.

16 See the *British Standard on Lightning Protection*, published by the British Standards Institute.

17 See Frazer, *The Golden Bough*, pp. 926–7.

18 See Thom, *Megalithic Lunar Observatories*, p. 115.

19 See Barry Marsden, *The Early Barrow-Diggers*; the relevant sections are quoted in Janet and Colin Bord, *The Secret Country*, pp. 205–9; along with some similar examples of apparent weather-control.

20 See L. V. Grinsell, *The Ancient Burial Mounds of England*.

21 For Reich's own summary of his work on orgone, see *Wilhelm Reich: Selected Writings*.

22 See Section VII-1, *DOR Removal and Cloud-busting*, pp. 433–46 of *Wilhelm Reich: Selected Writings*.

23 I'm perhaps being unfair here: since writing this I've been told that Reich was aware that UFOs had other aspects beyond the apparently physical one of 'nuts and bolts' flying saucers.

24 The Administration based its charge of fraud on the grounds that its scientists had found that Reich's orgone accumulators could not work with any of the physical energies they knew and understood, and therefore could not work at all. They never tested the accumulators in the way that Reich had designed them to be used: their approach to the workings of the accumulators was 'like that of a child with drum: cut it open to see what is inside it', as Watkins sourly commented about archaeologists and barrows.

25 Part of this material was published in the *Fortean Times* magazine, then titled *The News*. See *Portrait of a Fault Area*, by

Paul Devereux and Andrew York, in *The News* 11, pp. 5–10 and 14–19, and *The News* 12, pp. 12–13.

26 John Richards, *But Deliver Us From Evil*, p. 211.

27 Dom Robert Petitpierre (ed.), *Exorcism: the findings of a commission convened by the Bishop of Exeter*, pp. 21–2.

6 Ghosts and Ghouls

1 For a discussion of some interesting if depressing examples of prejudice and pseudo-science masquerading as proper scientific study, see *JSPR* XLVIII No. 770, pp. 412–21.

2 See particularly Lethbridge's *Ghost and Ghoul* and *Ghost and Divining Rod*.

3 See S. W. Tromp, *Psychical Physics* and J. C. Maby, *Physical Principles of Radiesthesia*; also the more recent work discussed in Francis Hitching, *Pendulum*, particularly Part II.

4 Someone did in fact jump over, but not until a few years later: see *A Step in the Dark*, pp. 94–6.

5 See Lethbridge, *Ghost and Divining Rod*, pp. 31–3.

6 For star-alignment, see Thom's *Megalithic Sites in Britain*, pp. 97–101; little material has been published on astronomically linked pulses at sacred sites other than what we've seen in this study.

7 See *A Step in the Dark*, pp. 110–11.

8 See *A Step in the Dark*, pp. 77–81.

9 For a more detailed discussion of this, see Dion Fortune, *Psychic Self-Defence*.

7 Magicians

1 See Lethbridge, *ESP*, pp. 111–12.

2 See Frazer, *The Golden Bough*, pp. 79–109; also Janet and Colin Bord, *The Secret Country*, p. 57.

3 See Brian Branston, *The Lost Gods of England*, and George Ewart Evans, *The Pattern Under the Plough*, for some of the many examples.

4 The full quote from Stubbe's *Anatomie of Abuses*, about twice as long as the version I have shown here, is in Frazer, *The Golden Bough*, p. 162.

5 The best-known example of this policy is expressed in the 'Mellitus letter' which Bede quotes in his *Ecclesiastical*

History – see Brian Branston, *The Lost Gods of England*, pp. 53–4 – but there are many others.

6 One set of examples is the Christianized 'charms': see *The Lost Gods of England*, pp. 48–51.

7 George Ewart Evans describes this in detail in his books on East Anglian traditions, including *The Pattern Under The Plough*.

8 A summary of the incident can be found in the leader to Dr G. V. Robins' article *Images in Stone* in *TLH* 76, p. 11.

9 I know that Castaneda's books are now no longer believed to be his personal diaries; but they are known to have been derived from accurate sources in any case, so the incident was certainly valid as *someone's* experience even if not Castaneda's.

10 This comment, cited in Feuchtwang, *Chinese Geomancy*, p. 221, is from Duke's article *Feng Shui* in *Encyclopaedia of Religion and Ethics*, Vol. V, published in Edinburgh in 1912.

11 See Feuchtwang, *Chinese Geomancy*, pp. 221–2.

12 Some has been published in various issues of the British dowsing journals, such as *JBSD* and the *Radionic Association Quarterly*, particularly under headings like 'the control of noxious earth rays'.

8 Angels and Demons

1 See Keel, *Operation Trojan Horse*, p. 252.

2 See Lyall Watson, *Supernature*, pp. 34–7 and 175.

3 The 'placebo effect' is that a 'dummy' drug – usually calcium lactate – will work as well as or better than the 'real' drug with up to half as many patients during drug tests. It has been known to work half as well, in these terms, as aspirin, or heroin, or anything which is the 'real' drug at the time. One of my mother's patients still asks for 'those tablets that made my arthritis better, because none of the others work so well': 'those tablets' were, of course, calcium lactate. The fact that chalky sugar – which is effectively what calcium lactate is – works better than the so-called 'wonder drugs' in many cases is quietly ignored in medical circles.

4 Two useful introductions to homoeopathy are Sharma, *A Manual of Homoeopathy and Natural Medicine*, and Wethered, *An Introduction to Medical Radiesthesia and Radionics* – the

latter deals mostly with its use in the medical applications of dowsing.

5 See John Wilcox, *Radionics in Theory and Practice*, pp. 85–6 and Figs. 20–1.

6 See *Radionics in Theory and Practice*, pp. 85 and Figs. 16 and 18.

7 This is discussed in Wethered, *An Introduction to Medical Radiesthesia and Radionics*.

8 There is a detailed article on the relationship between water-lines and arthritis in *JBSD* XXIV, No. 167, Mar 75.

9 The article was by Helmuth Hesserl, *The Earth Rays and Their Importance*, in *JBSD* IV, No. 26, Dec 39, pp. 52–60.

10 See, for example, the comments by the American dowser Jack Livingston in Francis Hitching, *Pendulum*, pp. 227–8.

11 Letter from Frau Anka von Knoblauch in *JBSD* III, No. 20, Jun 38.

12 From V. D. Wethered, *The Problem of Obnoxious Earth Rays*, in *JBSD* XVI, No. 113, Sept 61, p. 253.

13 This is something of a characteristic of religious 'visions' and 'apparitions', as well as many types of UFO incident, as Michell and Rickard show in their book *Phenomena*.

14 This is now recognized to be a risk that UFO researchers undertake, as John Keel discusses several times in his *UFOs: Operation Trojan Horse*.

15 See *Operation Trojan Horse*, pp. 273–90.

16 This kind of 'message' appears several times in the incidents described in Keel's and Vallee's studies.

17 For Lourdes and Fatima see *Operation Trojan Horse*, pp. 252 and 256–64 respectively; for Knock see Vallee, *Passport to Magonia*, pp. 132–9.

18 Keel gives several examples in *Operation Trojan Horse*: particularly on pp. 278–84.

19 Vallee gives an example of 'man-in-black'-style telephone disturbance in *Passport to Magonia*, p. 84; Keel describes several variants on the 'man-in-black' theme in *Operation Trojan Horse*.

20 These can all be found among Keel's reports in *Operation Trojan Horse*.

21 Aime Michel presented his main 'orthoteny' thesis in his book *The Truth About Flying Saucers*; it has also been dis-cussed in many issues of *The Ley Hunter* magazine.

22 The reports on these can be found in *TLH* 75, pp. 10–11 and *TLH* 72, p. 10 respectively.

9 The Return of Paganism

1 Adapted from *Elemental Ecology*, an interview with Dick Barton, in *Undercurrents* 19, pp. 15–16.

2 From the accounts I've read, the Council's behaviour was hardly one of religious piety. Fights broke out in the Council Hall as each faction struggled to prove that its system of belief was 'the Truth'. All the key concepts of early Christianity, including the doctrine of reincarnation, were swept aside when Constantine overruled this ludicrous squabble, constructing a version of Christianity more suitable to his political needs instead. Such was the birth of modern Roman Christianity.

3 From Bede's *Ecclesiastical History*, quoted in Brian Branston, *The Lost Gods of England*, pp. 53–4.

4 According to discussions I've had with Geoffrey Ashe, it's likely that those supposedly after the death of Christ are true to some extent: see his *Camelot and the Vision of Albion*, pp. 110–15.

5 This comes out most clearly in a horrific book on the Victorian attitude to sex, *The Anxiety Makers*, once published by Penguin.

6 Pope Boniface, in a letter to King Edwin of Northumbria around AD 625, quoted in Brian Branston, *The Lost Gods of England*, p. 54.

7 By far the best source on Findhorn's work is the community itself – best visited in person, but otherwise through their book *The Findhorn Garden*.

8 See *The Findhorn Garden*, p. 74.

9 This theme is developed in some detail in Tompkins and Bird, *The Secret Life of Plants*.

10 Fritjof Capra's *The Tao of Physics* gives an indication of the near-mystical state of modern nuclear physics.

11 See Charles Fort's *The Book of the Damned* for the classic description of this; see also the magazine *Fortean Times*, edited by Robert Rickard, for an ongoing summary of current Fortean phenomena and their implications. Spontaneous human combustion is a particularly nasty phenomenon in

which a person's body is reduced to ashes without apparent
heat, without much scorching the surroundings, and even, in
some cases, without scorching the person's clothes: Michell
and Rickard give several examples in their book *Phenomena*.
12 John Michell, *View Over Atlantis*, p. 35.
13 See Euan MacKie, *Science and Society in Prehistoric Britain*.
14 Alexander Thom, *Megalithic Sites in Britain*, pp. 148–50.

10 Healing the Land

1 The leader of the community, Reshad Feild, commented on
   this in an interview in *Seed* Magazine, Vol. V No. 9, pp. 21–3.
2 See Martin Puhvel, *The Lore of the Cross-Roads*, in *Folklore*
   1976 ii, pp. 167–77.
3 See, for example, V. D. Wethered, *The Problem of Obnoxious
   Earth Rays*, in *JBSD* XVI, No. 113, Sept 61, p. 253.
4 Articles on local versions of earth-acupuncture appear from
   time to time in the French dowsing magazine *Radiesthesie*
   and the German equivalent, *Radiasthesie, Geopathie, Strahlenbiologie*.
5 There have been dozens of articles on this over the years in
   JBSD. Two worth looking at are Wethered, *The Problem of
   Obnoxious Earth Rays*, in *JBSD* XVI, No. 113, Sept 61, p.
   253 and H. O. Busby, *Further Notes on Earth Radiations*,
   in *JBSD* II, No. 18, Dec 37, p. 32. See also A. D. Manning,
   The Neutralisation of Harmful Earth Rays, in Bell (ed.),
   Practical Dowsing: A Symposium.
6 Reich claimed that according to the results of his ORANUR
   experiment, radio-activity was a side-effect of the over-
   activation of orgone by radio-active substances, producing
   DOR. See Section VI in *Wilhelm Reich: Selected Writings*,
   pp. 351–431.
7 See the correspondence on this in *JBSD* XXIV No. 168, Jun
   75, pp. 282–3.
8 Adapted from *Old Magic, New Magic*, an unpublished manu-
   script by Richard Elen.
9 John Taylor discusses directed poltergeist in his book *Superminds*, and Batcheldor and Brookes-Smith have developed a
   technique for teaching people in groups to develop poltergeist
   skills, as described in several articles over the years in *JSPR*.
   The best recent example of a psychic capable of tampering

with computer tapes and memory-banks is Matthew Manning; Uri Geller claims to have done both poltergeist work as well as computer-jamming, but it seems probable that some of his methods are not magical in the sense that we're using the term here.

Further Reading

This list represents a minute fraction of the published material on the various aspects of this study: the books and magazines listed here are those that were mentioned in the text or notes.

Leslie Alcock, *By South Cadbury is that Camelot* (Thames and Hudson, pb, 1972)

Anonymous, *SSOTMBE: an essay on magic, its foundations, development and place in modern life* (The Mouse That Spins, pb, 1976)

Geoffrey Ashe, *Camelot and the Vision of Albion* (Panther, pb, 1975)

Mary Austin, *Acupuncture Therapy* (Turnstone, hc, 1974)

Colonel Bell (ed.), *Practical Dowsing: a symposium* (Bell, hc, 1965)

W. I. B. Beveridge, *The Art of Scientific Investigation* (Heinemann Education, pb, 1961)

Edward de Bono, *Practical Thinking* (Jonathan Cape, hc, 1971)

Janet and Colin Bord, *Mysterious Britain* (Paladin, pb, 1974)

Janet and Colin Bord, *The Secret Country* (Elek, hc, 1976)

Brian Branston, *The Lost Gods of England* (Thames and Hudson, hc, 1974)

John Coles, *Field Archaeology in Britain* (Methuen, hc, 1972)

Fritjof Capra, *The Tao of Physics* (Wildwood House, pb, 1975)

Charles Diot, *Les Sourciers et les Monuments Megalithiques* (private? France, 1935)

Reverend E. J. Eitel, *Feng Shui* (Trubner & Co., 1873/Cockaygne, pb, 1973)

George Ewart Evans, *The Pattern Under The Plough* (Faber, pb, 1971)

Stephen Feuchtwang, *Chinese Geomancy: an anthropological analysis* (Vithagna (Laos), pb, 1974)

The Findhorn Community, *The Findhorn Garden* (Turnstone/Wildwood House, pb, 1976)

J. G. Frazer, *The Golden Bough* (edited version: Macmillan, hc, 1922)

Charles Fort, *The Book of the Damned* (Abacus, pb, 1973; originally published in USA, 1919)

Dion Fortune, *Psychic Self-Defence* (Aquarian, hc, 1967)

Tom Graves, *Dowsing: Techniques and Applications* (Turnstone, pb, 1976)

L. V. Grinsell, *The Ancient Burial Mounds of England* (Methuen, hc, 1936)

Evan Hadingham, *Circles and Standing Stones* (Heinemann, hc, 1975)

Francis Hitching, *Earth Magic* (Cassell, hc, 1976)

Francis Hitching, *Pendulum: the Psi Connection* (Fontana, pb, 1977)

W. G. Hoskins, *Fieldwork in Local History* (Faber, pb, 1969)

John Keel, *UFOs: Operation Trojan Horse* (Abacus, pb, 1973)

Peter Laurie, *Beneath The City Streets* (Granada, pb, 1979)

J. T. Lesser, *Sacred Geometry* (Alec Tiranti, hc, 1957)

T. C. Lethbridge, *Ghost and Ghoul* (Routledge and Kegan Paul, hc, 1961)

T. C. Lethbridge, *Witches* (RKP, hc, 1962)

T. C. Lethbridge, *Ghost and Divining Rod* (RKP, hc, 1963)

T. C. Lethbridge, *ESP: beyond time and distance* (RKP, hc, 1965)

T. C. Lethbridge, *A Step in the Dark* (RKP, hc, 1967)

T. C. Lethbridge, *The Monkey's Tail* (RKP, hc, 1969)

T. C. Lethbridge, *The Legend of the Sons of God* (RKP, hc, 1972)

Sir Norman Lockyer, *Stonehenge and other British Stone Monuments Astronomically Considered* (Macmillan, hc, 1909)

J. C. Maby, *Physical Principles of Radiesthesia* (private, hc, 1966)

J. C. Maby/T. Bedford Franklin, *The Physics of the Divining Rod* (Bell, hc, 1939)

Euan MacKie, *Science and Society in Prehistoric Britain* (Elek, hc, 1977)

T. C. McLuhan, *Touch The Earth* (Abacus, pb, 1973)

Barry Marsden, *The Early Barrow-Diggers* (Shire Publications, hc, 1974)

Louis Merle, *Radiesthesie et Prehistoire* (private? France, 1933)

Aime Michel, *The Truth About Flying Saucers* (Robert Hale, hc, 1957)

John Michell, *View Over Atlantis* (Garnstone, hc, 1969)

John Michell, *City of Revelation* (Garnstone, hc, 1972)

John Michell, *The Old Stones of Land's End* (Garnstone, hc, 1974)

John Michell/Robert J. M. Rickard, *Phenomena: a book of wonders* (Thames and Hudson, pb, 1977)

S. Ostrander/L. Schroeder, *PSI: Psychic Discoveries Behind The Iron Curtain* (Abacus, pb, 1973)

Dom Robert Petitpierre (ed.), *Exorcism: the report of a commission convened by the Bishop of Exeter* (SPCK, pb, 1972)

John Cowper Powys, *A Glastonbury Romance* (Macdonald, hc, 1933)

Wilhelm Reich (ed.), *Wilhelm Reich: Selected Writings* (Noonday (USA), pb, 1960)

Colin Renfrew, *Before Civilization* (Penguin, pb, 1976)

Research Into Lost Knowledge Organisation (RILKO), *Glastonbury: a study in patterns* (RILKO, pb, 1969)

RILKO, *Britain: a study in patterns* (RILKO, pb, 1971)

RILKO, *Earth Mysteries: a study in patterns* (*RILKO, pb, 1977*)

John Richards, *But Deliver Us From Evil* (Darton Longman Todd, hc, 1974)

Paul Screeton, *Quicksilver Heritage* (Thorsons, hc, 1974)

Chandra Sharma, *A Manual of Homeopathy and Natural Medicine* (Turnstone, hc, 1975)

John Taylor, *Superminds* (Picador, pb, 1976)

Alexander Thom, *Megalithic Sites in Britain* (Oxford, hc, 1967)

Alexander Thom, *Megalithic Lunar Observatories* (Oxford, hc, 1971)

Peter Tompkins/Christopher Bird, *The Secret Life of Plants* (Penguin, pb, 1975)

W. H. Trinder, *Dowsing* (British Society of Dowsers, hc, 1939)

S. W. Tromp, *Psychical Physics* (Elsevier, hc, 1949)

Guy Underwood, *The Pattern of the Past* (Abacus, pb, 1974)

Jacques Vallee, *Passport to Magonia* (Tandem, pb, 1975)

Alfred Watkins, *Early British Trackways, Moats, Mounds, Camps and Sites* (private, pb, 1922)

Alfred Watkins, *The Old Straight Track* (Methuen, hc, 1925)

Alfred Watkins, *The Ley Hunter's Manual* (private, pb, 1927)

Lyall Watson, *Supernature* (Hodder and Stoughton, hc, 1973)

Vernon Wethered, *An Introduction to Medical Radiesthesia and Radionics* (C. W. Daniel, hc, 1957)

John Wilcox, *Radionics in Theory and Practice* (Herbert Jenkins, hc, 1960)

Magazines and Societies

Fortean Times (formerly *The News*), a quarterly journal that chronicles and discusses, with high standards of accuracy and scholarship, all Fortean-type events. Editor: R. J. M. Rickard; available from PO Box 152, London N10 1EP.

The Ley Hunter, a bi-monthly journal on all aspects of the 'earth mysteries', which also organizes serious research into these fields. Editor: Paul Devereux; available from PO Box 152, London N10 1EP.

Undercurrents, a bi-monthly journal on all aspects of the practice and theory of 'alternative technology'. Edited by a collective; available from 12 South Street, Uley, Dursley, Gloucestershire.

British Society of Dowsers deals with every aspect and application of dowsing. Quarterly journal; operates from 19 High Street, Eydon, Daventry, Northants.

Radionic Association specializes in the medical aspects and applications of dowsing. Quarterly journal; operates from 16a North Bar, Banbury, Oxfordshire.

Society for Psychical Research deals with all forms of research into psychical phenomena, but mostly from a 'scientific' angle. Quarterly journal; operates from 1 Adam and Eve Mews, Kensington, London W8 6UQ.

Index

MYSTERIES OF THE UNIVERSE – REVEALED

Pauwels & Bergier
Eternal Man   75p ☐
Impossible Possibilities   50p ☐
The Morning of the Magicians   £1.25 ☐

Guy Lyon Playfair
The Unknown Power   95p ☐
The Indefinite Boundary   95p ☐

Brinsley Le Poer Trench
Secret of the Ages   60p ☐

Eric & Craig Umland
Mystery of the Ancients   50p ☐

Jacques Vallee
UFOs: The Psychic Solution   85p ☐

Richard Mooney
Gods of Air and Darkness   75p ☐

MYSTERIES OF THE UNIVERSE – REVEALED

Charles Berlitz

Without a Trace   95p ☐
The Mystery of Atlantis   85p ☐
The Bermuda Triangle   95p ☐

Robert Chapman

Unidentified Flying Objects   95p ☐

Robin Collyns

Did Spacemen Colonise the Earth?   75p ☐

Rupert Furneaux

The Tungus Event   60p ☐

Adi-Kent Thomas Jeffrey

Terror Zones   75p ☐

John A Keel

The Cosmic Question   75p ☐

All these books are available at your local bookshop or newsagent, or can be ordered direct from the publisher. Just tick the titles you want and fill in the form below.

Name ....

Address ....

....

Write to Granada Cash Sales, PO Box 11, Falmouth, Cornwall TR10 9EN.

Please enclose remittance to the value of the cover price plus:

UK: 30p for the first book, 15p for the second book plus 12p per copy for each additional book ordered to a maximum charge of £1.29.

BFPO and EIRE: 30p for the first book, 15p for the second book plus 12p per copy for the next 7 books, thereafter 6p per book.

OVERSEAS: 50p for the first book and 15p for each additional book.

Granada Publishing reserve the right to show new retail prices on covers, which may differ from those previously advertised in the text or elsewhere.